Vikings and Mandarins

Verner Worm

Vikings and Mandarins

Sino-Scandinavian Business Cooperation in Cross-Cultural Settings

HANDELSHØJSKOLENS FORLAG
Distribution: Munksgaard International Publishers Ltd.
Copenhagen

© Handelshøjskolens Forlag 1997
Set in Plantin and printed by AKA-PRINT, Århus
Cover designed by Kontrapunkt
Book designed by Jørn Ekstrøm
Translation: Marianne Risberg and Doug Conner

ISBN 87-16-13360-9

Series D, No. 27

Contents

Contents

Preface and Acknowledgements

There are two kinds of books on research topics, those for the academic audience and those targeted for business executives. Is it possible to write a book that appeal to both audiences? This is at least the aim of this book. Drawing on my experience, I am convinced that academic research in many fields of applied science and especially business studies will also be of interest to business executives and others, when written in a not too academic jargon.

This book is a revised and abbreviated version of my Ph.D. thesis at the Faculty of Business Economics, the Copenhagen Business School. The Ph.D. degree was conferred in December, 1995. My interest in cross-cultural cooperation between Scandinavians and Chinese in business settings was developed during my work as an expatriate in Beijing in the 1980s. Returning to Denmark in late 1989, I continued to work as a consultant for Danish companies considering or in the process of setting up operations in China.

One Sunday morning in early 1990, my life took a positive turn. I received a telephone call from an old friend, Professor Kjeld Erik Brødsgaard, the Copenhagen University. He called from Beijing, of all places, where he was on a visit. Knowing I had an interest in academia, he suggested I applied for a Fulbright Scholar-in-residence position at the Business School of Washburn University, Topeka, Kansas, USA. I did not know a city of that name existed, but decided to apply and was accepted as a visiting scholar for one year. Brødsgaard's call brought me back to the academic world, which I had wished for some time after having worked in private companies for almost ten years. I am grateful to him for taking this initiative.

Returning to Denmark in 1991, I solicited the head of the Institute of International Economics and Management, Professor Lauge Stetting, and told him about my interest in conducting research into the different ways of doing business in Scandinavia and China. Stetting, being a man of action, realized immediately that the most appropriate way for a person with my background was to try to get a position as industrial researcher, a research position attached both to an academic institution and a private company and supported financially by the Committee on Industrial Ph.D. Fellowship administered by the Academy of Technical Sciences. Stetting even supplied me with names of Danish companies operating in China. Stetting has continuously supported my project as can also be seen from the fact that he, now director of »Copenhagen Business School Press«, is in charge of publishing this book.

Having written a project proposal, I contacted Professor Karsten Laursen, Chairman of J. Lauritzen Holding, one of the companies operating in China mentioned by Stetting. Again, I was in luck, Professor Laursen was a man of action and initiative. Like Stetting, he did not know me in advance, but his was short and clear. Lauritsen Holding would support the project and employ me for two and a half years, which eventually became three years, provided the Committee on Industrial Ph.D. Fellowship approved the project. Without the support I received from Karsten Laursen and others at Lauritzen Holding, the project would never have materialized.

The approval from the Committee on Industrial Ph.D. Fellowship came in February, 1992 and I started on March 1. During the three years, a large number of persons contributed to guiding me through the process of writing the Ph.D. thesis. It is impossible to mention all those, who deserve mentioning, but a few stand out. Especially during the first part of my research, Professor Poul Schultz, Institute for International Economics and Management, gave me invaluable support, and on numerous occasions contributed with constructive suggestions, when I was stuck and needed to get back on the track.

Another professor, or one might even say institution, at the Copenhagen Business School, is Flemming Agersnap. His inspiration and ideas have affected a whole generation, and I am one of them. He was my psychological mentor throughout all the years. Back in 1990, he introduced me to the people at the office of the Fulbright Commission in Denmark. While writing my thesis, he always found time for a chat and after leaving his office, I had to sit down for a while digesting all the ideas he had suggested in his own informal manner. His attitude has always been: catch the ideas you like and forget the others.

The final part of this journey was to translate, revise, and reduce the thesis, bringing it into a form suitable for publication. First of all I wish to express my gratitude to the Faculty of Economics at the Copenhagen Business School for providing the funding for the translation into English, which has been undertaken professionally by

Marianne Risberg and Doug Conner. Marianne Risberg is much more than a translator. On many occasions during the translation process, she came up with excellent suggestions for improvements. Susan Aagaard Petersen, who is an academic secretary at the Asia Research Unit, the Copenhagen Business School, has gone through the manuscript several times, checked the references, and suggested improvements continuously. She has been indispensable for the revision of the original thesis. My thanks goes to both of them.

It goes without saying that any error or mistake is my responsibility.

Finally, I wish to thank my family for giving me much support and all the time I needed. Apart from my wife Muxiu Worm and our two daughters, Vivi and Camilla, I also wish to thank my mother-in-law, who has contributed more to the whole project than she thinks by taking care of our house and children when Muxiu and I were busy.

I am aware that I should have been of greater support to my wife, physically and mentally, while she was expecting Camilla and afterward, but she has always encouraged me to continue with the project. Vivi would have preferred a father who had more time to talk and play, and Camilla, after she arrived in 1994, a father who simply had more time. This book is dedicated to our children. Being born of parents rooted in the Chinese and the Scandinavian cultures, I hope, or console myself with the hope, that one day, when they grow up, they will read this book and use it as one source to explain and consolidate their own identity.

Verner Worm
October 1996

1. Introduction

Personal Background

I was born and raised in a nuclear family in the small village Thy in the countryside of Northern Jutland, Denmark. Today, I am living in a traditional, though inter-cultural, nuclear family in Copenhagen.

I became interested in China during the cultural revolution which I, like many other young intellectuals, thought represented alternative attitudes to those prevailing in our society. This brought me to China for the first time in 1974 with a 'friendship delegation', and the same year I started to study Chinese. Since then I have lived in close contact with Chinese, even though the nature of these contacts has changed over the years. When studying Chinese at Peking University in the 1970s, I shared a room for three years with various Chinese students. Later on, in the 1980s, I managed a Danish business office in Beijing, during which time my main contacts were Chinese business people. In 1981 I married my wife, Hu Muxiu, who was born and raised in Shanghai, but has spent fifteen years in North China, eight of which we spent together in Beijing.

Living in close contact with the Chinese and being part of Chinese public life, with exposure to newspapers, films, and fiction literature, has made me continuously aware of and surprised at the differences between 'us and them'. This is the actual background for initiating the project on which the present book is based. Even though I have changed over the years, at least on the surface, and become more 'Chinese' at the same time that many Chinese have become more 'Western', I do not feel that either my basic values or those of the Chinese I am in contact with have changed significantly.

The purpose of this personal introduction is to say that differences in values have affected my contact with the Chinese in the three situations described above. Even though I am only analyzing cultural differences and inter-cultural contacts in commercial situations in the present book, my non-commercial contact with Chinese has also effected my understanding of Chinese business people and my attitude toward them, for better or for worse. Since commercial activities, inclusive of management, basically consist of interpersonal contact, it is not surprising that cultural differences become apparent in such situations.

Background of the Project

General background

This project would never have been launched had development in China not headed in the direction it did since the mid-seventies. When Mao Zedong died in 1976, China gradually started to change its economic structure away from planned economy toward market economy, and ever since the country's annual growth rate has been approx. 8.5% (Perkins, 1992:59), contrasting sharply with the economic growth of approx. 1% in the West and a negative growth in many East European countries during the same period.

Albeit the dream of supplying 'oil for China's oil lamps', with its population of 1,2 billion, has existed for decades, this sudden dramatic increase in commercial interests in China should be viewed in light of the country's own development and the economic situation characterizing our proximate markets.

Specific background

These growing commercial activities often resulted in the establishment of production through joint ventures in which both the Chinese and the Scandinavian parties participated actively, not only as board members but also in the day-to-day operations. Thus, by the end of 1995, foreign firms had invested approx. 140 billion dollars in China.[1]

This onset led to exponential growth in the number of expatriates in China. During the Mao reign, that is until 1976, only a hand-full of Scandinavian business people worked in China. By 1994, approx 100,000 expatriates work in China (Andersen, 1995) out of which many are Scandinavians with their specific cultural and managerial background. Westerners who worked in China under Mao were either invited by the Chinese government as experts or represented foreign firms and lived strictly isolated from the Chinese population. So, Westerners were in general totally unprepared for the challenge of having to cooperate with Chinese over a longer period. In addition, each firm with foreign capital had only one expatriate, which made the situation even more difficult for the individual expatriate.

Objective

The overall objective of this project was to investigate the effect of cultural differences on interpersonal relationships and the management of Scandinavian firms in China. This overall objective can be divided into research and application.

Research

The scientific objective was to improve our knowledge and understanding of relevant business related cultural differences between China and Scandinavia and the specific cultural conditions for interaction, which were important for Scandinavian firms establishing themselves in China.

Even though the firm is an open system, the focal issue is interaction within the firm, because here the inter-cultural contact is more intense and of a higher frequency than outside the firm. However, where relevant, external relationships between Scandinavian firms and surrounding Chinese society, including fully owned Chinese firms, are also covered.

First, the purpose is to examine and analyze the most important differences between Chinese and Scandinavian managers' interpersonal behaviour and how these differences effect their interrelationships. Second, the analysis focuses on how cultural differences effect selected aspects of managerial processes and organizational structures in Scandinavian firms in China. The aim is to shed light on to what extent and within which areas it would be beneficial for Scandinavian investors to adapt to the local culture, and within which areas Scandinavian managerial forms can be introduced in China, and finally in which cases a mixture of the two are to be preferred.

These two themes are illustrated by empirical data, but a more general description of the two cultural areas is required. Therefore, the sections describing the cultures are first and foremost intended to provide background for the empirical part of this book. However, the chapter on Chinese culture, politics and management is structured in such a way that it can be used independently by Scandinavian business people operating in China.

Application

In terms of applicability, the primary purpose is to increase the understanding of the conditions for inter-cultural contact between Chinese
and Scandinavians. Understanding here means predictability, internal
contextuality, and the absence of surprises. Through a better understanding of these conditions and how they change in the short and the
long run, it becomes possible to offer suggestions for how to achieve
still more efficient and constructive inter-cultural contact at the personal level, which takes into consideration the various layers of
Scandinavian and Chinese culture.

Based on these conditions for inter-cultural contact, the secondary
purpose is to clarify which cultural factors among Chinese and expatriate managers are changeable through selection and influence, and
which are unchangeable in the foreseeable future. In light of this clarification, and in combination with the problems, differences and syner-
gies caused by managerial cultural specific values, traditions, and
behaviours, expatriate managers in China are offered concrete suggestions for how to act and create more efficient managerial processes and
organizational structures in present and future Scandinavian firms in
China.

Delimitation of the project's objectives

The project is confined to analyzing conditions in fully owned
Scandinavian firms and joint ventures with Scandinavian partners in
China in which the Scandinavian investor participates actively in the
management and has one or several representatives stationed on site.
The term 'Scandinavian managers' implies managers of a Scandinavian cultural background. Similarly, 'Chinese managers' implies
Chinese who have lived in China all their lives, apart from short trips
abroad. Thus, expatriate backgrounds are more important than the
formal ownership, as Scandinavian firms often establish firms and joint
ventures in China through their subsidiaries in third world countries.
Thus, other types of penetration are not examined, such as trade,
establishment of agencies, and licence production, because in this context the Scandinavian party will often be less involved in managerial
processes, and inter-cultural contacts will hence be more limited than
in the production and service firms.

The purpose is not directly to compare the efficiency of inter-cultural contacts with the financial result, in part because the latter is often affected by many other conditions than inter-cultural contacts, and in part because I have not had access to the firms' accounts. However, the underlying assumption is that, all else being equal, inter-cultural interaction free of conflict is advantageous financially, just as the opposite, cultural clashes, affects the firms' financial results negatively.

In this project, efficiency refers to the degree of goal achievement as expressed by Scandinavian expatriates, implying personal satisfaction, and the purpose for the Scandinavian firms establishing themselves in China.

Research Questions

As it appears from the above, research questions can be divided in two themes: understanding and guidance. The first include questions such as:

1. What are the important differences between Chinese and Scandinavian managers' interpersonal behaviour?
2. To what extent can cultural differences explain the behaviour of expatriates and natives in view of Chinese and Scandinavian cultural values?
3. How are selected aspects of managerial functions effected by the cultural specific differences characterizing members ot the two cultures?

The second theme includes questions such as:

4. How to improve the inter-cultural interaction between representatives of the two cultures?
5. How to make more efficient selected aspects of managerial functions which are fully or partly affected by cultural specific differences?

Key Concepts

The basis for discussing the concept of culture and cultural differences is a modification of Hofstede's definition of 'culture' as the mind's collective programming, distinguishing one category of population from another (Hofstede, 1991:17). This means that culture is acquired and hence not inherited. Culture is divided into values, which are difficult to change, since they are incorporated in a early phase of socialization and already determined when the child is approximately 10 years old, and values of a more superficial nature, such a habits and traditions.

Interpersonal behaviour and interpersonal relationships are used synonymously, as they both refer to the actions of people who are related to one another through their work.

This book discusses both the respondents' own behaviours and attitudes and those they observe both in members of the other cultural group and in interactions between the two. The difference in behaviours and habits are explained on the basis of the author's interpretation of the cultural values as described in literature on each of the two cultural areas. In the event that the explanation is based on the respondent's own interpretation, this is mentioned specifically.

Cultural specific refers to phenomena which are more dominant is one of the two cultural areas, China or Scandinavia, but that are not necessarily traceable only in either Chinese or Scandinavian culture.

Inter-cultural interaction, or inter-cultural communication, is used synonymously, and primarily implies face-to-face interaction[2] between individuals from at least two cultures, including the use of interpreters. When relevant to the operation of Scandinavian firms in China, inter-relationships between Chinese are also discussed, even though this does not imply face-to-face interaction in relation to expatriates. Also, inter-cultural interaction is viewed as a process during which both parties are expected to change over time, more or less as a result of the interaction.

Managerial functions imply the traditional functions addressed in management literature, such as planning, organizing, human resource management, control, etc. However, only those aspects mostly effected by cultural differences are discussed. Other aspects, such as marketing strategy and product adaptation, are not included.

Inter-cultural management implies management involving individuals from at least two cultures, meaning that managers must function together with other managers or employees from different cultures, which makes inter-cultural communication decisive.

Research Issues

The analysis focuses on cultural specific differences between Chinese and Scandinavian managers at the personal level, and examines how differences in interpersonal relationships effect selected aspects of managerial functions in firms fully or partly owned by Scandinavians. Though the major concern of this book is the effect of cultural specific aspects on interpersonal relationships, this does not imply that cultural elements have greater impact than other, such as situational factors, when establishing interpersonal relationships between managers in firms, or management in general, but only that culture is one of the relevant factors deserving appropriate attention when studying interpersonal relationships and management.[3] On the other hand, cross-cultural and inter-cultural studies do not use culture to explain everything. They often include social and political factors to clarify major differences (Adler, 1983:40). What characterizes cross- and inter-cultural studies is that they include more than one culture.

There are multiple cultural differences between Scandinavians and Chinese, but only the most important are discussed in this book. The criteria for selecting those issues analyzed here have been partly determined by secondary literature on the two cultures, and partly the collected empirical data. Since the interviews started with open-ended questions in order to identify what the respondents perceived as the most pronounced behavioral differences between Chinese and Scandinavian managers, the interviewees were in a position to influence the remaining part of the interview.

Political differences, in particular, as well as occasional social differences between Scandinavians and Chinese, will be included in the analysis to the extent this is considered necessary. Other general factors, which may affect interpersonal relationships and managerial functions, will not be treated systematically but only mentioned to make the reader aware of the impact of other significant factors. Hicks and Redding predict that the scope of culture's impact on organizations will never be resolved, since this impact is almost impossible to test. They suggest rather focusing on applicability: 'we ask not whether a particular theoretical position is correct or incorrect, but how useful it is in explaining observed phenomena' (Hicks & Redding, 1983:20).

This book is not only concerned with explaining certain phenomena, but also with the possibility of predicting Scandinavian and

Chinese managers' behaviour in connection with inter-cultural interaction, based on values and practices in the two cultures. If reactions
are predictable, it will become increasingly possible to make reservations and plan actions in a way which takes into consideration certain
reactions. It is the assumption in this book that interaction with members of an alien culture presupposes understanding the background for
their pattern of reaction. The strongest proponent of the influence of
national culture on interpersonal relationships and management is
Hofstede (*Culture's Consequences*, published in 1980 and in an abbreviated version in 1984, followed by *Cultures and Organizations* in 1991).

Hofstede's research

One of the reasons for taking Hofstede's work as a point of departure
is that his empirical data are the most exhaustive ever used in a cross-
cultural study. His study is based on no less than 117,000 responses
from approx. 88,000 respondents, all employed in the multinational
IBM corporation. Some were interviewed twice (Hofstede, 1984:46).
Another reason is that Hofstede reduced the countless cultural differences to five dimensions covering half the variance in his data which is
worth noting. Half of the identified cultural differences are characteristic of the individual cultural area or fall outside the defined dimensions. His works comprise 53 countries and in recent years he has
included socialist countries and Eastern Europe. Thus, China was not
included in his original study.

Hoftede's study has been criticized for only including respondents
from one multinational corporation, the American IBM. Thus, a certain social imbalance cannot be excluded, but in this context it is more
important that the respondents' corporate culture is identical.
Therefore, it is rather to be assumed that the study underestimates
rather than overestimates the national cultural differences.

Before turning to the individual dimensions, it should be emphasized that they refer to values. Hofstede (1991:263) defines values as
'broad tendencies to prefer certain states of affairs over others'. Thus,
referring to Hofstede's definition of culture, values entail mental inclinations which, all else being equal, are reflected in corresponding inclinations to demonstrate certain behavioural patterns. Hofstede has later
added yet a dimension to reduce the Western focus of his study. The
fifth dimension is based on a Chinese Value Survey, taking as its point

of departure behavioural patterns in East Asia (cf. long-term versus short-term time perspective). The five dimensions are:

Individualism Versus Collectivism[4]

Individualism pertains to societies with loose ties between individuals. Every one is expected to take care of himself and his immediate family. In contrast, collectivism pertains to societies in which people from the moment they are born and for the rest of their lives are integrated into cohesive in-groups, which throughout their lives protect them in return for unconditional loyalty.

In this book, this dimension is further divided into universalism and particularism. In individualist cultures the norm is that everybody must be treated as equals (universalism), whereas the norm of collectivist societies is to treat members of in-groups better then others (particularism). In effect, collectivist cultures are more inclined than individualist cultures to show friends and acquaintances special consideration, leading to the paradox that in collectivist cultures it is more important than in individualist cultures to know whom one is in contact with in order give him or her particular treatment.

Power Distance

Power distance is defined as the extent to which weaker members of institutions and organizations in a country expect and accept unequal distribution of power. Hofstede's notion of institutions implies basic elements in society, such as family, school, and local community. Organizations are places where people work. Power distance can range from great to small. Power distance explains relationships of emotional dependence in a culture.

Masculinity Versus Femininity

Masculinity pertains to societies with very distinct patterns of sexual roles. In masculine cultures, men are expected to be self-assured, 'tough', competitive and focused on material success and performance; women are expected to be modest, 'soft', cooperative, considerate and interested in quality of life.

Femininity pertains to societies with overlapping patterns of sexual roles. Both men and women are expected to be modest, 'soft' and interested in quality of life. In masculine societies children learn to admire the strong ones, and in feminine to sympathize with the weak.

Uncertainty Avoidance
Uncertainty avoidance can be defined as the extent to which members
of a culture feel threatened in uncertain and unknown situations. This
feeling is, among other things, manifested in a need for predictability,
a need for written and unwritten rules (Hofstede, 1991:121). That a
people feel a need for rules does not necessarily imply they feel they
have to comply with the rules.

Long-term Versus Short-term Time Perspective
Characteristic of a long-term life perspective are persistence (persever-
ance), ordering of relationships according to status and observing this
order, as well as thrift, and having sense of shame.

The opposite pole, short-term life perspective, is characterized by
personal steadiness and stability, protecting one's 'face', respecting traditions, reciprocate greetings, favours and presents. This pole is oriented toward the present and the past, whereas a long-term life perspective is oriented toward the future.

The problem of undertaking applicable comparative culture studies
of two such different cultures as the Chinese and the Scandinavian is
that, at first, everything seems to be different. Hofstede's dimensions
can be applied to create an overview. On the other hand, Hofstede's
dimensions are too general to function as the framework for a country
specific comparative study, as the crystallization and effect of the identical position on a certain dimension will sometimes differ from country to country. One consequence of Hofstede's theory is that firms are
viewed as carriers of national cultures in almost the same way as individuals. To the extent that culture plays a role in management, it plays
an even greater role in inter-cultural management consisting of persons
from different cultures.

Geographic Delimitation

Cultural areas and countries are recurrent themes in this book.[5]
'Chinese culture' in a geographic sense only covers the People's
Republic of China, since the empirical data do not include overseas
Chinese. Nevertheless, the reader will find references to Chinese cul-
tural area, because some secondary literature is based on studies which

include overseas Chinese, especially in Hong Kong, Taiwan and Singapore.

Chinese culture is known for its homogeneity, and China is the world's oldest existing nation which justifies talking about this culture at a particular level of abstraction. Though the Chinese are very homogeneous, they are in general very parochial. 92% of the population in China are ethnic Han Chinese.[6]

The other culture, the Scandinavian, covers Denmark, Norway, Sweden and Finland, the total area and population of which are far smaller than China. Here too, it is justifiable to talk about a relatively homogeneous culture.

As will be demonstrated in chapters 2 and 3, at a certain level of abstraction it is justifiable to use Chinese culture interchangeably with the nation China, just as it is justifiable to talk about a Scandinavian culture pervading the Scandinavian countries mentioned above.

Type of Study

This inter-cultural study is a critical diagnosticating study (Andersen & Gamstrup, 1994:42), which resembles a doctor's diagnosis and subsequent suggestions for treatment. The study is not referred to as change oriented, since the suggestions for improving conditions are not focused on a specific firm, nor are they to be applied systematically to a given project.

The study is characterized as inter-cultural because, contrary to cross-cultural studies, which typically compare different cultures, it focuses on the interaction between actors from two different cultures, and the primary aim it not to compare these. Interaction being central to this study, it is practical to divide culture into several layers which mutually effect one another. Cultural values are more consistent than superficial practices, which are often adopted from other cultures.

Variables

This study views culture, i.e. primary cultural values, as the independent variable. Dependent variables are phenomena affected by cultural values and practices, that are in part interpersonal relationships and in part the organizational and managerial activities of the firm.

Figure 1.1 illustrates the relationships between the variables:

Figure 1.1 The relationship between variables

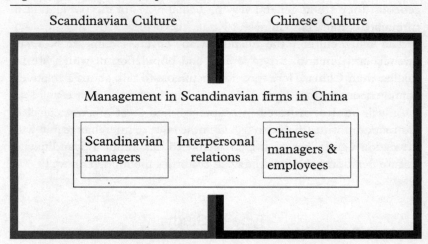

Having decided to focus on fully or partly owned Scandinavian firms which are physically located in China signifies that managers and employees represent both cultural areas, which has an impact on how managerial functions are conducted (see Figure 1.1). In keeping with this, Tayeb emphasizes that, apart from responding to their environment, organizations are also restricted by the cultural characteristics of the organizational members (Tayeb, 1988:5). Figure 1.1 illustrates the significance of the environment in that from a cultural perspective the firms are placed in two cultures. This also applies to firms fully owned by Scandinavians. The physical location in China and the fact that the majority of employees are Chinese will have an impact on Scandinavian firms toward becoming 'Chinese'.

Method

In a broad sense, method is a way of approaching things, or a way of attempting to realize one's goals. It comprises how data are collected and subsequently processed (Gullestrup, 1992:160).

Firms

The study comprises twenty-one firms of which nineteen have been visited, and in two of the latter I interviewed representatives of the firms' board members in Beijing and Hong Kong. Of the twenty-one firms, nineteen were registered as joint ventures. Another one was actually a joint venture, but since the Chinese partner had invested through his subsidiary in Hong Kong, the firm was not registered as such. Finally, one firm was fully owned by Scandinavians but had originally started as a joint venture (GN-Danavox, Xiamen). Thus, formally twenty firms were joint ventures. In one of these the Scandinavian partner owned 95% of the firm, and the Chinese did not interfere with the management. The firm had originally been a 50/50 joint venture, but the Chinese had withdrawn because they found the firm's yield deficient. For practical reasons, such as conditions of employment and renting factory premises, the Chinese had kept 5%. Of the twenty-one firms, sixteen operated within the production sector and five within the service sector (two hotels, two consultancies, and a transportation firm). Since I have not found any systematic variation in responses from the two sectors, I will not be indicating to which sector the respondents quoted belong. Thirteen of the firms had only one expatriate, and only three firms had more than one expatriate, two within the service sector and one within the production sector. Five had no expatriates when I visited them, but had earlier had expatriates for more than a year.

Respondents

The study includes forty-four interviews of which forty were taped. Twelve Chinese and twenty-eight Scandinavians were interviewed, four of the latter twice.

The majority of the twenty-three Western expatriate respondents had been in China for more than two years.[7] Most of the respondents quoted throughout the book have lived in China for more than two years, and when new expatriates or board members are quoted, this is stated specifically. Five board members, who have not lived permanently in China, have been interviewed.

Focusing on expatriates who have been in China for a longer period should outweigh the fact that new expatriates are often uncertain about what is going on. Statements from board members not living in China have been ascribed less importance since they cannot know the country as well as expatriates.

As to the Chinese respondents, all interviews were conducted in Chinese, and by and large they were all seconded by the Chinese partner in the joint venture, a state owned firm.

Transcribing Tapes

The taped interviews were transcribed, a time consuming process further complicated by the fact that twelve of the interviews were in Chinese. The interviews in Chinese were transcribed in Chinese and only quotes from these have been translated.

Subsequently, data were ordered thematically in order to facilitate comparisons of statements on identical subjects, and to identify common traits or patterns in the statements that might constitute a basis for more general assertions about the manifest culture.

The Analytical Process

The data analysis falls in two parts, interpretation and comparison.

The interpretation process

Based on the respondents answers to which cultural specific difference in behaviour they found in representatives of the two cultures, these differences and their consequences were analyzed comparatively. The type of interpretation applied here is intended to deduce general patterns from investigations of sequences of events. This implies that the researcher attempts to abstract from the unique situational traits by constructing 'ideal types' of anonymous sequences of actions and events. Concretely, this means that in the few cases where the answers did not fit into the general pattern, they were omitted. However this oonly applies to a few cases.

The conclusion aims to construct a holistic picture of the sub-conclusions, assuming that cultural characteristics affect one another, i.e., represent a system.

Based on the results of these open-ended interviews, the subjects to be analyzed were determined by a combination of the interview-guide, and what the respondents found to be the most important cultural differences.

The comparison process

In order to elaborate on the analysis and to suggest improvements, the respondents' statements are subsequently interpreted as sensemaking expressions, which in part show their perception of the other culture, and in part reflect their own cultural values.

On aspects where the answers by respondents from one culture differ from those of the other, these answers are compared in order to emphasize differences. In a study of this nature, it is justifiable to focus on differences, since the precondition for improving collaboration is to recognize differences. However, it should be noted that this approach gives a somewhat distorted picture of reality, since it underestimates similarities.

No attempt has been made to compare statements from respondents representing the same firm, since the purpose has not been to include firm or industry specific conditions. In addition, only a few mirror interviews have been conducted.

Finally, it should be mentioned that, in general, the Chinese were unable to distinguish between Scandinavians and Europeans, but tended to contrast Europeans with Americans and Japanese, which reflects their contacts so far.

The Structure of the Book

Chapter 2 is a general description of Chinese culture, which is meant as a background for the specific cultural differences discussed in the chapters 5 to 10. Chapter 2 concludes with an overview of the most relevant aspects of Chinese politics and management. Chapter 3 is a brief summary of the general aspects of Scandinavian culture. Like the previous chapter, the purpose of Chapter 3 is to provide a basis for discussing cultural differences between Scandinavia and China. Both chapters are based on secondary literature covering the two cultures and drawing on earlier studies and synoptical works.

Chapter 4 is a comparison of the two cultures, based on the differences identified in the two previous chapters. These comparisons only include dimensions into which both cultures can be fitted. Chapters 2 to 4 constitute the background for deriving certain phenomena which govern the presentation of the data collected in chapters 5 to 10.

Chapters 5 to 8 concentrate on various aspects affecting interpersonal relationships. In Chapter 5, aspects related to personalization are addressed. Chapter 6 treats networking and similar phenomena, and Chapter 7 discusses the concept of face. Chapter 8 focuses on the two cultural perspectives on time and related issues.

Chapter 9 and 10 concentrate on those aspects of management which are most affected by cultural differences. In Chapter 9, selected managerial processes in the firms are discussed, and in Chapter 10, selected aspects of managerial and organizational structures are considered. These chapters are in part based on how the individual aspects discussed in chapters 5 to 8 interact, and in part based on the respondents' statements about specific managerial aspects. Each of the chapters 5 to 10 are supplemented with a series of recommendation for Scandinavian expatriates.

Chapter 11 summarizes the most important results from the previous chapters and presents a model for optimal interaction between representatives of the two cultures. In continuation, the project's limitations and ideas for further studies are discussed. In a concluding section, the results from the study are put into perspective.

Recommendations

Recommendations on how to improve both interpersonal relationships and the handling of managerial functions are made based on analyses of the respondents' answers to questions within the two areas and, not least, by subjecting the answers to cross-analyses, both within and between the two levels analyzed. Thus the respondents' responses to interpersonal relationships also affect the way in which managerial functions are handled.

There are two different reasons for these recommendations, since interpersonal relationships are rather studied as a process in which two parties over time develop certain attitudes toward one another, whereas managerial functions basically are studied in view of the expatriates' comparisons with managerial forms in Scandinavia, and the Chinese comparisons with managerial forms in state owned firms in China.

Figure 1.2 Structure of the book

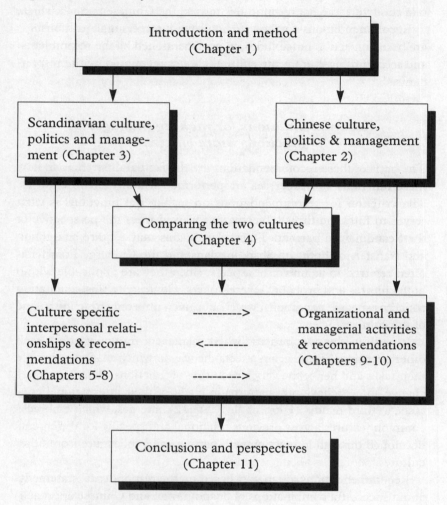

Recommendations for interpersonal relationships

The basis of recommendations for interpersonal relationships is what counteracts clashes and promotes cooperation between representatives of the two cultures. Taking into consideration how the relationships between the two parties have developed thus far, the question is to what extent expatriates should adapt to local traditions, and how they can actually do it. It is a process during which expatriates develop certain positive and negative attitudes toward the Chinese and vice versa.

Recommendations for how to improve interpersonal relationships are based on action possibilities, in part mentioned by the respondents, and in part derived from the cultural clashes recounted by the respondents.

Recommendations for making managerial functions more efficient

The basis of these recommendations are the factual differences in how these functions and processes are performed within the two cultures. The criterion for recommendations on managerial functions is what serves to fulfil the firms' objectives as viewed from the perspective of the Scandinavian partner. To start with, this may require adaptation and transfer for both the Scandinavians and the Chinese. Transfer is often referred to as universal aspects, since they are applicable within both cultures and probably several others. Contrary to this, adaptation concerns specific conditions, which at a given time only function in one of the cultures.

In reality, this is a process where managers mutually affect each other over time, which again affects the way in which managers handle their tasks and hence the very structuring of functions. Since managers change some behavioural patterns in effect of their international contacts, a 'third reality' (Hjort et al., 1993:12) emerges, which embraces common features across previous tractional and specific local elements developed through interaction with partners and colleagues from other cultures.

Recommendations are in part based on the respondents' statements about successful combinations of Scandinavian and Chinese approaches to management, and in part on an analysis of the causes of the managerial problems described by the respondents.

2. Chinese Culture, Politics, and Management

Introduction

To understand intercultural relationships and how they affect organizations one must understand the basic elements of such relationships. One of these basic elements is the Chinese character and their cultural disposition.

All people's behaviour is culturally determined, and cultures vary which is why North Europeans often find it difficult to acquaint themselves with what it means to be Han-Chinese, and what is meant by the Chinese tradition. Similarly, it is difficult for the Chinese to understand what it means to be Scandinavian.

The point of departure is thus to describe the basic values and belief structures, beginning with those of Confucianism and continuing with a description of the social structures and rules governing relationships. Finally, the rules governing interpersonal behaviour shall be addressed.

For a discussion of the background for the concrete aspects addressed in the empirically based chapters, I refer to chapters 5 to 8. Political and managerial conditions are discussed to a certain extent as well. No attempts will be made to provide a general overview of all value aspects of the Chinese culture. Only issues relevant for understanding and being able to relate to Chinese organizational behaviour will be addressed.

The Genesis of the Chinese Culture

China is the world's oldest nation. Since the country was first united around the year 200 B.C., it has never been totally dissolved. Nor has it been occupied by Western powers, which is why the country's culture is continual, homogeneous, and strong, thus distinguishing it from all other cultures. At the same time, Chinese society has always been deeply stratified, which has led to discussions about the big and the little tradition.

Even though tradition plays a central part, Chinese culture has witnessed vast changes during the last couple of decades, at least in the more superficial layers. An in-depth study of the Chinese tradition is a life-long project with the first traditions in Chinese history dating back to around year 2,700 B.C. China is also that county in the world which has the most voluminous written traditions, partly due to the fact that the Chinese mastered the art of printing 600 years before Gutenberg (Redding, 1990:47).

The Chinese wrote down their history for didactic reason: they wanted to learn from history. Chinese culture is retrospective. It draws wisdom from stories about legendary characters in former times. These stories were compiled for the first time by China's greatest philosopher, Confucius. Thus, the Chinese culture is fundamentally rather conservative (Eberhard, 1967).

The continuity of Chinese culture is maintable partly due to the fact that contemporary Chinese have no difficulties reading works that are 2,000 years old, because the written language has not changed much. In effect, the classical works, and hence the passing on of old values, play a much more central part in China than in the West.

Confucianism

The role and position of Confucianism is comparable to that of Christianity in Scandinavia, except for one great difference. Originally, Confucianism was not a religion and thus lacks an institutional structure, such as churches, priests, and ceremonies.[1] Since Confucianism is the dominant philosophical school in China, and is central to the Chinese in general and to their behaviour in particular, the most important aspects of this philosophy will be addressed below.

It is difficult, perhaps even impossible, to define Confucianism unequivocally, as the maxims and statements attributed to Confucius have been subject to various interpretations throughout history.[2] Viewed from the perspective of cultural history, Confucianism is temporal. It contains no divine or mystic origin. It focuses on the secular. Western religious higher powers have been replaced by detailed rules for interpersonal behaviour. Confucianism deals with what to do in this world and not with what one believes. In this respect, it goes very well with Capitalism.

Confucius (551 – 479 B.C.) was a common man who did not view himself as the founder of a philosophy, rather as the transmitter of the existent harmonious philosophy said to have dominated China origi- nally. Some 2,500 years ago, Confucius took his ideals from the leg- endary kings of that time, but his ideas still have a strong influence on the Chinese.

Confucianism has often been called the philosophy of those in power, as it primarily dwells on how to rule the country. It prescribes the behaviour of a good ruler and how the subjects must obey that ruler. Historically, emphasis has been on the latter.

Another characteristic of Confucianism is its emphasis on ethics, which has had a great impact on the Chinese people. Even though its influence has varied during different historical periods, it has, to a cer- tain extent, influenced the total Chinese hierarchy, from the emperor via the family system to the single individual. Man is viewed as a social being whose identity is determined by his position in relation to others in a network of social relationships. Literally translated, the Chinese word for 'wrong' (budui) means 'not a couple'. The individual can only be understood in relation to others (Sun, 1991:2-3).

This collectivist aspect places the community above the individual and is central to discussions of the wisdom and applicability of Confucianism in the 1990s. The principle of the individual's obligation to comply with society is the very opposite of modern individualism.

The most salient feature of Confucianism is its accentuation of the five relationships between man, viewed as the basic element of social stability, i.e., the relationships between ruler/subject, father/son, older/younger brother, husband/wife, and between friends. Most peo- ple interpret these relationships as unequal, implying that the latter in each relationship must obey the former, but they are reciprocal. The father must love his son to be worthy of his son's obedience.

As the ruler in his behaviour and virtues was to be the model for his subjects, one can deduce inversely that if the population did not behave properly, it was because the ruler was a poor model. Fundamentally, the system is thus 'government by man', and not an institutionalization of power as in the West.

It is remarkable that many interpretations of these relationships cat- egorize the latter four as family relations in that friends are perceived as individuals who can be taken into the family – 'family friends' (Lin 1989:170). Some scholars emphasize that all five are to be interpreted as family-like relations, since the nature of the relationship with the ruler is the same as that with the father (Fung, 1996:21). No matter whether Confucius viewed just the four, or all five relationships as family-like, they indicate something about the foundation of personalization discussed in *Personalization* page 48.

Confucianism's strain of ethics

Lin Yutang says that Confucius 'forgot' to define the relationship between man and the stranger (Lin 1989:185). Well, it is not that he forgot, just that in a world defined according to family relations, there was no need to consider such relationships. In the words of Confucius: 'Those who love their parents dare not show hatred to others. Those who respect their parents, dare not show rudeness to others.' (Lin, 1989:171).

From the above, it is evident that Confucianism is based on strong ethics as opposed to Western rationalism. Some scholars have described this as the most important difference between the Western and the Chinese concept of the state. The Confucian state was a 'super-family' whereas the Western was an abstraction, a universal idea (Redding, 1990:44).

Ethics was thus more important than power, though it was considered that virtue, and the public manifestation of virtue, would result in power. In continuation of this, correct behaviour was more important than efficiency, which can be witnessed in China to this day, (e.g., the discussion about 'red' or 'expert' in the 1960s and early 1970s).

Nobody ever succeeded in establishing such an ethical relationship or to restrain powers throughout most of China's long history, which is why the Chinese state has enjoyed unlimited power over the individual. Confucianism seems to be excessively idealistic. Hamilton (1984:411) explains the difference between the Western and the Confucian state by indicating that the Western state developed a legal system stipulating a framework for individual freedom without prescribing individual behaviour.

The Confucian state, on the other hand, concentrated on making the population understand prescribed behavioural rules and hence demonstrating self-discipline.

The result led not only to far more narrow restrictions on individual opportunities for self-expression, but combined with a group based social system, this ideology often implied that not only was the family of lawbreakers, or 'breakers of ethics', punished but also their neighbours who had neglected their obligation to improve these people's manners and watch over the 'lost'.

The Communists often applied a modified version of the same principles by depriving the spouse and children of a lawbreaker to lose their possibilities for education. On the other hand, a family member's extraordinary efforts resulted in proudness and higher status for the entire family, not just the one in question. The point here is to emphasize the immense pressures to conform in Chinese society.

The idea was that people were supposed to be attentive to what others thought about their behaviour. The purpose of life was to fill one's place, meaning to comply with the environment's expectations rather than realize oneself or achieve inner salvation. This compliance is a key concept in Confucianism. The ruler governed the country and his subjects were not in a position to make demands. This is one of the aspects that contemporary Chinese scholars criticize since many wish to promote commercial initiatives among the Chinese.[3]

The Chinese are often characterized as passive and fatalistic which, to a certain extent, stems from the Confucian doctrine of filling one's place. Yet, it has always been possible to reach the top of the pyramid by passing the imperial examinations. As the costs involved in such projects demanded the total excess income from the average middle class family, only a few had the means to let their sons pursue this route to the top.

The Confucian tradition strongly emphasized what in modern language is called status. The word, which in Chinese is 'mingfen', is a combination of the words 'name' and 'duty'. A name is a designation assigning to the individual his place in society and hence defining his relationship to others. Therefore, the individual must know his place, or position, in society in order to behave concordantly, which is why the Chinese tend to perceive what we call status as something natural.

The original Confucianism did not commit itself to whether man by nature was good or evil, even though the issue was raised, and scholars have compared the dispute between Mencius and Xunzi about the nature of man two thousand years ago with the discussion in Europe between Freud and Maslow (Lin, 1988). Ng (1990:317) says that according to many Confucians, human nature is 'plastic'. What is more decisive is the emphasis on the preconditions required in order for man to be able to behave right: proper training, resulting in a tendency to emphasize 'cultivation' or disciplinary education.

The purpose of education was to improve man's moral character, which historically was done by learning the classical works by heart. In traditional China, a relationship between education and science was never established.

Confucianism's classification of the population

The population was classified either as the learned (junzi), or those who had not acquired knowledge of the classical works (xiaoren), which literally translated means 'petty man'. What distinguishes these two groups from one another is, according to Confucius, their moral character. 'Great Man is conscious only of justice; petty Man only of self-interest.' (Legge, 1994:Analects 170).

The learned have always been admired, and according to the Confucian tradition they were to rule the others, but by and large everybody had the right to sit for the imperial examinations and hence had the possibility of becoming learned and subsequently a public servant. China has no tradition of hereditary aristocracy.

Confucianism divides society into four classes according to their social status: Scholars, Farmers, Artisans, and Merchants of which the latter is the lowest class (Lin, 1989:182). Merchants are a broad category of people including all those who do not belong to the other classes.

Contemporary Confucianism

To achieve higher status, a Chinese merchant, or firm owner, will often pretend to be learned. He will often refer to himself as a Confucianist, even though most of them only have a superficial knowledge of the Confucian classics, and their way of living differs from traditional Confucian values (Redding, 1990:Ch. 8). Confucianism looks down on business people who view Confucianism as being superior to other philosophical traditions, which indicates they strong postion of Confucianism even today.

Until 1979, Confucianism was blamed for China not having been industrialized, yet since 1979 it has been credited for the current industrialization of China (see *In-groups* page 47). In this context, Tu Wei-ming emphasizes that the Confucianism referred to today has incorporated some Western practices, such as competition, autonomy, and certain individual rights. Thus, it is a synthesis of Western practices and classical Confucian values such as conscientiousness, personal development, and discipline.[4]

It is noteworthy that for two thousand years, Confucianism has praised the art of government and looked down on commercial activities, because Chinese both inside and outside China have done well commercially, whereas attempts to modernize the political system have failed. The system is still dependent on single individuals. This puts Confucianism into perspective as one can probably say that Confucianism as political ideology is incompatible with a modern political system, since it is based on 'state ethics' that requires a high degree of consensus among the population, a consensus which is absent in a modern fragmented society.

Thus, only some of the Confucian values, not the entire Confucian system, are relevant to understanding contemporary China.

Key concepts

Confucianism has a series of key concepts such as the five virtues[5], but only those of particular relevance to commercial activities are mentioned here. Confucianism, and Taoism for that matter, is built around the concept Tao 'the way'. In his translation of the four classical Confucian works, James Legge writes: 'It occurs everywhere with a moral application, meaning the way or course to be pursued, the path of reason, of principle, of truth, etc.' (Legge, 1994:579).

Another key concept of Confucian philosophy is harmony, which some scholars interpret as the concept superior to all other concepts (Westwood, 1992:49). In modern times, harmony refers to appearance rather than essence. 'Ren' means human, or benevolence. The sign is a combination of the sign for 'human beings' and that for 'two'. Man only becomes human when he enters into social relationships. What leads from 'ren' to action is 'li', civilized behaviour. This means that one is capable of assessing the situation correctly and acting in accordance.

The original sense of the word was to act according to the rituals, but gradually it has come to signify that one is capable of showing appropriate behaviour.[6] 'Xin' means keeping one's word, or being reliable, which is also decisive in commercial relationships (Redding, 1990:67-68). Finally, there is 'bao' which translates into reciprocity, meaning a favour must be reciprocated to maintain harmonious relationships. 'Bao' can also be negative reciprocity, such as the necessity to revenge injustice (Yang, 1987:21).

Other Philosophical Schools

Traditional and often extremely stratified societies, are often divided philosophically in a 'big tradition' and a 'little tradition', a concept borrowed from anthropology. The big tradition, political Confucianism, is first and foremost the philosophy of those in power, but through its ideas about the family it has influenced every Chinese.

However, Confucianism never enjoyed societal monopoly. The 'little tradition', which in terms of ideas is much more mixed, was originally the peasant's philosophy. They tried to maintain a reasonable life and a good income by ensuring security for themselves and their successors. The most important schools of the 'little tradition' in this context are Taoism, Buddhism, and Legalism. Historically and politically, the 'little tradition' has tended towards manifesting itself in opposition to the big tradition. As the saying goes, which became popular under Communism: 'The Government has its politics, we have our countermeasures.'[7]

China's other great political philosophy, the Legalistic school, had a different attitude toward the nature of man. Confucianism emphasized moral honesty, whereas Legalism emphasized reward and punishment. Thus, Legalism emphasizes control and clear rules with which the population must comply. When they did, they were to be rewarded, and when not, punished.

Confucianism did not consider the nature of man whereas the other philosophical schools tended mainly to view the human nature negatively, i.e., man is an egoistic materialist. This is understandable given the Confucian public servants' exploitation of morality to serve their own purposes. Another old saying often quoted in China runs like this: 'If one leans against the mountain, it topples down; if one leans against the river, it dries out.' The conclusion is that one can only lean against oneself and one's family.

The 'little tradition' did not look down on trade as classical Confucianism did. On the contrary, it emphasized material wealth, social stability, and operated with a relatively short time perspective, something which has characterized business relationships in Hong

Kong for a number of years and is currently spreading throughout China. China is a commercial nation. Few other societies are more alien to Socialist planned economy than the Chinese. As soon as they are set free, their spirit of entrepreneurship materializes as we have witnessed in other parts of Asia.

Religions

Historically, China has been dominated by Taoism and Buddhism, two religions that do not view one another as opposites. More importantly, religion has always played a minor role in Chinese life. The Chinese are often said to be less religious, and more superstitious. What is referred to here as superstition, (beliefs in the meanings of certain colours, numbers, directions, etc.), is of crucial import to most Chinese, even though we have gradually accustomed ourselves to Communist disavowing superstition. However, concurrent with the new religious liberty in China, we will witness a return to the superstitions of former times. Taiwan and Singapore are good examples of this.

Fatalism has been an important feature of Chinese superstition, which has made people passive, though it seems to be on the decline, at least among people of higher education (Tan, 1990:282-283). However, the common Chinese, both in China and in Hong Kong, is still a fatalist. In connection with interpersonal relationships, in the sense 'fates meet', the original Buddhist expression 'karma' (Chinese: 'yuan') is often used.[8]

The foundation of Confucianism was that everybody occupied a well-defined place in society, which also contributed to the strong sense of fatalism. The Chinese still refer to 'fate' more often than Scandinavians. Nevertheless, it would be a mistake to view the Chinese belief in fate as absolutely deterministic. One's fortune may change for better or for worse. Fate has often been employed as an intellectual post-rationalization in making sense of having to live a wretched life.

The Chinese have always tried to improve their lives to the best of their abilities. As mentioned earlier, a European sense of aristocracy has never existed in China, so in principle even the poorest could obtain high positions, both under the traditional system through imperial examination, and later through being a member of the Communist Party.[9]

The Family

The most central institution in the Chinese tradition and society is the family. Apart from being the most important social unit, it was the model for the entire structure of society. The most important relation is that between a father and his son, and second that between the older and the younger brother. The least important family relationship is that between husband and wife, which explains a great deal about the woman's role. According to Confucius, 'filial piety is the basis of virtue, and the origin of culture.'(Lin, 1989:171).

A person is not primarily an individual but a member of the family. The Chinese starts by being his parents child, and as life passes he takes on commitments to his own family, his wife's family, and his friends. Lin (1989:172), who wrote his book in the early 1930s, called the family a genuine Communist unit in China with the principle 'do what you can and take what you need'.

The family is perceived as the most important stabilising factor in society, and various welfare arrangements are thus left to the family. One explanation is the size of China and its centralized government. Chinese who lived far from the capital had practically no contact with the state.

It is a general custom in China that members of the family hand over their income to the family. The act is not particularly commendable, but taken for granted, which is why nepotism is an intrinsic part of the Chinese tradition. It is stated in the Chinese constitution that adult children are responsible for caring for and supporting their parents when they can no longer take care of themselves. Old people's homes are exclusively for those without children.

The only support in the life of Chinese is the family. This explains why it has been impossible for many Chinese to accept the one child policy. If this one child was a daughter, there would be nobody to support them and care for them in their old age, and when the parents were gone, the daughter would be alone in the world.

A country's language often reflects important phenomena. The Chinese language probably contains the world's richest vocabulary for describing family relations. As an example, there are different words for cousins, depending on whether they are from the father's or the mother's side.

The family and economic growth

The family pattern is often viewed as a function of economic development, i.e., higher levels of economic development lead to smaller families (the nuclear family) and to higher degrees of individualism, which in the sociology of the family is often referred to as functional draining. In general, this development pattern is true, and the extended family in the physical sense is also disappearing in the big cities, but so far it has not changed significantly in the Chinese countryside. This is not the same as saying that the family in China has not changed at all. Both the father-son axis and the parent's influence on their children's choice of spouse have been weakened. But the emotional ties, which in China are mainly expressed in economic ties and other forms of help between family members, do not appear to have weakened. This shows that the form of the family may change without affecting the underlying value, i.e., spirit of solidarity, at least in the short run. This applies to the family as well as other phenomena of a deeper structure.

As early as 1979, Herman Kahn used the concept 'neo-Confucian ethics' to explain the dynamic economic growth in the Far East. He emphasized the following characteristics: 'Socialization within the family unit and the way it promotes (a) sobriety; (b) education; (c) the acquisition of skills, (d) seriousness about tasks, job, family and obligations.'[10] As the citation demonstrates, he ascribes a decisive role to the family. His argument is an oversimplification, but it gives reason to emphasize the dominant role of kinship in China. Without discussing the conditions for economic development in depth, it should be mentioned that when China, as opposed to other Chinese communities, did not become dynamic until the 1980s, it was probably due to the fact that a market did not exist until then for the exchange of production goods.

Aside from resting on traditional values, the family in contemporary China must be viewed in an economic context. In addition, in the People's Republic of China, as opposed to other Chinese societies, women continue to work, and young couples thus need the grandparents to look after their child. Thus, where the extended family still exists, it is probably just as much the young ones who choose to continue this traditional way of living, whereas many elderly people would not mind living by themselves. However, an increasing number of Chinese prefer living in nuclear families.

Even though the family appears to be a harmonious unit on the surface, members often lead a cat-and-dog life, and many of the young wives would like to move away from their husband's parents if the housing situation made it possible. The Chinese tendency to feel jealous and their reluctance to resolve conflicts openly make internal strife unavoidable. In addition to this, prior to the 1990s premarital contacts were very limited and condemned socially. There are few empirical studies of marital relations in China, but it is symptomatic that the art is full of stories about unhappy marriages. The best known examples in the Western world are Zhang Yimou's films 'Ju Dou', 'The Red Lanterns', and 'To Live'.

However, during the 1980s it has become easier to obtain divorce, which is in line with the general tendency of the state to interfere less in people's private lives. The above description of the family and its material basis makes it evident that Chinese managers' incentive structures differ from those of Scandinavian managers. The prospect of getting a larger apartment often motivates managers to make an extra effort.

Respect for age

Within the family, and in society in general, age is of decisive import which is an almost logical consequence of the retrospective philosophy of Confucianism. Wisdom is drawn from the past, not through development. The significance of age is reflected in the two dominant roles in any Chinese family: the oldest man in the family is head of the family (jiazhang), meaning the family's formal representative to the outside world, and is 'the family director' (dangjia), organizing the family and its finances. In small families, the father occupies both roles, but as he gets older, one of his sons gradually takes over the role as 'family director', usually the oldest one (Cohen, 1991:116). In today's China, the latter is sometimes a woman who thus controls the family's finances.

When the state started to change the seniority hierarchy in the 1980s, the older managers and party secretaries strongly opposed this initiative, as the wage system was based on seniority exclusively. The purpose of the reform was to recruit younger and technically better qualified persons for managerial positions in the large firms and to make those above 55 retire (Henley, & Nyaw, 1990:283-284). Even though factory managers today, particularly in firms with foreign capital, are in general in their forties, the firms still hold the old 'masters' in respect. Furthermore, in China formal positions do not always entail real power.

Family owned firms

The significant position of the family in Chinese society meant that extended families competed for appropriating as many of society's resources as possible, which again meant pronounced rivalry between families. One family tried to get rich at the expense of another, which has been called the Chinese 'magnified selfishness' (Lin, 1989:164), as opposed to the social commitment characterizing Scandinavian societies.

Chinese firms tend to be small. Rather than building up large firms that can handle the total production process, the Chinese contract work out to other family firms using middlemen, which makes trade more important than management (Redding, 1990:138)[11] Traditional Chinese firms, including private firms owned by Chinese both inside and outside China, are typically centred around the family. Important positions in the firms are occupied by members of the family as they are the only ones in whom one trusts. The manager of the firm, who is usually also the owner, behaves paternalistically and didactically towards his employees.[12]

Traditional Chinese management style has been called didactic because the manager uses information as power, whereby he gradually leaks information to his subordinates thus making them dependent on him. Chinese managers are typically autocratic, tending to prevent others further down the hierarchy from making visible personal efforts which might indicate the possession of managerial abilities. The Chinese management style is based on clear authoritarian traits. The manager's personal character strongly affects the employees. The pattern of behaviour is rooted in the family, and in the more traditional Confucian communities, which are reemerging in China, the manager cannot be promoted if he divorces or if his family life is miserable. If he cannot even run his own family, how should he be able to run a firm (Chen, 1991:179).

Redding (1990:155) finds Chinese family firms to be characterized by 'patrimonialism which relates to paternalism, hierarchy, responsibility, mutual obligations, family atmosphere, personalism and protection.' Patrimonialism signifies that power and proprietary rights are inseparable. Family firms are handed down.

Many of these issues, but not the right of inheritance, have spread to the state owned firms in China which are also operated in a paternalistic fashion with the workers dependent on the factory director in almost all aspects of life. Far into the 1980s, it was common practice for state owned firms to reserve jobs for the children of the workers.

By the end of 1992, the Communist Party gave its cadres the green light to establish private firms while simultaneously maintaining their Government posts. Many cadres exploited this opportunity, drawing on their connections in the Chinese bureaucracy. Thus, even within the Communist system, family firms prevail. Being in general pragmatic, the Chinese do not find Communism and Capitalism incompatible, nor do they find it inappropriate to use position of power to obtain advantages at the expense of other entrepreneurs. These cadres are in a position to pressure other cadres, as they have connections with units supplying raw materials or public goods, such as electricity, water, etc. One example is cadres who, upon receiving their 'business licence', mail invitations to friends. The firm's new account number is printed in the bottom corner, signifying that since one is expected to bring a present, one might as well pay it into the account. The invitee has no choice. If he fails to bring a present or stays away, the new entrepreneur will instigate sanctions against the culprit.[13]

This example shows that the Chinese are not passive under all circumstances. They are passive if they gain nothing from working or demonstrating initiative, but industrious if they can see the purpose of it. Thus, many overseas Chinese, who have invested in firms in the People's Republic of China, have filled managerial positions in their firms with family members who had remained in China. Knowing the significance and structure of the family, it is understandable that the Chinese tend to construct hierarchical systems, or to conceive systems or organizations as hierarchical, which implies that the ideal manager is a charitable autocrat, i.e., a 'good father' or a 'good teacher'. Passivity in work-related situations will often be due to inappropriate incentive structures.

Personalization

The concept most adequately characterizing Chinese culture is probably personalism or personal obligations (renqing) which will be considered a superior trait to subsequent characteristics. The phenomenon can be viewed as a combination of Chinese collectivism and power distance. The concept of personalization (personalism) stems from Redding (1990:82-83) who explains it by referring to the tension between the Confucian ideals of family in society and the real insecurity generated in a society accustomed to despotism and autocracy. In this context, Redding's despotism can be replaced with anti-social attitudes as this, to a large extent, is a matter of the individual Chinese attitude and not only the insecure society. Society is insecure due to the individual's attitude toward his fellow man which, as Redding points out, is far from the Confucian ideals.[14] Personalization means that one tries to turn all relationships into specific relationships between particular individuals. Personalization of power creates mutual dependency in interpersonal relationships.

In-groups

To the extent that a Chinese is not defined in relation to his/her own family, s/he will view himself/herself in relation to groups of peers at the psychological level. Such groups are limited in terms of size and usually include only a few people and not, say, an entire firm. For example, within work teams, or units, the Chinese may form small friendship groups of very strong interrelationships. Such groups are often referred to as cliques. In-groups, or friendship groups in Lin's (1989:170) terminology, are explained in Confucianism as special family relations ('family friends').

The Chinese anti-social attitude

It is important to be aware of the anti-social attitude because it is easily ignored on account of the focus on family, in-groups, networks, etc. The ties between friends in in-groups sometimes become very strong precisely because the Chinese basic attitude is anti-social. What we call a social attitude is perceived by Chinese families as interference with their internal affairs. This phenomenon is vividly described by Lin

(1989:172), referring to what he calls the Chinese lack of 'samaritan virtue'. According to Lin (1989:166), he who advocates social reforms or engages himself in social issues is perceived as somewhat ridiculous, and people think, why does he not help his own family rather than meddling with other people's business.

In the last century, Smith (1986:196) talked about the Chinese lack of sympathy for others. He claimed this was particularly true for people who were different, such as the physically handicapped. Furthermore, Smith pointed out that until modern times, the Chinese language had no word for 'society' or 'social', and group work was unknown in China. He referred to the Chinese as preferring poker and mayong to bridge. They even favour individual games in sports.

The lack of sociability, combined with competition against neighbouring families over who does best, leads to jealousy and snobbishness characterizing Chinese interpersonal, or rather interfamily, relationships. Thus, the Chinese are known for both lack of interpersonal trust and an absence of cooperative spirit outside their in-group. On the other hand, these propensities reinforce the orientation towards one's in-group.

In-group affiliation is very binding because the Chinese are willing to go to such extreme lengths to help their friends. It is not unusual for friends to look after one another's children for up to a year, if the parents are out of town (Chu, 1994:154). If one has a friend in China who is a doctor or a lawyer, he will never think of charging you for his services, just as the salesman gives friends better goods than others. Friendship is more binding on the Chinese than Westerners. The Chinese feel that not only are they committed to help their friends, they also have a right to use or demand help from them, which is why the Chinese often prefer not to have too many friends. Having a large circle of friends may prove expensive. As a result of this strong attachment to small in-groups, loyalty in an abstract sense is almost unknown. The Chinese are only loyal to concrete groups or relationships.

Network

The Chinese word for network, 'guanxi', is described in *The Concept of Guanxi* in chapter 6 and is only discussed briefly in the following. Translating 'guanxi' into network is problematic, but there is no more appropriate Western concept. Contrary to Western networks, the Chinese are much more focused on persons and what we characterize as friendships. Thus, friendships without 'guanxi' are inconceivable (Pye, 1982:89-91), whereas the opposite is possible since network relationships are more utilitarian than emotional, and do not necessarily have to be based on friendship.

The Chinese tradition has no concept of justice and laws did not exist, which is why favour and its counterpart gratitude became concepts used in place of justice in this society based on ethics, not law (Lin, 1989:186-187). For this reason, the administration of justice by officials and other leaders has traditionally been looked upon as favour, and one who had granted another a favour was remembered with gratitude for ever, and naturally there was willingness to reciprocate the favour. Therefore, most had a circle of people to whom they owed favours, resulting in the emergence of what in this context is referred to as networks.

The Chinese indeed have extraordinary ways of socializing, within and outside their networks. However, it should be emphasized that whether we talk about networks, cliques or anything else, Chinese society is more bonded and entangled than Western societies which is due in great part to the vast flow of informal communication among the Chinese (see Chapter 6).

Middlemen

Middlemen are often used to establish relationship between two people who do not know one another, one of whom wishes to establish network relationship with the other. Middlemen hold a key position in Chinese society, representing the only possible way to resolve conflicts. This is also the case with firms, at least to a certain extent. Their role is declining in large organizations which are characterized by more complex relationships. The increasingly open labour market points in the same direction (Tan, 1990:280).

Face

The fear of losing face is a universal human phenomenon in any society. It is discussed here, because it is more important in China than in

the West and thus is worthy of consideration when trying to understand Chinese organizational behaviour. Chinese culture is often
referred to as a culture of shame as opposed to the West's culture of
guilt.

The fundamental difference between face and other concepts such as
self-esteem and self-respect, which reflect the individual's perception of
himself, is that face is the individual's evaluation of how others look upon
him. The Chinese talk just as much about giving face as losing face,
which is not the case in the Western world. Furthermore, the Chinese
have two different concepts for face, 'lian' and 'mianzi' (see *The Concept
of Face in China, chapter 7,* for a more detailed discussion).

'Lian'

Philosophically, the most important concept of face is 'lian' which
refers to the ethical aspect of one's personal behaviour, i.e., behaving
as a decent human being. 'Lian' is something which is ascribed to one
rather than something one can acquire. To lose one's 'lian' means that
one has no integrity, which is the worst condemnation of a Chinese.

'Mianzi'

'Mianzi' refers to one's reputation based on one's own efforts. It is
good to have but not decisive for one's life. Not having 'mianzi' means
to have failed to achieve success (Redding & Ng, 1983:100). 'Mianzi'
contributes to regulating negotiations, etc., in that aggressive
behaviour by one party will cause the other party to suffer loss of face,
which tallies well with the Confucian principles described in *The
Doctrine of the Mean,* advising one to control one's emotions and to
avoid conflict. (Chen, 1992:89-90). Given that the Chinese do not
wish others to lose face, 'mianzi' implies that they are reluctant to
refuse anything openly or to say something that others do not want to
hear, as this would lead to the other party suffering loss of face. This is
one of the reasons for the extensive use of middlemen everywhere in
the Chinese society.

Time

In Hofstede and Bond's study, the time perspective points towards the Chinese being much more prone to think in the long-term, but this is only partly true (Hofstede & Bond, 1988:20). But like other of Hofstede's dimensions, the time perspective has a specific objective. In terms of family, the Chinese do indeed apply a long-term perspective whereas in other contexts their perspective is short-term (see Chapter 8). By the same token, China's existence as the oldest country in the world indicates a strong retrospective orientation. This can be seen in the strong historical consciousness and ancestor worship. The Chinese are proud of their history and they all know historical anecdotes and allegories, even though they may be difficult for a Western sinologist to understand. Yet another aspect is the Chinese polychronic perception of time, which is why organizing time is of little importance in their lives. Time is considered to be a holistic element and is not given priority over other elements.

Cognitive Aspects

The following summarizes certain concepts describing the Chinese notion of reality affecting the population's behaviour.

Causality

The Western world developed a type of logic based on the relationship between cause and effect, whereas the Chinese way of reasoning is much more synthesizing. A particle's behaviour is controlled by the force-field in which it co-exists with other particles. In the words of Needham 'causation is not »responsive« but 'environmental'« (Ronan & Nedham, 1988:166). The result of this is that the Chinese tend to emphasize what is concrete, special, practical, and harmonized, whereas Western thinking leans toward the abstract, the universal and formal logic.

In an organizational context, these differences result in, for example, a more contextual, intuitive kind of decision making (Redding, 1980:138). So, according to Hofstede and Bond (1988:20), whereas Western thinking has advanced the natural sciences and hence technological development, the East layed the groundwork for establishing the preconditions required for exploiting the natural sciences, which are based on the ability to combine various ideas into syntheses.

Truth

According to Hofstede and Bond (Hofstede & Bond, 1988:19), one of the great epistemological differences between the Chinese and Westerners is that the former have never developed a belief in one absolute Truth which, based on the Western religious axiom of one God, became the foundation of Western thinking. Therefore, the religions of the East, such as Buddhism and Taoism, have no need to exclude one another.

According to the original Taoist tradition, 'truth can never be proved, it can only be suggested' (Lin, 1989:83), thus invalidating the axiom of truth in the Western sense. Lin Yutang furthermore emphasizes that rather than cultivating logic, the Chinese have always cultivated intuition and 'common sense'. In continuation of this, he claims the Chinese prioritize sensibility over rationality. Rationality is abstract, analytical, and idealistic with a tendency to logical extremes, whereas the spirit of common sense is more realistic, human, in closer contact with reality, and yields a much more genuine understanding and evaluation of the actual situation (Lin, 1989:86-86).

The Chinese Understanding of Privacy

The Chinese are not accustomed to private life. Both in traditional and Communist China, neighbours are encouraged to socialize as this has been part of informal social control. Thus, most neighbours know one another from a previous quarrel. Poor housing conditions combined with a high population density have created a situation where the only place for the Chinese to enjoy privacy is the parks, which indeed are crowded but not with people one knows.

According to Selingman (1989:53), the Chinese language does not even have a word for privacy. He points to the Chinese not being conscious of this, and says foreigners are often surprised to learn that guest houses in the countryside have no locks. Also, if members of the staff walk into a room without knocking first, they are not perceived as impolite. The Chinese are used to such manners, and it does not even occur to them that they are walking into someone else's private space.

Materialism

The Chinese population attaches great importance to material things, money in particular. Even though the major part of the philosophical tradition points in a different direction, the scarcity of physical goods, which the majority of the population has experienced throughout most of China's history, has made people think differently.

One aspect of this materialism is the Chinese frugality, which has been a topic of interest for Europeans ever since they first arrived in China. In 1890, Smith (1986: Chapter 2) described the Chinese frugality as based on three elements: first, they reduced their needs by eating simple and cheap food on week-days; second, they avoided waste; and third by adapting, such as by using existing materials with extreme efficiency. Even though it may be difficult to detect the difference between the latter two, he pointed to a significant disposition among the Chinese, which still characterizes them today.

A second aspect of the Chinese frugality is their high inclination for saving. Chinese, both in the People's Republic of China and in other places, have the highest rates of savings in the world. The Chinese prioritize affluence over other values, such as leisure or personal development. This is often used to explain their entrepreneurial spirit. The Chinese are used to having to survive under hard and poor conditions.

Tactics

What in the following is referred to as the Chinese disposition for thinking tactically is often referred to as strategic thinking by the Chinese. But since it primarily concerns short-term optimization, I prefer the term tactics. Tactics here are discussed from a cultural perspective, referring to the general use of tactical thinking inherent to all Asians and forming part of all everyday activities to a much greater degree than in the West. Right from the childhood, the Chinese learn how to obtain benefits through acting tactically.[15] The major point in this context is to emphasize the popular use of tactical thinking in Asia, as many Western business people tend to neglect this aspect. For more than 2,000 years, the Chinese have developed tactical thinking and applied it to both military and business purposes. Sunzi's classic work 'The Art of War' is still widely studied by business people in the Far East and in China[16] on the grounds that the marketplace is viewed as a battlefield. By contrast few Western managers find it relevant to read Clausewitz today.

The underlying principles of Asian tactical thinking seem simple and pragmatic. Due to considerations of space it is not possible to go through the individual axioms here, but the essence of it is to 'know yourself and know your adversary'. Thus, the Chinese find it imperative to know their opponents. They spend much more time than Westerners getting information about people with whom they contemplate establishing business relationships.

An important tactical method is delusion, which is also widely used in commercial negotiations with Western partners (consider the Chinese attitude about truth). When Western business people admit to a weakness in order to appear open and honest, the Chinese typically think that they do so to conceal nine others, which is an example of how the Chinese have internalized tactical thinking. The Chinese find cheating the other party admirable, whereas Westerners find such behaviour unethical. In all fairness it should be mentioned that the goal must be justifiable ethically.

Chinese tactical behaviour gives reason to attach great importance to discipline and strong management. Both elements are still central to the Chinese way of thinking, but like many other ideas, they have been subject to 40 years of socialist government.

The Chinese Attitude Towards Foreigners

Viewed from an historical perspective, the Chinese have been introverted and self-important. Even today, they feel they are unique. Foreigners have been viewed as uncultivated because they had not learned the Chinese classics and hence did not know how to behave. China has always had strict rules regulating relationships between Chinese and foreigners. Foreigners were only welcome when they were paying their attributes, often of symbolic value, but signifying that the foreign countries subjugated themselves to 'the Middle Empire' (Liao, 1986:Chapter 2). Mao Zedong continued this tradition and rigorously kept track of who was allowed to socialize with foreigners, and it did not take much to be accused of sympathizing with foreigners, which of course was a crime. During the Cultural Revolution, this attitude towards foreigners became reinforced due to the party's extremely negative propaganda on conditions in other countries.

The subject of foreigners were, and to a certain extent still is, a category all to itself. On the surface they were to be treated decently, while always bearing in mind that they might be foreign spies and thus were to receive as little information as possible. One explanation of why the Communists developed this attitude could be that the state did not have the same possibilities for instigating sanctions against foreigners as it did against Chinese citizens. Contrary to the Soviet Union under Stalin, the Chinese never extended this lack of legal rights to include foreign visitors, which is an evidence of the Asian politeness.

When firms seriously began establishing themselves in China in the mid-1980s, the Chinese interpreters were often accused of sympathising too much with the foreign party if they tried to explain his points of view.

Foreign friends

In relation to foreigners, the Chinese concept of friendship has two meanings. The best known is the tactical, using the word to obtain those advantages that internal Chinese friendship relations entail, but which in reality is no friendship. Clearly, when foreigners after two meetings are called 'old friends', it is not because the two parties have developed a friendship, but because the Chinese hope to make the foreign party act as if a friendship existed between them.

Even though friendship is a two-edged concept, it is important not to reject it a priori. In China, it is fashionable to have a foreign friend, and one can count on genuine Chinese friends to do much more to help than we are accustomed to in the West. But it takes time to build up such friendships, and Westerners often find it difficult to distinguish between the real friendship and the make-believe.

Pye (1982:32-33) mentions examples of Chinese who have abandoned their friends because they felt that others could offer them more advanced products. Thus, in the 1980s many cadres experienced a clash of interests between feeling bound by friendship relations and their wish to import the most advanced technology.

Xenophilia

This xenophobia, or at least unnatural attitude toward foreigners, still characterizes many Chinese cadres. On the other hand, a countercurrent has emerged over the last hundred years, reflected in a kind of xenophilia, viewing everything of foreign origin as good. For example, young Chinese, in particular, eagerly adopted Western advertising when it appeared in the 1980s.

The Chinese's enthusiasm for foreign goods is reflected in consumption patterns. Imported goods sell best, followed by goods produced by foreign firms in China, while Chinese goods are only sellable if the Chinese have no other choice. In addition, the Chinese have been strongly exposed to Western influence since 1979, in part because of growing personal contact with foreigners. Many Chinese have been allowed to visit Western countries, which is still a top priority among the Chinese, and even more have met Westerners in China. Furthermore, through radio, TV, books, and journals the Chinese are indirectly influenced by Western ideas. People in the habit of reading have had access to a comprehensive range of fictional and non-fictional literature translated into Chinese.

It is important to pay attention to the ambivalent Chinese attitude toward foreigners. Often, the Chinese exhibit simultaneously both xenophobia and xenophilia during negotiations, attempting to turn the West invasion of China in the last century to an advance. They demand special agreements with Western firms, and then appeal to their emotions by saying that the West is rich whereas China is poor, all the while praising Western products and technology to the skies (Pye, 1982:81-82). Yet, Chinese have never accepted that China is no longer the world's leading power, as it had been until the industrialization of Europe. They view it as unnatural for their country to be underdeveloped. Combined with their historical consciousness, the Chinese are somewhat more culturally bound than the North Europeans, which in part gives rise to a deep-rooted resistance to and difficulty in accepting Western organizational forms and behavioural patterns, particularly among older people.

In conclusion, foreign goods are primarily to be used for modernizing China. Since the end of the previous century, the catch word has been: 'Chinese learning is the basis, Western learning is for practical use.'(Rodzinski, 1988:215). Studying Chinese history, one cannot help questioning if the Chinese will ever find their place among peers in the global society.

Holism

The Chinese view the world from a holistic perspective, influenced partly by the traditional family, and partly by the Marxist state's municipal control over the population. But Chinese philosophy has always had a strain of holism. One of the best known classic works, Yijing (The Book of Change)[17], dating from before Confucius, builds on a holistic thought. Taoism is characterized by emphasising the relationship between man and nature, understood as a unity, which is a trait of holism.

In recent times, the holistic view has been stressed in connection with their negotiating techniques, implying that they want everything to fall into place at once, whereas Westerners are accustomed to resolving one problem at a time (Withane, 1992:68-69).

The Chinese are famous for seeking out a compromise, viewing compromise as an optimal solution which is the result of reuniting common interests based on a mutual objective (Kirkbride & Tang, 1990:5).

China's Political System

Since the Communists came to power, politics has largely been isolated from Chinese culture. The major reason is that it was considered to be in the interest of the population to break with tradition. For a very long time, many Western scholars seemed to believe in the reality of this break. Not until the 1980s did these scholars seriously begin to view China as a continuum, reflected in new concepts such as 'Confucian-Leninism' (Pye, 1991:443-66), clearly demonstrating the connection between tradition and Communism.

This new awareness reflects, to a certain extent, the political liberalization in China throughout the 1980s. Since the Socialist revolution in 1949, introducing one-party dictatorship, the Communist Party of China has played a dominant role. Therefore, in dealing with industrial China, it is imperative to understand the Communist Party's political role in shaping the operation and management of Chinese firms.

In many ways, Marxist ideas, which build on European philosophy, run counter to the Chinese tradition. Communist ideas are built on the belief in an absolute truth, and their utopian concepts about future social order are far from the down-to-earth materialistic attitudes among the Chinese. The idea of utopia as part of Chinese thinking refers to the past rather than to the future.

The Communist Party

The core of political leadership in China is the dictatorship of the proletariat, which has actually meant the dictatorship of the party. The organizational principle of the party is called democratic centralism, a term meant to describe what in reality is, simply, central planning. The idea of democratic centralism is that the individual is subordinated to the organization, minorities are subordinated to the majority, lower levels subordinated to higher levels, and the entire party is subordinated the Central Committee. In addition to this official version, the Central Committee and its politburo have been subordinated to the party leader, or the party's strong man. Deng Xiaoping has not had any leadership position since 1989, but in practice he governs like Mao did until he died. The government constructed by the Communist Party is a continuation of the old 'governance of the people, not 'governance by law'. The old communists at the top of the party can govern the country through their personal connections.

The most important change in the Communist Party's politics occurred in 1978 when the party leaders announced that the party's major task no longer was to carry on the class struggle, but to modernize the country. This new policy is known as the four modernizations: modernization of industry, agriculture, defence, science, and technology. Even though the modernization programme has been adjusted currently, its basic objective is still the same.

This change in political prioritization has led to a series of reforms and reformational experiments within all sectors of the Chinese society.[18] Arbitrary persecutions of cadres during Mao's regime made them passive and spineless. Cadres simply repeated official opinions without committing themselves. Criticism was prohibited, and those who ventured to air their own opinions were deported into the country-side or sent to prison.

China still harbours political prisoners even though this is rejected officially, but this should not overshadow the fact that conditions have turned much more liberal than under Mao Zedong. Persecutions have declined significantly and are considerably less arbitrary, than previously, and as a result of opening up the country to foreigners, the outside world learns about more cases than earlier. However, it is still prohibited to criticise the party in general and Deng Xiaoping in particular. This prohibition does not mean, however, that people do not discuss and criticize the party when meeting in the streets. But contrary to earlier, public bodies no longer interfere quite as much in people's private affairs. Critical opinions only become criminal if published and, even worse, if published in foreign media.

Party and Firm

Since 1950, Chinese firms have in reality been controlled by the Communist Party. The party secretariat in a firm has functioned as a working board of directors. In principle, the communists' tasks were to formulate the overall strategy and to monitor the implementation of Party policies and regulations. But in reality, they engaged in the day-to-day running of the factory which was supposed to be the managing director's domain.

Starting around 1980, it became evident that the principle of 'the non-expert leading the expert' was erroneous, and this principle has gradually been abandoned as reforms accelerated. Thus, throughout the 1980s, management has been strengthened at the expense of the Party. However, Lockett (1988:476) points out the mistake of only considering the relationship between Party and management as a clash of interests. The mere fact that the party secretary and the managing director often was, and is, the same person makes this interpretation problematic.

According to the Communist Party, Chinese enterprises were facing two major problems in the mid-1980s: (1) by and large they had no autonomy and were managed top-down by administrative supervising bodies, and (2) management had too little power internally. These problems were emphasized at the Central Committee's plenary meeting in 1984, which was the first time members of the Central Committee talked about giving directors full responsibility for running factories (Factory Director Responsibility System).[19] Previous administrative changes had moved the decision right between the central ministries and the local province or county authorities, whereas the core of the 1980s reform of state owned enterprises was to expand management's self-determination, implying that the decision right was now decentralized and given to the individual enterprises (Jackson, 1992:1). As a result of the Central Committee's decision in 1984, enterprises are themselves now allowed to sell new products that they develop, products not purchased by the public commercial firms. Furthermore, they can keep a certain percentage of their profits which, however, must be earmarked for specific purposes. Also, the enterprises can keep most of their depreciations.

Chinese Management

In the following, China's firm structure and managerial forms are briefly discussed, focusing on the conditions of state owned enterprises, since they are the ones with which Scandinavian firms primarily engage in joint ventures. Apart from one firm fully owned by Danes, all other firms in the study are joint ventures. State owned firms are enterprises governed either directly by central ministries or by provincial or county authorities.

Types of enterprises

After the Communist take over in 1949, existing traditional enterprises were nationalized throughout the 1950s, and China entered into an agreement of cooperation with the Soviet Union which primarily entailed assisting the Chinese in establishing industrial conglomerates, mainly within the heavy industries, imitating the Soviet pattern. In addition, agricultural collectives were encouraged to build up local industries, in part to absorb redundant manpower, and in part to make each province self-sufficient in case of war.

Great changes took place during the 1980s when the state allowed the establishment of private enterprises, foreign firms, and various hybrid forms in which state owned enterprises joined forces with collectively owned enterprises and other institutions, or in which state owned enterprises were leased to private persons.[20] Some state owned enterprises and other institutions established fictitious companies in Hong Kong, enabling them to have new enterprises registered as joint ventures, which meant tax benefits. In recent years, a large number of holding companies have been established, veiling subsidiaries with various forms of property rights. Thus, it is impossible to draw a sharp line between the various forms of ownership, particularly in southern China, as they become increasingly interwoven (Lee, 1993:17).

The business structure in China is a combination of traditional small Chinese enterprises and socialist conglomerates. Ninety-five per cent have less than 500 employees and produce only 37% of the GNP (Feng, 1992:113-123). Out of approximately 8 million enterprises, around 100,000 are state owned. Of these, 13,415, or 7%, are classified as large or medium-sized enterprises.[21]

Even though state owned enterprises represent a negligible share of China's 8 million enterprises (1.25%), they produced 54% of the total industrial production in 1990.[22] The state owned enterprises' share of production is, however, declining continuously. In 1978, it represented 80%, whereas it had dropped to 50% in 1992 and is expected to be around 25% by the year 2000 (Shaw & Woetzel, 1992:37-51).

The private sector has thus re-emerged. In 1993, China had 237,900 private enterprises employing 3.7 million. China distinguishes between private and individual enterprises. Individual enterprises represented 17.6 million independents, employing 29 million.[23]

The organizing of state owned enterprises

Just as China harbours a variety of enterprise forms, the organizational forms of these vary correspondingly, in part because form of enterprise has to match organizational form, and in part because the firm has to adapt to its environment. Among these environmental factors, the changing policies of the Communist Party are essential.

The major components in Chinese enterprise organization stem from both traditional Chinese organizations and the Socialist economic system. Traditional Chinese family centred enterprises are characterized by a low degree of structuring. Roles are not as clearly defined as in the West, they operate with less standard procedures and the boundary between white and blue collar workers is more blurred. On the other hand, centralization of decision making is higher. Only in the formalization of paperwork procedures do they resemble Western firms. Many enterprises are so small that they have no division into departments (Redding & Wong, 1986:276). Strategic planning is replaced by personal intuition (Silin, 1976:118).

What characterized the socialist system, originally constructed under Stalin, was state ownership of enterprises, planned economy, centralization of decision rights above enterprise level, and vertical communication in all matters. Enterprises were managed top-down with quotas[24] for output, quality, consumption of materials, production costs, productivity, numbers of employees, total payroll expenditures, and size of profits. Other functions, such as logistics, sales, investments, and renewal of equipment were handled by bodies above the enterprise level. In return for handing over their income to the state including profits, enterprises were allocated the means for running themselves. Aside from the general five-year plans, one-year plans were drawn up for each enterprise after consultations with the directors in question.

Due to China's backward economy, such plans never became fully effective, forcing the directors themselves to try to get the necessary materials. On the other hand, the director only needed to fulfill some of the expectations, of which the quantitative output was the most important, whereas less emphasis was placed on quality and sales (Henley & Nyaw, 1986:10-15). The result was over-production of certain goods and shortages of others, as well as inefficient use of energy and raw materials. The latter is an important cause for the decline in productivity still troubling state owned enterprises (Perkins, 1992:22).

Not until 1988 were three quarters of state owned enterprises classified as independent accounting units, implying that they had their own bank accounts, in principle were responsible for their own income and costs, and had the right to sign contracts with other enterprises (Hsu, 1992:75)). It was furthermore indicated that enterprises could negotiate with foreign business people and keep their share of earnings in foreign currency, hire and fire workers, decide the size of their labour force, and fix the prices of their products.

The implementation of these new policies caused far greater problems than assumed originally. The latter issues in particular were not yet fully implemented by the middle of 1993, almost ten years after they were introduced. One reason is the experimental nature of the reforms implying that some enterprises, the most profitable, acquired a high degree of self-determination and are generally able to function on market conditions whereas others do not. This means that many enterprises still fail to respond to market signals, and the weaknesses of the original system, where management is more production oriented than market oriented, have not been removed. There are many stories about management being more interested in paying bonuses to their employees than in increasing profitability.

The state attempted to put a curb on the Chinese economy in the Summer of 1993 to prevent it from becoming too overheated. This was in response to bonus payments having risen by 38% in the first part of that year, when economy had grown by 'only' 13.9% and living expenses only by 17% (Walker, 1993:1). Thus, the size and rate of expanding managers' autonomy are a decisive factor for whether China succeeds in introducing a market economy, which was made the official political goal at the 14th Communist Party Congress in 1992.

Management

During the period of planned economy, management's most important function was to decide methods and procedures for meeting quotas, which is why long-term planning and other managerial skills in a Western sense were never developed in contemporary China. Managers saw it as their principal task to satisfy the cadres occupying the responsible governing bodies. Chinese directors never needed to develop managerial skills. In fact, under Mao, the Communists criticized Western management styles, viewing them as an integral part of the capitalist system (Chan, 1990:84). Mao felt that Western management theory was directed primarily at exploiting the worker. But when Deng Xiaoping came to power, management theories were presented as non-political and could thus be employed under both a socialist and a capitalist system.

The general characteristics of state owned Chinese enterprises are the extensive differentiation of functions and the lack of effective mechanisms for integrating these various functions, resulting in inefficiency (Lockett, 1988:476). In general, there are no positive incentives to make operations more efficient. During the period of planned economy, the major tool was coercion. The director was replaced if he proved incapable of meeting quotas, which is why managerial tasks increasingly focused on making the authorities accept low target figures.

Middle managers

The distance between top level managers and middle mangers in Chinese enterprises is greater than in Western. Middle managers and foremen have less influence and their domain of responsibility is not clearly defined as in Western firms. They tend to be required to ask their superiors for advice all the time.

As a result of this centralist tendency, hierarchical channels are over-stretched, which especially applies to the managing director, since he is then involved in various tedious affairs. In consequence, the greater the enterprise, the greater the problems of efficiency. Staff and line functions are often overlapping and lack a clear division of responsibility, causing friction between production workshops and specialized staff functions. Lockett quotes a cadre saying: 'In an enterprise it seems that everyone is responsible, but also no one is responsible.' (Lockett, 1988:478).

Another problem in Chinese organizations is the typical lack of formalized flow of information which also overburdens top managers. The problems of external coordination are caused by the sharp distinctions between ministries and between provinces. An enterprise, receiving its raw materials from another province or a supplier belonging under another ministry, often encounters coordination problems. These problems are strongly reinforced by all the vertical communication required.

Chinese Managers

Chinese political leaders and scholars increasingly recognize the Chinese manager's lack of technical and managerial qualifications, as described very clearly by one Chinese analyst: 'the bureaucratic system of economic management in China is the most backward in the whole world.' (Wan, 1980:3-8). Aside from the Chinese system itself, another explanation may be the poor education of managers. Lockett (1988:489) quotes a study from the mid-1980s of 134 state owned enterprises in Shenyang, showing that only 6% of the managers had higher education. The percentage was even lower among middle managers where in some cases their proficiency in writing could be questioned. Economic reforms have reinforced the problems of management by creating a need for more and better qualified managers. As enterprises gradually obtain greater autonomy, they have to undertake more functions, such as marketing, accounting, product development, etc.

By the end of 1986, the Politburo decided to implement a 'Contract Management Responsibility System', the aim of which was to fix a progressive amount which enterprises were to hand over to the state after having paid assessed taxes. This system was to function as a positive incentive for managers to increase profits. According to certain stipulations, managers were to have disposal of any remaining profits. But one weakness in this contract system was that contracts were negotiated individually between the enterprise management and the supervising bodies, making room for individual benefits. A positive effect was that the Government encouraged local authorities to lease small enterprises to individuals through public invitations to submit tenders. In principle, anyone could tender, but in most cases the present director was awarded the contract.

Despite these attempt to raise efficiency, between 65% and 80% of state owned enterprises lost money in the summer of 1993[25], primarily because the financial market did not function. When state owned enterprises do have available funds, managers either invest these or spend them on various forms of fringe benefits for the employees. Public investments in fixed assets were actually 70% higher in May 1993 than in the previous year.[26] The state owned banks control 85% of all financial assets, which are used in general to make up for state owned enterprise deficits. Only 20% of bank loans go to the non-state sector, which produces more than half the industrial output, and in general the total production within other sectors of the economy.[27]

An obsolete financial system combined with reluctancy to let enterprises go bankrupt for fear of political unrest has meant that it has been in the interest of enterprises to get rid of their savings as quickly as possible, as they could always rely on the state to put up security, should they later get into financial troubles. Albeit, enterprises have obtained a certain degree of autonomy over production, marketing, and finances, this has not led to substantially higher economic efficiency.

The Chinese manager's attitude toward management

Based on the above, it is hardly surprising that Davidson finds the following attitudes to be widespread among Chinese managers:

1. They do not worry about the relationship between incomes and costs.
2. They are risk aversive due to the negative consequences if mistakes are made.
3. All communication goes through headquarters.
4. Negative relationship between employees and management. (Davidson, 1987).

In 1984, Mun (1990:314-15) examined the possible discrepancy between what 50 Chinese managers wanted and the actual situation they had to live with. The study showed that management goals had become more comprehensive than prior to the reform policy, when meeting quotas and attending to the welfare of workers were the domineering issues. Now the goals included issues such as higher profits, satisfying consumer needs, and improving technology through collaborating with foreign firms. However, the respondents found the objective was still too narrow. For example, they found that too little emphasis was placed on aspects such as growth, rational utilization of available funds and public relationships. According to the managers, the major task of management was to meet target figures representing the basis for the authorities' assessment of the enterprise. On the other hand, they found the growth of the enterprise, employees welfare and the evaluation of managerial performance to have too little effect on decision making. Also, the managers mentioned that minimizing risk was given too great an importance.

The interdependency between employees and managers is well-known. It shows when employees attempt to make the enterprise employ a family member rather than trying to have their own wage increased. Since the extended family is still the basic financial unit, it is more advantageous financially to get one more member of the family employed than getting a higher bonus.[28] However, it seems surprising managers find that too little is done for the employees. In previous studies, managers have often pointed to inadequate influence on central aspects, such as personnel policy, hiring and firing, and wage systems (Campbell, 1987:59). This indicates that in some cases, the directors have wanted to use their influence to improve conditions for their employees, but in other cases certainly also to lay off redundant labour.

In his study of manager prioritization of personal incentives, conducted from 1981 to 1983, Cragin (1990:333) found their first priority to be better housing, and second better basic wages. However, Punnett and Zhao's study from 1989 (1992:86) shows that, at least in an organizational context, managers preferred low basic wages and high bonuses based on individual performance. No matter if this study is compared with Cragin's or with Mun's, variations are pronounced indicating that managers have changed their attitudes during the 1980s. Mun's (1990:314) study showed that managers viewed employee affiliation with the enterprise as moderate and found it should be strengthened. This confirms assumptions about a relatively weak organizational culture in China's state owned sector.

In general, the employee work ethos presents a problem for managers of state owned enterprises. Due to the pragmatic Chinese attitude, they are little motivated to work, something which the State Council attempted to ameliorate in 1986 by formally introducing a contract system to the effect that new recruits were employed for a fixed period of time.[29] Mun found managers placed stronger emphasis on the 'hard' facts of management, which is explicable in view of the Chinese Government's decision in the seventies to take an interest in certain aspects of Western management theory and to view management as 'scientific management', i.e., Taylorism and Fordism (Howard, 1992:48 cont.). On the other hand, managers did not attach much importance to the 'soft' areas, such as managerial style and qualification. Not attaching importance to the qualifications of management is perhaps the most pronounced difference between Western and Chinese management.

Max Boisot's study

Max Boisot's (Boisot & Liang, 1992:161-184) study from 1990 of how Chinese managers spend their time, developing his ideas based on Mintzberg's study of how American managers spend their time, offers a rare opportunity for comparing Chinese managerial activities with managerial activities in the U.S.A. Thirty per cent of a Chinese director's incoming mail is from supervising bodies, in the US only 6%. This confirms that Chinese enterprises to a much larger extent are governed by administrative regulations than by laws. The supervising authorities, in China referred to as 'mothers-in-law', constantly and arbitrarily interfere with the operation of enterprises, and often place a representative in the enterprise whom the enterprise is to provide for in terms of wage and housing. Many 'mothers-in-law' undertake social functions, such as monitoring family planning programmes, health and school systems, and the local militia. According to Boisot, it is not unusual for a medium-sized factory to house up to 22 such persons. Representing superior bodies, their instructions are in reality law for the managers since they take part in appointing him and thus can also have him dismissed.

Compared to American managers, Chinese directors may spend the same amount of time on contact with subordinates, but four times as much on contact with superiors and half as much on external contacts. The Chinese director receives five times as much paperwork from superior bodies than his American colleague, but only sends a twelfth of the amount of paperwork to these bodies compared with American managers. This, in connection with the extensive personal contact maintained with superiors, demonstrates that the manager is able to widest possible extent to avoid committing himself in writing. This is in keeping with the Chinese tradition, but is also due to the fact that supervising bodies often present the director with conflicting demands, which is why he has to negotiate his way out of the situation. In state owned enterprises, the director is expected to simultaneously represent the interests not only of the state, but also of the enterprise, the employees, and other organizations, whereas the Western manager is expected to maximize profits.

The personalized managerial style of Chinese managers is also reflected in that they spend less time at their desks than American managers, 9% and 20% respectively. Another characteristic is that only 7% of the Chinese manager's verbal contact is planned and only 35% takes place at his initiative. Most often others seek him out. The Chinese manager often participates in numerous meetings by walking to and fro, confirming a lack of willingness to delegate responsibility, characterizing a personalized managerial style.

Boisot and Liang (1992:177) explain the directors' personalized and centralized managerial style by referring to the organizational environments. For career reasons, managers attempt unrelentingly to satisfy their 'mothers-in-law' to the best of their abilities, simultaneously committing themselves as little as possible by avoiding written decisions which might be used against them. They refer to this system as patrimonial bureaucracy. Chinese directors cannot reduce uncertainty, only absorb it as there are no free resources available for screening functions. In reality, organizational and managerial processes in state owned enterprises are conflicting, which tempts many Chinese managers to choose opportunism as a survival strategy in this system which simultaneously rejects and mistrusts them (Boisot & Liang, 1992:178-179).

Decision Making

The tendency toward group identification is apparent in the decision making process which is almost always collective and unanimous. No single Chinese is willing to take the responsibility for a given decision. Historically, status and responsibility have been separated. In many cases, the individual with high status and great influence on decision making was not the one held responsible for the decisions. High status implied that one had subordinates to blame, which is still widely the case in China.

One area of great discrepancy between desire and reality is the rate at which decisions are made in Chinese enterprises. Decision making is slow, in part due to manager risk aversion, and partly because more important decisions have to be approved by superior bodies. Poor coordination inside the enterprise between the various units probably explains the slow implementation. This would seem to be something that management should be capable of ameliorating, which makes it a critique of themselves, but this is apparently not management's perception of the situation. Previous studies have indicated that Chinese directors tend to delay implementing orders from the top, fearing that they will soon receive counterorders. Changing policies caused by the experimental nature of reforms led to a situation where managers never really knew what to do.

Mun writes that decision making is collective formally, but in reality authoritarian, which is explicable in terms of the collective responsibility for decisions made by the individual person.[30] The lack of individual responsibility for authoritarian decisions is probably the greatest weakness of Chinese management.

Conclusion

The purpose of this chapter has been to discuss the concrete manifestations of Chinese culture, politics and management. Thus, this chapter constitutes a background for further analysis of cultural variations.

Chinese collectivism was, first and foremost, found to be tied to the family, and secondarily to other smaller groups of friends, excluding the workplace. Chinese tend to have little confidence in people who are not members of their in-group. The salient role of the family is also reflected in the language and in the Chinese constitution. Family responsibility goes beyond the nuclear family to include the extended family, which is seen in practice through various means of support for family members. The Chinese are indeed characterized by a high degree of materialism and thrift. And through the establishment of personal relationships by exchange of services, the Chinese gain protection in a hostile, hierarchical society, characterized by tough competition and scarce resources. Personalization is reflected in a series of derived phenomena such as network, corruption, cliques, use of middlemen, etc.

Confucianism viewed the family as a model for the construction of the entire society. As a result, Chinese society reflects a series of central characteristics, such as affiliation with smaller in-groups, an antisocial attitude, networking, face consciousness, indirect communication, etc. These phenomena have affected Chinese interpersonal relationships throughout history and still do.

The Chinese attitude toward time, honesty, tactics, and foreigners reflect features specific to the Chinese culture. Long-term orientation is linked strongly to the family, and in general time is viewed as more contextual than in our culture. Deadlines are rarely kept. Plus the Chinese lack of belief in an absolute truth makes them view situations tactically. It is generally considered that they relate in a different and more pragmatic way to honesty than Scandinavians do.

The political system is centralized and dominated by the

Communist Party, which attempts to maintain political dominance, while at the same time declaring that since 1992 the intent has been to reintroduce market economy. Even though the Chinese economy cannot be characterized as a fully developed market economy, the significance of planned economy and the national sector is declining, though state owned enterprises still dominate as joint venture partners.

Chinese state owned enterprises lack autonomy, since decision power is placed above the enterprise level. Despite attempts to introduce positive incentive structures, their efficiency is declining. Due to the planned economy system, management in the Western sense hardly exists. Within all areas, state owned enterprises have been governed by administrative agencies. In consequence, Chinese managers received no education prior to the emergence of the market economy in the 1980s. Factory directors were used to functioning within the planned economy system where the relationship between income and cost was of less importance than being on good terms with superiors. Studies throughout the 1980s show, however, that Chinese managers have expanded their perspective considerably during this period. Dissatisfaction with the inefficiency of the Chinese bureaucracy rose, and internally managers began showing interest in strategy, formal structures, and information systems. One of the problems managers in the state owned sector face is that they represent not only the interests of the state, but also other organizations and the employees.

Communication in Chinese enterprises is primarily top-down, and administrative bureaus still attempt to control state owned enterprises. Internal communication is mainly verbal. In addition, even though the management style is still personal and centralized, individual, personal responsibility for decisions made by the often authoritarian manager is still lacking. This evasion of responsibility is the greatest weakness in Chinese management.

3. Scandinavian Culture, Politics, and Management

Introduction

This chapter on the Scandinavian countries has a dual purpose. First to describe the Scandinavian respondents' cultural background in a broad sense, such as dominant cultural values, practices, and these cultural dispositions affect on the political system. Scandinavian management is also discussed briefly. Since the target culture is Chinese, depictions of Scandinavian conditions are more limited than corresponding portrayals of Chinese conditions. The point of departure is Hofstede's dimensions and how they manifest themselves in the Scandinavian countries.

The second purpose is to make scholars more attentive to their own cultural inclinations. Belonging to the same culture as the respondents in my study, I find it important to explicate my own cultural biases. As mentioned earlier, almost no Chinese were able to characterize what distinguishes Scandinavians from other Europeans, which is why the Chinese tend to view Scandinavian culture as part of European culture. In the following, I shall confine my characterization of culture to the Scandinavian, since the behavioural pattern of Scandinavians is independent of whether the Chinese can distinguish them from others, and the focal issue of this book is the Scandinavian expatriate's perception of the Chinese and how this perception is affected by cultural values from the Scandinavian countries.

This following review is mainly based on Swedish and Danish data. In general, Sweden is perceived as representative of the Scandinavian countries, which is why most of the literature is on Sweden. Though there are differences between the Scandinavian countries, these differentiations are of little consequence in this context, because the purpose is to draw comparisons to Chinese culture.

Review of the Scandinavian Region

The history of the Scandinavian countries

The Scandinavian countries are shaped by more than 1,000 years of war and collaboration. For a long period, Finland was subject to Sweden, and Norway was at first subject to Denmark, then later to Sweden. In consequence, outsiders view the Scandinavian countries as a unity, and the countries' populations feel closely related culturally.[1] The same applies to other areas affected by Scandinavian cultural values, such as the legal system, which is built on Scandinavian and Germanic law and which is basically identical in all Scandinavian countries. All Scandinavian countries are highly developed. The populations have mainly survived and developed by working materials into products that were exchanged or sold. Thus, from early on in history, the Scandinavian economies have been relatively open.

Language and geography

The populace of the three Scandinavian countries, (Denmark, Norway and Sweden) understand each other's languages. Finland is not viewed as part of Scandinavia but as part of the North, and though its language differs from the others, having been subject to Sweden for 400 years, many Finns have a certain knowledge of the language. All the Scandinavian countries have small populations, and the total for the area is approximately 23 million, corresponding to the population of just Shanghai and Beijing combined. Being small countries with small populations is said to have affected the mentality of these countries towards preferring small units. 'Small is beautiful' is an expression often used. With few exceptions, the area is dominated by small enterprises. An implication of this extensive use of small enterprises is a relatively high rate of trade, inclusive of foreign trade, which means that it is important to learn foreign languages. Almost everybody can manage in English or German, more or less proficiently.

Religion

All Scandinavian countries belong to the Christian religion which, like other Western religions, is characterized by an emphasis on the existence of only one God, with all others being mere idols to be combatted. According to Hofstede and Bond (1989:19), this is the basis for the Western belief in an absolute Truth and the victory of rationalism. Unlike the Chinese, whose way of thinking is more synthetic and associative, the Scandinavians' is more analytical and abstract.

Protestantism

Since the emergence of Lutheran Protestantism in the 16th century, this religion has been predominant in the Scandinavian countries.[2] Protestantism is characterized by a high degree of internalization in religious matters. It is faith alone that leads to salvation, and not diverse external institutions or dogmas. It is central to Protestantism that only if one is free can one have faith, which is why spiritual and secular powers were separated. Protestantism contains no ideas for using secular powers to settle spiritual disputes. Religious revivals, such as Evangelism, enhanced the religious experience, but without involving other institutions in such attempts. Protestantism underlines the direct connection between the individual and God.

Today most citizens in Scandinavian countries consider it natural to be a member of the Protestant Church, even though many are just as suspicious of religious authorities as of other authorities. Protestantism fitted well into the previous worship of nature and the Scandinavian gods, such as Odin and Thor.

Individualism

Compared to China and the third world, the Scandinavian countries would appear to have a relatively high degree of individualism combined with very strong female traits. There is also an absence of significant power being placed in the hands of a few. Thus, Scandinavian individualism includes a sense of caring for the weak and a general rejection of self-promoting impetuous individuals. Therefore, in Scandinavian countries, individualism points towards self-realization rather than towards selfishness. Self-realization implies that the Scandinavians attach great importance to their working conditions and to their leisure time, much of which is spent with the family in a cheerful atmosphere. The latter is an almost unknown phenomenon in

China, where spending time with the family most often means doing practical things and helping the child with its homework. The closest resemblance to this phenomenon in China is a family walk in a public park in connection with festivals.

Socializing to individualism

Historically, rationalism has had an effect on trust in the individual's judgment in all matters, including religious and political issues. Thus, the degree of interpersonal trust and solidarity is relatively high in the Scandinavian countries. In consequence, trust in the individual's judgement, development, and self-development with the purpose of being able to act independently are important ingredients in the Scandinavian socialization process. Within certain social confinements, the individual is encouraged to act independently without necessarily considering the family.

In bringing up their children, the family finds it more important to encourage independence and humanity, the latter reflecting that the population is still deeply rooted in the morals of Christianity. The Danish Primary Education Act, (which is fairly similar to other Scandinavian education acts), states that the school must attempt to develop the pupil's abilities for independent evaluation and attitude.[3] Educational policy in the Scandinavian countries aims at the majority of children as opposed to the élite. Equal importance is ascribed to the development of attitudes, social capabilities and knowledge, and in relation to the latter how to find and apply this knowledge. However, rather than employing coercion and threats, as in China, the teachers appeal to the children's sensibility and interests. Therefore, Chinese moving to Denmark tend to find their children learn too little and have too much leisure time.[4]

The spirit of self-help implies life-long education and emphasis on continuous training. Thus, in general, managers at various levels in Scandinavian firms regularly attend courses throughout their career. In Scandinavia, education and knowledge lead to action and not systems building, and inductive analysis based on empirical data or cases is preferred to logical deduction based on theory, indicating the pragmatic trait characterizing the Scandinavian countries. 'To know is to do' as the saying goes.

Low Uncertainty Avoidance

As illustrated in Table 4.1, uncertainty avoidance tends to be low in the Scandinavian countries, such as can be seen in the Scandinavian mentality resembling English pragmatism rather than German idealism. Emphasis is placed on experience, empiricism, and utilitarianism. The Scandinavian people's overall positive attitude towards others differs from the Chinese suspicion of those they do not know. This attitude implies that Scandinavians take it for granted that others do what they are expected to do. Control measures are not instigated unless this is discovered not to be the case. Scandinavians are known for being tolerant of other opinions and of those who are different, which should make it easier to operate among people preferring more structured situations.

Scandinavians, inclusive of Scandinavian managers, tend to search for pragmatic solutions and to place emphasis on practical results. In Scandinavia and other North European countries, pragmatism is action-oriented, both in relation to managerial tasks and the learning process.[5] Pragmatism also implies that the nature of goals is often determined by the persons involved and the methods available. Thus, the basis for action is not which goals to achieve but the resources available (Fievelsdal & Schramm-Nielsen, 1993:32).

Greater Distribution of Power

Informal behaviour

The horizontal distribution of power contributes toward the Scandinavians' informal behaviour and dress as compared with most other societies. Thus, social convention is egalitarian, and people who know one another use first names and omit titles, even when talking about a third person. Mr. and Mrs. are only used in writing and often only when addressing people whom one does not like (Schramm-Nielsen, 1993: Part 3:31). Organizationally, this distribution of authority can be seen where boldness is more appropriate than being deferential. Informality also applies to the Scandinavians' manner of dress. Of all the populations in the Western world, they spend the least money on clothes.

As this applies to an organizational setting, a dynamic Scandinavian manager has no use for formalities and kowtowing. One is expected to have the courage to express one's opinions and stick to them, no matter what one's superior thinks, but not to do it in a self-promoting way. First and foremost, managers must be able to cooperate.

Interestingly enough, Czarniawska-Joerges talks about the end of informal social conventions in Scandinavia since the 1940s as a part of what she describes to be the current change in doctrine (Czarniawska-Joerges, 1993:236). She refers to a growing tendency to use civil forms of address and titles being observed in Scandinavia during recent years. However, it is questionable to what extent this tendency will continue. Anyhow, it is difficult to deduce much from this type of tendency. It may reflect a change in values, be a temporary trend, or be a reaction to egalitarianism having been stretched too far.

Mediocrity

Another characteristic feature of the Scandinavian population is mediocrity. The 'Jante Law' (the principle of 'just who do you think you are?'), formulated by the Danish-born Norwegian Axel Sandemose, reflects this mediocrity. The essence of the 'Jante Law' is:

> *Do not think you are anything.*
> *Do not think you are worth just as much as we are.*
> *Do not think you are wiser than we are.*
> *Do not think you are better than we are.*

An immediate implication of this attitude is the risk that individuals withhold initiatives, since this would mean standing out from others.[6] However, in general the 'Jante Law' functions to prevent people's success from going to their heads, helping them remember their social obligations which wealth entails in the feminine Scandinavia. However, since the state has taken over the social obligations, this primarily entails high taxation of personal incomes.

Status

Another function of the 'Jante Law' is that people are disinclined to show their wealth. It is thus a peculiarity that status symbols play a relatively modest role in the Scandinavia. Chinese, and many others, find it difficult to understand that it is almost impossible to buy twentyfour-carat gold in Scandinavia, this being the genuine product for the prestige-conscious but though not the most practical. In general, visible status symbols are of little importance in the Scandinavian societies. One illustration of this is open-space office settings, in which even the department manager has his desk.

Egalitarianism

The small power distance can also be seen in the high degree of egalitarianism in the Scandinavian societies, implying little difference between people, groups, classes, and even sexes. This limited differentiation adds to the homogeneity of society. The goal is to achieve uniformity in firms, creating a situation where each person, while fulfilling a certain role or function, can be replaced just as well by another. In principle, everybody is to be treated equally.

Naturally, competition and power exist, but have a negative connotation. The population in the Scandinavian countries primarily talk about cooperation and responsibility. There is a tendency to forgive, and everybody is equal no matter what their position is in society or at work. Naturally, many of these statements are ideological, meant to make subordinates feel more satisfied with their jobs. There is no totally egalitarian society in the world.

Time

The Scandinavian perception of time is strictly monochron. Time is perceived as being at least as important as money. Increased efficiency is often viewed as a question of reducing time consumption, implying that planning is the focus of all life situations. This attitude about time affects organizations in that, if a firms is organized inadequately, the staff is considered to be wasting time. It is not only stated, for example, when a planning meeting will start, but at what time it is expected to end. In China and many other foreign cultures, the latter is perceived as particularly inconvenient.

The Scandinavians are known for being of few words, which they themselves perceive as positive, not 'wasting time with idle talk'.

Contrary to many other cultures, there is nothing wrong with being silent in Scandinavia. 'Speech is silver, silence is golden.' (Selmer, 1993:129). The Scandinavian behaviour is quiet, slow, non-emotional, non-aggressive and they have difficulties in expressing feelings. Thus, compared to other cultures, Scandinavian often appear to be closed (Hofstede, 1982:99).

As the Chinese are also emotionally closed in many areas, this is of little importance in this context. However, the Chinese do generally talk more than the Scandinavians.

As for the time dimension, Scandinavians are oriented towards the present. History is of little importance in everyday life. Similarly, they do not talk much about the future. Society is primarily interested in the present. This is in keeping with Hofstede's placing of Scandinavia in the middle of his time-orientation dimension. Scandinavians are not as short-term as the Americans, nor are they particularly long-term oriented.

Internalization of the Driving Force

The belief in individual judgement has led to a strong internalization of norms among Scandinavians. Contrary to collectivist cultures, inner driving forces are relatively important to behaviour and activity. This is the underlying reason for the indirect control which is typical in Scandinavian societies, and for the great extent of codetermination in Scandinavian firms, in which the workers have representatives on the board of directors.

Political Conditions in Scandinavia

Independence and trust in individual judgement are central concepts in Scandinavia and one of the explanations for the early consolidation of parliamentarianism in this region. Parliamentarism is deeply rooted in the Scandinavian tradition, even though Norway, Denmark, and Sweden are monarchies, but the royal heads of state have no political power. Dating back to the time of the Vikings, the king in certain areas of Scandinavia was elected (Selmer, 1993:114). Individualism here entails a tradition for freedom of speech and freedom to organize without interference from the state.

The Scandinavian model

The foundation of the Scandinavian model has been described as the Protestant ethic of honest disciplined hard work combined with a typical Scandinavian endeavour to realize consensus democracy.[7] Individualism, egalitarianism, and humanity are the values on which this rests. This model is the basis for all political-social systems in all of Scandinavia, implying that Finland too must be viewed as resting on the Scandinavian model, even though the country is not part of Scandinavia.

The combined social forces, which provide the material basis for welfare and high levels of consumption are a private business life and a strong labour movement, comprised of 90% of the labour force and which defends the living conditions of the workers. The political arm of the labour movement, the Social Democratic Party, or the Labour Party, has dominated the political scene in building the welfare society which more than anything distinguishes the Scandinavian model. The social state plays a key role in realizing positive objectives in society. A relatively large part of the national income is derived from transfer payments, securing the social welfare of the population.

The society is designed in a way that makes individual independent of help from family, neighbours, or friends, because there are no intimate groups such as the clans or extended families existing in more collectivist societies. It is considered a positive social objective that the state secures the individual. Free public services, such as the health sector, education, national pension, and the entire social sector are financed through high taxes. Thus, the state holds a large part of the finances, though not a large part of the production.

Despite the fact that transfer income is often criticized by the population, claiming it does not pay to work, the majority supports political parties sustaining the welfare model. Thus, during the ten years of non-Socialist government in Denmark (1982 – 1992), the size of transfer income increased. The other Scandinavian countries have been dominated by Social Democratic governments since the Second World War. This indicates that on the whole, the Scandinavians are satisfied with the welfare state despite the fact that taxation appropriates half their income. The state welfare system indicates great confidence in the fairness of collective decisions made by central authorities. This again leads to deep respect for the law and regulations adopted by the authorities, something which also affects employee attitudes to the internal regulations of the firm.

However, as indicated, the state plays a limited part in relation to the labour market. The two sides of industry view it as ideal to be able to negotiate labour market conditions without interference from the state. Nevertheless, there is an increasing tendency toward government representation in large organizations constituting the two sides of industry, making the boundaries less clear and indicating a move toward corporatism. Thus, Scandinavia is characterized by high incomes and a well-educated, but expensive, labour force which forces industry either to invest in advanced technology, or to move less advanced production processes to other areas of the world and then sell know-how. The major trend is, however, to invest in advanced technology. Sweden houses more robots per capita than any other country in the world.

Attitude towards foreigners

The Scandinavian attitude towards others is, as mentioned, in general positive. This also applies to foreigners. However, during recent years the potential 'threat' caused by immigrants to Scandinavian values, society and welfare state, has currently been a topical issue. Possibly the most conspicuous expression of Scandinavian political ideology is the Scandinavians' ambiguous attitude towards the European Union – half of the population is against the Union. Thus, large parts of the Scandinavian population are extremely skeptical of the centralist tendencies displayed by the European Union. Nevertheless, the Scandinavian countries remain in the Union out of 'financial necessity'.

Historically, the Scandinavian countries have often found it difficult to collaborate, which is perhaps why they are afraid of losing their independence in unifying with the large European nations. In addition, many Scandinavians feel that money and finances are not to determine everything, which is typical of feminine cultures. Not knowing very much in general about the Chinese, Scandinavians in the main start by being positive. The Chinese are still that group of immigrants afforded the best treatment in everyday contact with Scandinavians in the shops and streets.

Management

The Scandinavian countries are populated by a multitude of small and medium-sized enterprises, albeit Sweden and Finland also harbour a number of large, transnational companies. Being of a limited size, each economy is open, with about one third of the GNP derived from exports. These open economies have given Scandinavian managers considerable international experience. They are bound to spend some time abroad, as opposed to Chinese managers, most of whom have never had the opportunity to even associate with foreigners, let alone travel or work abroad.

Egalitarianism in a managerial context

According to Fivelsdal and Schramm-Nielsen, Danish managers share a set of common values, such as egalitarianism, collaboration, and professionalism (Fivelsdal & Schramm-Nielsen, 1993:28 cont.).

Interpersonal relations are characterized by such a fundamental sense of egalitarianism that there is a strong tendency to treat people universally. The aim is to treat people, or groups of people, on the same footing, and, as far as possible, to avoid discrimination on grounds of sex, age, status, friendship, etc.

There is very little or no personal control of subordinates who are assumed to be responsible for their domain. It is acceptable to point out errors, which are often interpreted as mistakes. On the other hand, lying is totally unacceptable which is almost a function of the very limited direct control. If too many cheat, this system is not sustainable. And the use of power has negative social connotations related to superiority, cohesion, and dominance. This is why Danes tend rather to talk about responsibility, which has positive connotations, such as obligation, competency, etc.

Decision-making

In relation to the firm, egalitarianism means that the ideal organization is flat, containing as few hierarchical levels as possible. Since the Vikings, the leader has been considered the foremost of his peers. Decision-making is usually delegated to a large number of people who can make determinations within their field of responsibility. A common principle characterizing Scandinavian firms is participative management. According to Lindkvist, all employees demonstrate a certain amount of managerial behaviour (Lindkvist, 1991:34). An effect of this decision-making structure is that managers must constantly collaborate with others at lower levels of the hierarchy, which makes everybody interdependent on one another.

The strong egalitarian traits characterizing the Scandinavian countries, combined with an emphasis on good interpersonal relationships, results in efforts to reach consensus in decision-making situations, the outcome of which is often a compromise. One gets as far as one can in the given situation.

Thus, decision-making becomes a mixture of top-down and bottom-up. The firms harbour many middle managers who play an important role as coordinators, motivators, and decision-makers. This, accompanying a relatively modest pursuit for status, typically results in good cooperation between the firm's various departments, efficient teamwork, and eases the introduction of new measures with which the involved parties typically comply (Selmer, 1993:121).

Anti-hierarchical and anti-authoritarian attitude

Egalitarianism involves an anti-hierarchical and anti-authoritarian attitude. Hierarchy is viewed as a necessary evil needed to make organizations function. But in Scandinavia, attempts are made to minimize hierarchies. The anti-authoritarian attitude is a natural consequence of the belief in the individual's capacity to evaluate situations independently at any level.

These egalitarian and anti-authoritarian values can explain the informal relations for which the Scandinavians are known both within and between different layers of hierarchy. According to Fivelsdal and Schramm-Nielsen (1993:29-30), relating to one another informally is a way of hiding differences that exist due to job, education, and income.

Informal relations are perceived to facilitate creativity. That which in other countries is considered to be initiative is in Scandinavia referred to as creativity, which to Scandinavians have more positive connotations than initiative, though both concepts are understood to be fairly positive. The lack of authoritarianism also enables students, workers, and other subordinates to air their dissatisfaction. There are few places in the world where students file as many complaints about their grades as in Scandinavia.

Consensus and collaboration

Collaboration is central in the feminine Scandinavia, but in a formalistic and superficial way, implying that the major purpose of collaboration often seems to be to obtain consent over certain measures. In an organization consisting of anti-authoritarian individual, it takes a high degree of consensus to make the organization function. Most Scandinavian managers will consult their relevant employees prior to making decisions, as it is imperative that decisions are supported by those employees who have to implement them. Decisions made by the managing director are no more right than other decisions.

Therefore, a decisive managerial skill is the ability to explain ideas to employees and argue convincingly, just as the ability to persuade them is central. Dialogue becomes an important managerial tool which is difficult to transfer to another country with a greater power distance.[8]

Cooperation is often crucial when applying for a job whereas everything resembling nepotism is viewed with extreme negativity.

The above factors imply a very close relationship between decision and implementation, or that the organization appears as a combination of talk and action. This managerial style has been referred to as action-oriented (Selmer, 1993:126). The consultative style characterizing Scandinavian management is time consuming, but attempts of streamlining are made through a high degree of formalized procedures and a strong monochron time schedule.

Individual ambitions are considered relatively negative, whereas collectivist ambitions are well-accepted in line with collective wage and salary systems. Teamwork is widely used. The fact that individual ambitions are not in general sanctioned by society does not mean that individuals do not pursue their own ambitions. Otherwise there would be no leaders.

Professionalism

Scandinavian managers tend to search for pragmatic or practical solutions based on expertise, which is why Scandinavia harbours many 'experts'. Authority which cannot be grounded in the manager as a person can only be grounded in competence which in principle everyone can achieve, thus making knowledge the only acceptable basis for classifying people. Decisions based on knowledge and competence give no cause for discussion since they are indisputable due to objective circumstances. Consequently, the rate of abstract knowledge is low. It must be transformed into expertise that can guide action in the rationalist, pragmatic Scandinavian countries. The manager transforms his competence into concrete results. Therefore, most Scandinavian managers have graduated either from a business school or a technical university. The ideal is both. Large firms, of which there are relative few in Scandinavia, harbour relatively few entrepreneurial types who have worked their way from the bottom to the top.

Changes in the perception of managerial functions

When reading descriptions of Scandinavian management styles from a cultural perspective, the authors tend to ignore changes over time. One positive exception to this is Barbara Czarniawska-Joerges, who discusses what she refers to as doctrinaire changes in relation to Sweden. Summarizing these doctrinaire changes shows that relatively greater emphasis is placed on the market rather than on production, implying a growing focus on firm external relationships compared with firm internal, and a growing commercialization of society. The customer's central position in relation to the firm leads to, in general, stronger emphasis on people in the firm, both internally and externally. This becomes manifest in increased localization of both competencies and negotiations, and in increased participation and profit-sharing among the employees. Management entails creating ideas rather than offering recommendations. Organizations are perceived as super-human, with their own identity. They are born, learn, mature, and die.

Finally, in Scandinavia there is an increasing tendency to question planning. Business life is showing a growing interest in chaos theory, and Czarniawska-Joerges tells of a management guru who was accused of being too rational (Czarniawska-Joerges, 1993:238). It should be stressed that these are trends that have not yet finalized, and it is difficult to say if they will continue. They might as well be a reaction to the youth revolt around 1970 that placed anarchism on the agenda for a short period. However, similar trends characterize other European countries and the U.S.A.

Managerial behaviour

Among other things, egalitarianism makes managers hand over power in many cases, enabling them to live a more quiet life. The Scandinavians are increasingly trying to strike a balance between work and family life, and sometimes family life is given priority over money (Selmer, 193:121). This, combined with a graduated taxation system, further indicates that those reaching the top in business life are rather driven by inner forces than by external reasons.

Life quality and leisure time thus play an increasingly important role to managers and others in the Scandinavia. As a result, weekends are viewed almost as sacred, and banquets, business lunches, entertainment, etc., are reduced, on the whole, confined to foreign business associates and the annual Christmas lunch. In general, after working hours most Scandinavians prefer going home to their families over participating in social activities at the workplace.

Long working hours are often viewed as unreasonable to the working spouse. The fact that the spouse of many managers works outside the home, and there is no maid to take care of the children, further results in managers trying to limit long visits abroad. The latter is quite opposite to the predominant attitude among Chinese managers who can depend on the extended family to a much greater extent.

Managerial style

In consequence of the informal behaviour and manner of dress, the Scandinavian management style appears to be extremely 'soft' to many foreigners. But there is a difference between form and content. Often the content is fairly 'hard', resulting in the Swedish management style being described as 'an iron fist in a child's glove'.[9]

Informal behaviour also applies to managers who must learn to make themselves respected despite informal manners. A Swede describes management in Scandinavia as 'to create such prerequisites in an organization that everybody should be happy to give their utmost to produce a result as good as it ever can be.'[10] Scandinavian management style is also characterized by a relatively high degree of informal communication. The telephone is preferred, being faster than using memos or letters and requires no secretarial assistance. Compared to China, the formal part of communication is relatively comprehensive.

To stay in contact with their employees, management tends to be very visible and to walk around in the factory. The purpose is not so much control as to get input from the employees. Czarniawska-Joerges describes Swedish management style in the following way:

> 'I do not know whether there is a »Swedish management style«, but if I were forced to describe typical organizational practices in one word I would choose »pragmatism«. It means balancing rituals with rational choices so that the former acquire instrumental uses, while the latter – rational choices – expresses important values.' (Czarniawska-Joerges, 1993:236).

Her point is that, as a result of the Swedes' pragmatism, they fluctuate between rationalism and ritualism. One example is the strong emphasis on consensus in the decision-making process, often leading to situations where foreigners do not find that any decisions are made at meetings because the only thing that happens is a discussion leading to consensus. This process indicates the relationship between rituals and Scandinavian values. When a Swede doubts the existence of a Swedish management style, it is even more questionable if a Scandinavian management style exists. Thus, it is not surprising that the Chinese find it difficult to identify such a style.

Conclusion

The purpose of this integrated description of key values, political system, and managerial issues is to emphasize that the three aspects are interrelated. This first and foremost implies that management must be viewed in a larger context in which values and the social system affect management style and the organization of the firm. From this short review of Scandinavian history and values it is clear that the countries are sufficiently homogeneous to be viewed as one cultural area. The most divergent country is Finland, primarily because of its language, though the Finns have a fairly solid knowledge of Swedish.

The basis for describing the Scandinavian countries has been their unique form of individualism, femininety, small power distance, and their low uncertainty avoidance. The latter does not, however, apply to Finland which is placed in the middle on the dimension uncertainty avoidance. The time perspective in the Scandinavian countries is assessed to be medium, but the foundation of this is moderate and intuitive. Pragmatism is a common feature of the Scandinavians, both in terms of their belief and their attitude in general.

Being small countries with small homogeneous populations has probably added to the mediocrity which contributes to other's perceiving Scandinavians as grey and boring, and the Swedes as the most boring ones. Scandinavia has relatively few charismatic leaders. Simultaneously, it is viewed as a positive quality to be able to create one's own image, and despite mediocrity and the rejection of competition, 'being pushy' is a favourable characteristic. Mediocrity and egalitarianism are thus combined with some individualism and small uncertainty avoidance. It is viewed as very positive if people themselves take initiatives. On the other hand, from a Scandinavian point of view, egalitarianism as a too ostentatious or straight forward presentation of individualism is problematic. Collective wage and salary systems are more common than individual.

Egalitarianism has led to very informal social conventions, but those have tended to become more formal in recent years, probably as a reaction to the 1970s revolt against authority rather than as a change in doctrine.

Pragmatism implies emphasis on action and practical results. Available resources form the basis for objectives, and planning time is viewed as important. Trust in the individual and his/her judgement is widespread and, combined with egalitarianism, results in an anti-authoritarian attitude. Simultaneously, the individual is socialized into not being dependent on family or friends or the opinions of others. This is then combined with high interpersonal trust and solidarity.

Education and development is a life long process internalized in the individual. Greatest importance is attached to the development of analytical skills and the ability to collaborate. In principle, competition is rejected, even though it exists everywhere in society.

Scandinavians are, in general, tolerant towards people of a different opinion, the political result of which is a long parliamentary tradition and employee representation on many boards of directors. The aim is for everybody to enjoy the same universal conditions. Trust in the individual's judgement allows widespread decentralization, and attempts are made to reach consensus in the firms, which makes the decision-making process fairly protracted and almost invisible to outsiders.

Debates go on until everybody agree, and then a decision is made. Like Scandinavian behaviour, decisions are informal.

As an aspect of decentralization, middle managers hold a central position in the firm, also in terms of financial transactions. Managers below the level of chief executive are often themselves responsible for budgets. The basis is a trust in employee ability to fulfill responsibility, which is why control is not instigated until mismanagement occurs, and this is often merely interpreted as a mistake.

Leisure time is important to the Scandinavians (characterized by Trompennars as a specific culture).[11] Efficiency, and hence saving time, is a key value in Scandinavia. The managerial style is consultative and participative. The informal tone implies that those who succeed in becoming managers do it by making themselves respected indirectly in a society viewing direct communication as positive. Acting as mediator is an important part of the management role in Scandinavia.

4. Comparing the Two Cultures

Introduction

In the following, Chinese and Danish culture are compared, discussing differences and similarities in relation to the dimensions addressed earlier. Based on the issues addressed in chapters 2 and 3, the following discussion mainly concentrates on comparing the values of the two cultures. A culture's superficial layers are fairly volatile, and the customs of one culture can be adopted by another, which is why it is difficult to determine what stems from which culture. Based on an index comparing the two area's scores on different cultural dimensions, cultural differences and similarities are reviewed, with an emphasis on the differences (see tables 4.1 and 4.2).

Comparing the Two Cultures Based on Hofstede's Dimensions

The starting point for discussing the two cultures is their scores on Hofstede's dimensions. However, the differences addressed are more complex than Hofstede's dimensions.[1] In addition, a specific interpersonal or firm relationship is seldom affected by just one dimension.

The Scope of Power Distance in Scandinavia and in China

All Scandinavian countries rank among the lower third of the 53 countries included in Hofstede's study of the dimension power distance. China, on the other hand, is estimated to rank among the upper third, which seems likely based on Hong Kong's ranking. As an effect of China's large power distance, firms are centralized and the distance is great between managers and subordinates in China.

The structure of Chinese society is hierarchical, and its model is the Chinese extended family. According to Chinese tradition, the subordinate must always obey his boss who, on the other hand, is committed morally to protect the employee. In reality, this patriarchal aspect is

Table 4.1 Cultural dimensions of the five involved countries and Hong Kong

	PD	IN	MA	UA	LO
Denmark	18 (L)	74 (U)	16 (L)	23 (L)	
Sweden	31 (L)	71 (U)	5 (L)	29 (L)	33 (M)
Norway	31 (L)	69 (U)	8 (L)	50 (L)	
Finland	33 (L)	63 (U)	26 (L)	59 (M)	
Hong Kong	68 (U)	25 (L)	67 (U)	29 (L)	96 (U)
China	80*(U)	20*(L)	66 (U)	60*(M)	118 (U)

* Hofstede's estimation.

PD = power distance; IN = individualism; MA = masculinity); UA = uncertainty avoidance; LO = long-term orientation; U = upper third; M = middle third; L = lower third (among 54 countries and regions for the first four dimensions and among 23 countries for the fifth).

ascribed less importance in favour of didactic managers who make sure that the employees become dependent on them.

Organizational structures in Scandinavia are flat and anti-hierarchical, and managers are not much different from other employees. Managers are democratic and consultative. Delegating responsibility and employee decision competence is high. Both in speech and attire, the Scandinavians are unpretentious and informal. Contrary to China, titles and family name are rarely used. Egalitarianism is customary, but people's way of socializing indicates greater equality than is actually the case. Hofstede has pointed out that it is easier to move from an area of small power distance, such as Scandinavia, to an area of larger power distance, such as China.

Degree of Collectivism in China and in Scandinavia

The dimension individualism differs strongly. All the Scandinavian countries rank relatively high compared to China, which is estimated to rank low on a par with Hong Kong. In China collectivism is linked to in-groups, the most important of which is the extended family supplemented with other small groups of friends. Because of this close attachment to family and other groups of friends, Chinese employees are less committed to their workplace than Scandinavians. The loose association with the workplace in China makes it more difficult to develop a corporate culture in China than in Scandinavia. Chinese loyalty is tied to specific persons, which is why their loyalty to the firm depends on whether it is in their own or their family's interest to work for the firm.

Personalization versus roles

A key aspect of Chinese collectivism is the inclination to establish personal relationships. Personalization implies that concerning work relationships, the Chinese tend to relate to specific persons and their attitudes and characteristics. Chinese personalization has a resemblance to the relationships which Scandinavians form part of, such as the relationship between the members of a nuclear family. Contrary to this, work related roles are emphasized in Scandinavia, roles which are characterized by not being tied to a specific person. Different persons can perform the same function.

In China, personalization causes the organization of networks, a series of personal relationships connecting the members in relationships of trust. This, and other personalized relationships, such as cliques, mentors, behind-the-scene activities, is reinforced by a general anti-social Chinese attitude toward strangers. An effect of these particularistic relationships is that they focus on the specifics of a given situation. In contrast, Scandinavians tend towards universal attitudes, such as treating people of different functions equally. Everybody is equal before the law and general rules must be complied with.

Degrees of interpersonal trust within the two cultures

Another difference between the Chinese and the Scandinavians is the degree of interpersonal trust. Scandinavians have relatively great confidence in strangers and their judgement. Control is mainly internalized. Control is only utilized after numerous erroneous actions. There is a tendency to explain away such actions as mistakes. With the Chinese, low interpersonal trust entails widespread personal or external control. Personal control adds to reinforce the construction of particularistic relationships between people.

Indirect versus direct communication

In consequence of this particularism, the Chinese have a greater face awareness than the Scandinavians, resulting in a higher degree of ambiguous communication. By expressing themselves ambiguously, the Chinese attempt to avoid getting into situations where they themselves, or others, risk losing face. Comparatively, Scandinavians are not very sensitive to others losing face, though it is important to draw attention to the positive aspects of people's actions and measures, which in Chinese society could be interpreted as a kind of giving face. However, by no means does it assume dimensions similar to the Chinese.

Scandinavians prefer people to express themselves directly. Scandinavia is a typical example of what Hall refers to as low context societies in which information is expressed as explicitly as possible (Hall, 1990:9). Information must be understood without requiring extensive previous background knowledge. Chinese society, however, is a high context society, where part of the information is not expressed explicitly, but is implicit. Living in a high context society takes a high degree of common knowledge to understand a given piece of information. One factor is the Chinese language itself, which adds considerable context to communication.

When moving from a low context culture, such as the Scandinavian, to a high context culture, such as the Chinese, one has to be 'contextualized', meaning to acquire the knowledge necessary for understanding information in a high context society. This process takes a long time. Until Scandinavians acquire an understanding of the Chinese context, their mutual communication is bound to be characterized by numerous misunderstandings. Members of low the context cultures are more likely to misunderstand Chinese information or signals than vice versa, since they express themselves more explicitly.

Differences in the Degree of Masculinity
Between the Two Cultures

The two cultures are located at their opposite ends of a pole, Scandinavia being characterized by feminine values, and China by masculine. Even though China falls within the upper third of Hofstede's masculinity dimension, this does not imply extremely high masculinity, such as in Japan. In China, masculinity is expressed through competition between households or extended families, and, as mentioned, in anti-social attitudes to strangers. The Chinese find it difficult to collaborate with others outside their in-group. Another manifestation of their masculine attitude is the importance of status, reflected in status symbols such as access to a car or the like.

The femininity of the Scandinavians implies care for the weak and rejection of the individualist. On the other hand, collaboration between employees is widespread both horizontally and vertically. Femininity combined with low uncertainty avoidance and small power distance generates the basis for mediocrity. Also, as a result of the above combination, little emphasis is placed on status and status symbols. Wealth is almost concealed in Scandinavian societies.

Differences in Attitude Toward Uncertainty Avoidance

The Scandinavian ranking on the dimension uncertainty avoidance is more diffuse than the first three dimensions. Denmark, Sweden, and Norway rank in the lower third, whereas Finland ranks in the middle. China is estimated to rank at a level with Finland.

It is difficult to assess Chinese uncertainty avoidance as Hong Kong ranks low, being mainly populated by people who have either left China legally or have fled the country, i.e., on a par with Denmark and Sweden. When the Chinese are estimated to rank in the middle third of this dimension it is probably, in part, due to political conditions. The many shifts in the totalitarian political line have made cadres uncertain and passive. In addition, poor countries tend to rank higher on the scale than developed countries which is understandable. However, the Chinese eagerness to free their entrepreneurial spirit points in the opposite direction. These tendencies have become increasingly clear in recent years with the introduction of a market economy in China.

China's score on the uncertainty dimension is in itself uncertain, in part because Chinese elements are spread over most of the dimension which concerns a culture's search for truth. Truth is not a key concept in Chinese culture, which is far more focused on sensibility and synthesis based on reason. This explains the Chinese conditioned honesty, which is tied to specific persons (discussed in detail in Chapter 5). This is essentially different from Scandinavians' unconditional demand for honesty without which the high level of general interpersonal trust is unsustainable. Thus, there is no reason to doubt the relatively low score of the Scandinavian countries, even though there are differences between Denmark and Sweden on the one side, and between Norway and Finland on the other.

Consensus, characterizing Scandinavia, only exists formally in China and in relation to responsibility. In reality, important decisions are made by the leader. Often, decisions have been made solely by the chairman of the Communist party committee while the whole party committee was responsible for the decision collectively. In Scandinavia, the tendency toward low uncertainty avoidance contributed to reinforce the anti-authoritarian attitude characterizing the Scandinavians' relationship with their managers.

Differences in Life Orientation

China scores extremely high on long-term life orientation, which is confirmed by the Chinese attitude toward the family, thinking not only of the next generation but of generations beyond. The Chinese thus ascribe great importance to money and other material goods. They lead a simple economical life and the savings rate is high. It is considered important to improve the wealth of the family, and the Chinese are known for their persistence.

This dimension was developed by Chinese scholars to identify certain Chinese or Asian values that the first four dimensions neglected. Looking at the characteristics used to determine the dimension (see Chapter 1), the difficulty of placing Scandinavia understandable. The immediate reaction is that Scandinavia does not relate much to any of the features characterizing the dimension. Furthermore, the empirical basis for placing Scandinavia is thin. Sweden is placed in the middle third of the 23 countries studied, and this may be interpreted as Scandinavia neither tending towards one or the other pole. On the one hand, Scandinavians do not place much emphasis on the feeling of shame, but rather on guilt which is not included in the dimension. On the other hand, neither respect for traditions nor personal tranquillity are especially characteristic of Scandinavia.

Orientation Toward the Past Versus the Present

The long-term Chinese orientation is inseparable from that culture's orientation to the past. Chinese philosophers, such as Confucius, took their ideals from legendary kings, believing in the existence of harmony. Thus, consciously or unconsciously the Chinese are attempting to reestablish the golden age of earlier times. The Chinese possess the world's greatest historical treasure and are very conscious of their history. In effect, they are perceived as a proud people.

Scandinavians are more oriented towards the present. They are not inclined to save, and in terms of material goods they neither think of the previous nor the next generation. This orientation towards the present means that Scandinavians are very occupied with their leisure time, which is to be enjoyed here and now. Their historical awareness, as well as expectations of the future, are in general very low.

Diffuse Versus Specific

Emphasis on leisure time and the Scandinavian distinction between working life and leisure indicates their specific life style. Scandinavians divide their life into various segments, each independent of the other. Chinese life style is more diffuse and less divided. Thus, it is not unusual for the Chinese to try to get members of their family a job at their own workplace, or to use their network to this end, whereas nepotism is viewed negatively in Scandinavia. The Chinese attitude indicates a difference in the importance of the family member's occupational experience. Experience, or performance in the terminology of Trompenaars (1993:82), means relatively less in China than in Scandinavia. In China, good relationships may be more valuable than performance, or a condition of high performance.

As a result of this diffuse life style, Chinese managers involve themselves in their employees' private problems and visit them privately. The diffuse orientation in China also affects how one gets to know other people. Basically, the Chinese have little trust in strangers whom they will associate with only at a superficial level in the beginning, gradually developing trust. The approach is very indirect. They give high priority to time spent on getting to know business partners, and they are reluctant to enter into business relationships with people whom they do not know. Scandinavians, on the other hand, are straight forward and their reasons for contacting a stranger are transparent. If the stranger is interested, one gets to know him by gradually expanding one's knowledge about him.

Monochronic Versus Polychronic
Perception of Time

The Scandinavian way of organizing time is distinctly monochronic, placing a strong emphasis on solving problems one by one and keeping time schedules. Contrary to this, the Chinese way of organizing life is polychronic, which means that meeting deadlines are given less priority than in the West. Deadlines are probably more often missed than met in China, causing many problems for Scandinavians working with the Chinese. Due to this polychronic view of life, managers often participate in several meetings at once, and all day long people walk in and out of the manager's office.

Cognitive Differences Between the Cultures

The Chinese way of thinking is rather associative, whereas the Scandinavian is abstract. Chinese associative thinking allows them to see connections between events that are not necessarily founded in logic. Context is very important, and their way of thinking is basically holistic. The Chinese tend to emphasize what is concrete, specific, and practical, which is why they prefer new things to be visualized. Contrary to this, the Scandinavian way of thinking is more abstract and analytical, categorizing phenomena and viewing them as separate. As opposed to the Chinese, Scandinavians combine the parts into a whole. Thus, pragmatism characterizes both China and Scandinavia, but the kinds of pragmatism are quite dissimilar. One similarity, however, is that both cultures are founded on the practical and the concrete. Differences stem from contrasting attitudes toward harmony and face. The greatest divergence of attitudes is with respect to honesty. In the Chinese tradition, honesty is conditioned by and specifically associated with a specific person. This is probably related to the fact that the

Chinese have never worshipped one god, and thus never developed a belief in an absolute truth. In their tradition, the truth is contextual and hence concrete. Abstract truths become irrelevant. Whereas in Scandinavia, the demand for honesty is universal, though this does not imply that all Scandinavians are honest. This universal honesty can be traced back to the belief in an absolute truth, which again stems from the Scandinavians belief in one god.

Conclusion

Table 4.2 summarizes the scores on a series of dimensions based on the Chinese and Scandinavian cultures. Not all dimensions are equally important in this context, so only those dimensions referred to in the subsequent empirical chapters are included.

In Table 4.2 'researcher' refers to those who have used these dimensions in the literature. It should be mentioned that this does not always mean that the person was the first to apply the dimension. The criterion has relied upon who applied the dimension to China. My own name is mentioned, where no one so far, to my knowledge, has placed China or Scandinavia on the given dimension. Thus, these are my own deductions from country specific chapters and sections. As mentioned earlier, these dimensions are not independent of one another, but I have made no attempt to cluster them. As appeared from Chapter 1, the dimensions particularism versus universalism and diffuse versus specific can be viewed as aspects of the dimension collectivism. The same applies to other dimensions, such as diffuse versus specific, guilt versus shame, and high context versus low context communication.

Table 4.2 Summarizing dimensions used in comparing China and the North. The dimensions are categorized: high (H), middle (M), and low (L).

Dimension	China	Scand.	Researcher
Collectivism (vs individualism)	H	L	Hofstede
Power distance	H	L	Hofstede
Masculinity (vs femininity)	H	L	Hofstede
Uncertainty avoidance	M	L(M)	Hofstede
Long-term orientation	H	M	Hofstede
Interpersonal trust (M-nature)	L	H	Tayeb/Worm
Relationship to workplace	L	M	Tayeb/Worm
Particularism (vs universalism)	H	L	Trompenaars
Personalization (vs roles)	H	L	Redding
Diffuse (vs specific)	H	L	Trompenaars
Performance (vs allocation)	L	H	Trompenaars
Past orientation (vs future)	H	L(M)	Trompenaars
Shame (vs guilt)	H	L	Benedict
Polychronic time (vs monochronic)	H	L	Hall
External (vs internal) control	H	L	Trompenaars
High context communication (vs low context comm.	H	L	Hall
Associative (vs abstract) thinking	H	L	Kedia/Bhagat

5. Personalization

Introduction

In the following a distinction is made personalization and network, which requires a clarification. Albeit the distinction may seem hairfine, it is relevant when studying China since the personal plays a decisive part in all contexts. According to Redding (1990:83), personalization exists at all levels in Chinese society: at the individual level where there is a need for personal control and for controlling, and hence abhorrence of being employed; at the level of relationships in networks and other similar relationships; at the organizational level through the obligation to be the benevolent autocrat and in non-rational applications of power and control; at the societal level in deficient horizontal collaboration.[1] The latter also applies at the level of the firm, as will become evident during the course of this book.

Thus, networking is an element of personalization, but the concept of network and similar concepts are discussed separately in Chapter 6 due to their central position in China. In this chapter, the discussion focuses on the concepts of loyalty, status, and degree of honesty relevant to the two culturally different attitudes to personalization. Personalization is also tied to the Chinese view of themselves and others, such as expatriates, which is particularly important in this context. Therefore, a considerable part of this chapter is devoted to the discussion of the two culturally different views of expatiates and foreigners.

Personalization and Roles

At the personal level, the greatest and most important difference between the Chinese and the Scandinavians seems to be the phenomenon referred to here as personalization, the cause of most cultural clashes. Personalization implies that Chinese tend to perceive the behaviour of others as particularistic, meaning they focus on the specifics in each situation or are attached to specific persons. Contrary to this, Scandinavians tend to evaluate other's behaviour as universal, as roles that can be filled by different role-owners. Thus, Scandinavians do not focus much on the person performing the role. Roles exist independently of certain persons.

Personalization means making relationships personal as opposed to neutral relationships determined by norms. Redding views the personalization of relationships in Chinese society as a mechanism for creating ties and loyalty between employee and employer in a society characterized by mistrust. It eases the tension created by the strong vertical order and latent mistrust (Redding, 1990:82).

In Chapter 2, personalization as a characteristic of Chinese culture was discussed in general. This chapter focuses on the Chinese disposition of making relationships personal based on empirical accounts. In more individualist cultures, such as the Scandinavian, depersonalization of roles has a positive connotation and means that ideally everybody should be treated equally. Accodring to law, regulations, etc., this is not the case in collectivist cultures such as the Chinese, where consideration is focused on specific persons. The difference is hard to point out, because in individualist cultures, the individual should be considered based on common, universal rules and regulations. In collectivist societies, it is the other way around. The point of departure is personaization, which is minimized by the common rules and laws.[2]

Personalization of the negotiation process

Here, negotiation process does not refer to a specific type of negotiating, but naturally the respondents drew on their own experiences. As stated in Chapter 4, China has a high context culture distinguished by implicit communication, whereas the Scandinavian countries are identified as having low context relationships or direct relationsships.

An experienced Scandinavian negotiator and member of the board who has lived in China for many years, says:

> 'The Chinese do not want to do business with people who appear stressed because they do not find them trustworthy. The Chinese interpretation is that such people are not in control of things. A preliminary negotiation requires a minimum of seven to ten days, and one talks for at least two weeks before mentioning the price.'

When negotiating with the Chinese for the first time, the initial period is usually spent on getting to know one another, no matter whether the discussion deals with joint tourist visits or pseudo-negotiations. This phenomenon is not unique to China, it exists in most collectivist countries or high context societies. A prerequisite for doing business is the establishment of a relationship of trust. The Chinese attempt to 'contextualize' foreigners, in order to understand their specific characteristics.

By contrast, low context countries, such as the Scandinavian, have a predictable legal system for enforcing contracts, making trust redundant to a certain extent. In effect, it is unnecessary to know the specific chracteristics of those people with whom one negotiates. This makes for difficulties in understanding when people from low context societies try to adapt to Chinese conditions. One problem is that they perceive the first week's negotiations as a waste of time, and the negotiators are often subject to pressure from their superiors who cannot understand why it takes so long just to get started.

Some expatriates view the Chinese negotiation style as tactical, wanting to get to know the foreigners but not wanting the foreigners to understand them.

Another Scandinavian respondent views it this way:

> *'In China we are always negotiating with a whole group of people. They are uncomfortable if we bring along some one who speaks Chinese. The best thing is to bring along people who speak Chinese. We always do.'*

This is in keeping with the Chinese tactical disposition. However, it should be added that if the Chinese seldom appear alone it is due to political conditions. In most cases, authorities will not allow only one person to negotiate, and if they do, the individual person does not want sole responsibility. However, it has not been my experience that the Chinese object if a delegation brings along a Chinese interpreter. The Chinese have ample opportunity to talk other than during the meeting, or they can ask for a break during which they can withdraw to discuss matters internally. Yet, the Chinese often view it as upgrading the status of negotiations if the foreign party brings along its own interpreter. This can be interpreted as a way of giving the Chinese more face. In addition, it is easier for the interpreter to establish good personal relationships with the Chinese than for the negotiators who work through an interpreter. Furthermore, after the meeting the interpreter can explicate the process.

The Chinese personalization of the negotiating process seems to include a tactical element which should not, however, be exaggerated. Tactical maneuvers are elements of any negotiation. The Chinese wish to spend time on getting to know people, especially in the preliminary phase. This is primarily a function of personalization.

In conclusion, it is a fact that during the first part of the negotiation phase, much time must be spent on getting to know one another, even though to the Scandinavians this 'socialization process' seems superficial and a waste of time. The Chinese do not protract negotiation purely for tactical reasons. Indirect communication requires the construction of a certain measure of common context prior to discussing the points of fact. The Chinese follow the same pattern when negotiating with fellow-countrymen whom they do not know.

Foreign negotiators should be aware of the high contextual conditions and use them to learn as much as possible about the Chinese and their system. Like the Chinese, foreigners will be able to benefit by personalizing the negotiation process when in China. If the process turns out differently than expected after having signed the contract, it is often difficult, or very costly, to take countermeasures in China. This being the case, it is to be recommended that Scandinavian negotiators bring along a Chinese interpreter if the size of the contract justifies this financially. The chances of gaining insight and establishing personalized relationships increase, and for the Chinese, the presence of an interpreter can be justified as a reflection of the importance the Scandinavian firm assigns to the negotiations.

Personalization of employee relationships to managers

The personalization of relationships exists at all levels in Chinese society and is one of the phenomena most often referred to by expatriates.

> 'The Chinese work for me. They are all my employees. The Chinese feel they do something for me and not for the firm or themselves. Personal contacts are inheritable. Ensuring succession is important and happens by the outgoing himself presenting his successor.' (Scandinavian respondent)

Thus, personalization is a phenomenon representing both negotiation situations and long-term relationships of collaboration, such as the establishment of firms. It is essential to be attentive to the Chinese way of thinking in terms of personal relationships, even though it is possible to replace expatriates. Successors can inherit personal relationships. But with Scandinavians replacing individuals is not a big deal. They view positions as roles, which in principle can be performed by anybody possing the necessary technical and linguistic proficiency. In China, however, it is more difficult to replace expatriates, which is why long-term stationing is most beneficial to the firm.

The Chinese View of Expatriates

After a firm has been established, the interpersonal relationships of collaboration and conflict change form.

> *'Problems pertaining to collaboration are primarily internal in the firm. One of the problems is wage differences between the Chinese and the expatriates. If the expatriate is competent there are no serious problems; however, if he is incompetent, does not know how to behave (zenyang weiren), and is incapable of maintaining good relationships with his Chinese colleagues, quarrels are unavoidable.'* (Chinese cadre)

It is remarkable, but in keeping with the Chinese tradition for personalization, that Chinese respondents place the greatest emphasis on a manager's attitude toward others, giving technical skills second priority. According to the Chinese respondents, a competent expatriate is first and foremost expected to be able to socialize with the Chinese in a way they find acceptable.

Another Chinese respondent gave this response when asked what was most important, job experience or being knowledgeable about China:

> *'Naturally, it depends on the particular person, but if he is bright and a fast learner, I would choose the one who knows China. He will soon make himself acquainted with the circumstances. An experienced [expatriate] with little knowledge about China will tend to think he knows it all and in every aspect is better than the Chinese, which will cause problems because his*

*experience is derived from conditions abroad [outside China]. It
is necessary to know something about Chinese tradition, politics,
and economic development. For example, we care more about
human obligations (renqing) and family than the Europeans,
for whom four generations all living simultaneously in the same
house/flat would be almost inconceivable.'*

This respondent was extremely well-educated and had lived abroad for
several years. The statement shows that collaboration is perceived to be
more important than professional qualifications. It is also typical of
many Chinese to distinguish between experiences gained abroad and
those gained in China. Implicitly, the Chinese feel that experience
gained abroad is not immediately applicable to the environment in
China.[3]

Human obligations, or the concept of *renqing*, create the background
for personalization and other particularist relationships, such as *quanxi*,
etc., (see Chapter 6). The quotations above indicate that, viewed from
the Chinese perspective, Western firms should give social qualifications
a higher priority than professional experience when selecting expatriates for positions in China. The most ideal ability would be intercultural competence combined with specific knowledge about China.

The Scandinavian View of Expatriates

Even though the Scandinavians' view of their own role as expatriates is
not characterized by personalization, the following section aims at contrasting theirs with the Chinese attitude.

It is a common experience among Western managers that recruiting
sinologists as expatriates in China is no solution to the problems mentioned above. The challenge is to find expatriates who not only have
experience with similar cultures, but also in managing a firm because
the Chinese have no knowledge or understanding of the soft aspects of
management which are given such a high priority by Scandinavians.
Evidently, one is not qualified to manage a firm merely because one
speaks Chinese. But in situations involving sizeable investments, it is
recommendable to supplement Western management with a sinologist
who can interpret and explain Chinese behaviour and statements and
who, to a great extent, can be taught certain firm specific functions.

*'It is important that the foreign managers participate and help
and do not feel too superior to get involved themselves in anything. I have also wall-papered and layed down flooring. The
Chinese appreciate that highly.'* (Scandinavian respondent)

This statement, which is not unique, placates the status conscious
Chinese. Historically, the distinction between people engaged in intellectual and manual work has been clear in China. Apparently it is
deeply rooted not to mix the two types of work, and it is considered
superior not to do physical work. The Chinese assume foreigners will
be unwilling to participate in physical work, but are positively surprised
when they do. In this respect, there does not seem to be any difference
between managers and subordinate Chinese. The Scandinavian
respondent continues:

*'Common sense and being a talker are important qualifications.
I spend an incredible amount of time talking to people. In addition, one must be willing to compromise on one's own ideas and
live with it.'*

On the whole, all respondents emphasize the necessity of technical
experience. Even the few expatriate managers who have no technical
background emphasize themselves that they have vast problem in controlling how the Chinese handle the equipment. Viewed from the perspective of the Scandinavian culture, the expectation that managers
possess technical skills and are 'talkative' should not be alien to Scandinavians. Thus, most expatriates have both practical experience and
good verbalizing skills, although usually not in Chinese, causing both
parties problems and misunderstandings. The reason is that, apart
from the language barrier, the two cultures have different ways of verbalizing. The Chinese expect personalized communication whereas
Scandinavians are used to universal communication.

An expatriate touches upon why so many go home before their contract expires:

*'You have to have an inherited talent for managing in China.
We have had six who have left. What happens is that they start
to interpret events personally: »they are victimizing me.« »It is
me, they do not like.« In such a situation one becomes irrational.*

The Chinese become irrational too, and the situation ends up in total confrontation.'

Even though I have only ever met expatriates who have remained in China, a majority of them are discontented with living there, which is perhaps not surprising given the unfamiliar circumstances. One reason for this discontent seems to be the Chinese habit of attacking people personally, which makes them break down. According to the respondents, expatriates must be able to depersonalize current conflict with the Chinese if they are to survive in China for a longer period.

Naturally, there are other reasons as well for expatriates going home before their contracts expire but they are less China-specific. Apart from the linguistic isolation, the typical reasons for expatriate discontent are the unfamiliar surroundings, the food, family affairs, etc.[4] Some of the respondents also mentioned more traditional idiosyncrasies neccessary in order to live in China, such as a good personality profile, a cheerful mood, etc.

On the other hand, only one respondent (with a background in sinology) emphasized the need for knowledge about China. However, some mention that they would like to be able to speak Chinese, but find the task too overwhelming. Furthermore, some expatriates have no desire to spend any more time than is necessary in China. Perhaps they do not learn Chinese in order to avoid becoming the firm's 'Chinaman'.

Whatever the case, it is evident from the above that the Chinese and the expatriates have different expectations of the expatriate. Western managers believe that the Chinese emphasize practical technical skills too much, whereas the Chinese rather emphasize behavioural aspects, which is traceable to the dichotomy between the particularistic and the universal.

Chinese Managers' Interrelationship

One serious problem is getting Chinese managers to collaborate.

'The biggest problem is getting the Chinese to collaborate among themselves. They will not collaborate [with this person or that], etc. It really takes time.' (Scandinavian respondent)

Expatriates complain about insufficient cooperativeness both among Chinese top managers and middle managers. Most Chinese seem to have problems in collaborating, though it is less important to the firm if the workers cannot collaborate, than if the managers cannot. Workers are often able to construct a system requiring a minimum of collaboration.

Viewed from a Western perspective, the greatest challenge facing Chinese managers is a change of mental attitude, rather than acquiring technical skills. The typical Chinese manager in a Scandinavian firm comes from the state owned sector and is used to top-down communication, which is why he avoids taking any initiative or accepting any responsibility (Child, 1994:255).

'Changing their mental attitude' implicitly suggests that one cannot expect Chinese managers themselves to recognize the need for change immediately. If they did, the problem would, in part, have been resolved. It is to be expected, however, that as market economy gradually penetrates society and becomes more widespread, managers in the People's Republic will develop different attitudes and become just as dynamic as managers in other parts of the Far East.

The Chinese Attitude About Honesty

Apart from being linked to particularistic relationships, honesty also plays a central role in the expatriates' perception of the Chinese personalization of relationships with foreigners, which is why the concept is discussed in this chapter. The alledged Chinese propensity for dishonesty is linked to many aspects of the culture. To a certain extent, this phenomenon is characteristic of all collectivist cultures. The low interpersonal trust prevailing in such societies makes it less reprehensible to be dishonest with people from whom one does not expect honesty in return. Other factors pointing in the same direction are the lack of belief in one truth and the desire to sustain superficial harmony (see Chapter 7).

What is here referred to as dishonesty, or lack of honesty, approximates what other scholars have called situational orientation, or pragmatism.[5] Here, dishonesty is used instead of pragmatism as the latter is an important element in describing Scandinavians. Dishonesty is biased by emphasizing the negative, whereas pragmatism can be both positive and negative, implying a sense of making the best of any situation (cf. persistence). The purpose is not to reject pragmatic Chinese qualities, merely to note that these are not essential in this context.

Thus, Yau argues that the Chinese are not very dogmatic and have a flexible attitude about the principles they have learned. The reason is, in his opinion, that the Chinese have been brought up by several members of their extended family (Yau, 1994:71). But as pointed out by Tung, engaging in deception to gain strategic advantages is acceptable in the East Asia, including China. Deception is considered a neutral term, which is acceptable if embracing »the greater good«, i.e., the well-being of the family or the self (Tung, 1994:60). This attitude is in sharp contrast to the Christian tradition dominating in Scandinavia, where deception is a sin.

> *'According to Chinese ethics, lying is not wrong. They lie to our faces, which we are not used to. They say one thing one day and another the next. The situation is another.'*
> (Scandinavian respondent)

All the respondents agree that:

> *'Honesty in China is not the same as in Scandinavia. The Chinese often tell white lies and when caught in doing so, they stick out their tongue at you.'*

Sticking out one's tongue is a widespread phenomenon in the area around the Jangze river, and clicking one's tongue is a way of apologizing. However, expatriated who had spent several years in China did not even know what it meant.

The limited honesty has other effects, too.

> *'If the Chinese [salesmen] are dissatisfied with something they will lower sales until they get what they want. They tell the distributors that we have no products which is why we receive no orders.'*

The expatriates indicated that cadres in the political system had told the salesmen to sabotage the system until they got what they desired. When this happens, it is important to distinguish between the interests of the state and that of individuals, as these will often be conflicting.

This makes it possible to ally oneself with individuals who are negative toward the system. This is not fully recognized by many expatriates, probably because the Chinese receive orders from their leaders or party divisions which they must obey, and they thus appear to be united.

> *'When you suggest something to the Chinese they tell you it's impossible. What they do is tell a lie.'*

When the expatriates find the Chinese relatively dishonest it is an effect of an opaque political system which pursues, or perhaps even reinforces, the cultural inclination toward establishing particularistic relationships of trust with individual persons. Particularistic relationships justify dishonesty to others outside the relationship. Evidently, if the Chinese were as dishonest as the expatriates proclaim, it would simply be impossible to run a firm in China or do any kind of business with the Chinese. Therefore, it is important to further elucidate on the Chinese attitude to honesty.

The Chinese focus on practical results leads to the end justifying the means. As a result, making the Chinese comply with rules requires very strict measures as they have no internalized code telling them to comply with laws and rules. Morals are primarily tied to family and friends. Thus, in Chinese dominated areas, and other societies in the Far East, ethics in business life is in general given a low priority. If the other party is stupid enough to be taken in, it is all right doing so.[6]

Therefore trust and trustworthiness *(shou xinyong)* in relation to personal relationships are key concepts among the Chinese (Silin, 1976:128). The preconditions for expecting honesty and sincerity from Chinese is the establishment of a relationship of trust. The degree of honesty is conditioned by whether or not they trust the other party, which they do not to start with. Trust must be built up. One expatriate stated that if one has succeeded in establishing a friendship (trust) with a Chinese, the ties are much stronger than those between friends in Scandinavia. This is in keeping with my own experience and many literary descriptions of friendships. A few expatriates did not find dishonesty to be a problem. However, it is surprising that the majority of expatriates have not given much thought to this phenomenon even after several years in China. This indicates the importance of understanding the Chinese language and tradition, and of being very open minded. Another Scandinavian respondent puts it like this:

'The Chinese are not trying to bend the rules, but they ignore those they do not like, or forget them. They say yes and ignore them.'

The distinction may seem subtle as the consequence of bending or ignoring the rule is the same, but the statement is an attempt to put the Chinese in a better light.

On the whole, the other Scandinavian respondents focused on the Chinese being dishonest in the beginning of a relationship. There is no time limit set for these situations because they only comes to an end when one has won their trust. The Canadian psychologist, Bond (1991:59), refers to a study of Carment which indicates that it is less reprehensible morally to lie in China than in Canada, and those Chinese who lie exhibit fewer behavioural changes than Canadians when lying. Sustaining harmony is what matters most to the Chinese.

In view of the particularistic Chinese attitudes, it probably seems that they are more inclined to tell 'white lies' than Scandinavians, especially to foreigners. This is viewed as a way of maintaining harmony. However, several respondents stated that the Chinese smile when caught in telling a lie, which reflects a certain modest embarrassment. In Scandinavian culture, it is viewed as totally unacceptable to lie under any circumstance since honesty is the basis for the very limited direct control of employees (Fivelsdal & Schramm-Nielsen, 1993:29).

Several studies have indicated widespread low moral standards and a lack of general honesty among business people in China and among many overseas Chinese, which is quite contrary to teachings from the Confucian tradition accentuating moral standards (Redding, 1990:193). This could indicate that a revival of Confucian values might improve the ethical situation in China. However, the likelihood of this is uncertain and does not seem to be the case right now.

Some Scandinavian respondents offered a more positive interpretation of the Chinese behavioural pattern, which does not claim that they do not tell 'white lies', but rather that they resolve the problems they create.

'My employees are good at making the best of surprises. They often find solutions that cause few problems.'

By 'surprises', he means unpredicted situations, indicating that the Chinese are clever at saving the situation at the last minute, i.e., they are good at improvising, which is enhanced by their unwillingness to give up.

White lies, which are used not only in relation to foreigners, result in problems not being discovered until very late, which has caused the Chinese to improve their ability to improvise. The Chinese are used to making the best of any situation. Just keep in mind that their dishonesty should be combatted by establishing personal particularistic relationships, rather than resorting to increased control. The latter may be interpreted as accepting their behaviour.

The Chinese Attitude About Loyalty

Loyalty can be viewed as an expression of the opposite of dishonesty. Those to whom one is loyal, one is also honest to.

The are two concepts in Chinese for loyalty: *xiao* (filial piety), and *zhong* (loyalty to the emperor or other tangible authority). Thus, there is no term expressing loyalty to society. In China, loyalty exists primarily in relation to specific persons, which is why it is viewed as a form of personalization. The firm and its managers must be worthy of the employees' loyalty through offering them protection, promotion or something else, which is why Silin (1976:128; Redding, 1990:66) talks about conditioned loyalty in relation to the firm.

> *'The Chinese are loyal to people, but you cannot make them loyal to something abstract, such as a firm.'*
> (Scandinavian respondent)

Again, this statement indicates the aspect of personalization characterizing by and large all aspects of socializing in China.

During the 1950s, the socialist unit replaced family enterprises, resulting in employees becoming almost tied to the firms which, on the other hand, provided for almost all aspects of their life.

> *'In the West we assume employees are loyal to the firm, but in China it is the other way around. Firms are for the benefit of the*

people. They are to keep people alive no matter what happens.
This is of course crazy.'

The Chinese tend to bring this attitude with them when working for foreign firms, at least in the beginning. However, this attitude is changing rapidly in the 1990s with the Chinese government attempts to make state owned enterprises more efficient.

In an empirical study of the Chinese, Lasserre and Probert (1994:5) found a low degree of loyalty to the firm in China, which is a logical consequence of the conflict between *xiao* and *zhong* mentioned earlier. If a Chinese works in a firm not owned by his own family, he will basically be inclined to show little loyalty, being suspicious of people whom he does not know. A Scandinavian diplomat says:

> *'In Japan, your old friend will still buy from you even though*
> *your goods are more expensive, whereas in China you will have*
> *to wait until the others have stated their prices.*

This is an indication of the Chinese practical attitude toward loyalty. Compared to the Scandinavian perception, it is unacceptable to show your friends what others can offer. But again, it is a matter of adapting to the conditions and trying to win loyalty. However, it is important to emphasize that there is a connection between honesty and loyalty.

Loyalty Among the Chinese

According to one Scandinavian manager, the greatest problem among the Chinese is their lack of loyalty, or trust, and he illustrates it with the following example:

> *'Second quality is put in store to be sold later at a lower price.*
> *The party secretary, who worked in the financial department,*
> *said that the production manager sold the materials and pock-*
> *eted the money. I do not believe it, nor does the Chinese vice*
> *director, but the story never died out.*
>
> *It is a typical example of a case that can never be proven. Its*
> *function is to create bad feelings. The party secretary and the*
> *production manager did not get along.*

Finally, I asked impartial auditors to examine the accounts together with the party secretary. The auditors could not find anything, but the party secretary would not recognize the result. She is no longer employed with the firm, and our partner took her back, but she is married to a colleague of the chairman of the board.

The story may seem banal, but it is a typical example of how Westerners experience Chinese and their interrelationships. Also, the last sentence indicates a certain fear of what she might be able to accomplish through her connections. Lasserre and Probert (1994:18) use the term 'poison pen' to describe the actions of people who hurt one another indirectly.

The Scandinavian Perception of the Chinese View of Foreigners

As mentioned several times, the Chinese are perceived as being suspicious of people they do not know, which is reinforced by the fact that, historically, foreigners are considered barbarians. Scandinavian expatriates certainly perceive the Chinese as suspicious of foreigners:

'I never know what the Chinese think. No matter what we say they are suspicious. No matter what we do, the Chinese think they are being fooled. The attitude is: the Danes are probably telling lies.'

The often negative attitude aired by Chinese Communists during the 1970s has been somewhat reduced, and the young are more positive towards foreigners and foreign ideas. To bridge the distrust, many expatriates attempt to make suggestions for change appear as if they are the Chinese's own suggestion:

'Patience is decisive. The best is if they themselves make suggestions. Sometime they suggest something I mentioned half a year ago.' (Expatriate)

This is the positive way where the expatriate succeeds in making the Chinese feel that ideas accepted originate from themselves. If such attempts fail, the Chinese tend to be suspicious of suggestions from expatriates. This is also related to the concept of face, because it gives more face to the Chinese if their suggestions are accepted.

Different Attitudes Toward Age

It is to be expected that the Chinese attitude toward age differs from that of Scandinavian managers. About age, a Chinese manger says, referring to his colleagues:

> *'The number of competent Chinese managers is increasing. You have to try to recruit people around fifty. If they are much younger, they are not adequately experienced, and if they are above sixty years they do not have the strength (sufficient energy) to handle the job as manager.'*

The essence being that managers have to be between forty and sixty, which is possible since they do not have to leave their native home like expatriates do. Thus, the Chinese set more narrow age limits and bottom limits higher than Scandinavian firms, which tend to recruit either very young or fairly old expatriates. Many expatriates are above sixty. Few expatriates are between forty and fifty, probably because many people of this age have children in school and therefore do not wish to be stationed abroad. Also, many firms start in small and are disinclined to send their best employees to China in the initial phase. Interesting enough, the Chinese do not prefer older expatriates anyhow, feeling that experienced foreigners think they can manage everything. They can not anyway, as many conditions are specific to China.

Status

Status refers to differences of social honour and prestige assigned to social groups by others (Westwood & Chua, 1992:150). In China, personalized relationships combined with great power distance tend to result in greater emphasis on status and status symbols than in

Scandinavian countries where status symbols are viewed as suspicious and negative by other employees.

China's high degree of masculinity compared to Scandinavia also points towards greater emphasis on status and status symbols, material as well as immaterial, such as honour.

> *'Fine titles are important, so we are one director, two vice-directors and a secretary. That is the total staff of the joint venture.'*
> (Scandinavian respondent)

Another Scandinavian respondent said he called his employees technicians instead of workers. Knowing the importance which Chinese ascribe to status, it is relatively easy for the Scandinavian expatriates to give them fine titles and other symbols signifying status or enhancing their face, which is both sides of the same coin. Thus, the importance of status can be used as a motivational means.

However, not knowing the Chinese cultural proclivity in this area, there is every chance of getting into trouble. Another respondent describes Chinese reactions upon visiting Denmark:

> *'The Chinese could not understand that their expatriate Danish director did not have a large elegant office and thought that he occupied a low position with the firm in Denmark. Thus, they felt that the Danish parent company had sent a second-rate director to their joint venture in China. The Chinese are used to large offices and cars with chauffeurs.'*

Especially during the 1980s, when the Chinese had little knowledge of the West, there was a gap in understanding one another. The Chinese could not comprehend that business managers from Scandinavia drove their own cars, and their offices were often modest, or they did not even have an office but sat in an office landscape. One way of helping the Chinese understand the small power distance is to explain to them the principles of egalitarianism. During the reign of Mao, the socialist system operated with some of the same principles, e.g., cadres had to work and wage differences were reduced. Particularly during the Cultural Revolution great emphasis was placed on reducing the importance of status and status symbols, but it failed. In want of other things, the Chinese turned Mao badges into status symbols and competed for who had the largest and most extravagant badge. This shows how difficult it is to change proclivities deeply rooted in a culture.

Conclusion

In consequence of the universal attitude characterizing Scandinavia, the individual is less important because Scandinavians think in terms of roles and not specific persons. Roles can be performed by various individuals. Contrary to this, Chinese personalization creates particularistic relationships. In effect, they are more inclined to perceive people as individuals and not as role owners. Even though there are examples of both attitudes in both cultures, their dominance varies. Given that the two attitudes contrast, they are in principle incompatible.

The Chinese want to know people prior to entering into collaborative relationships or doing business with them. This period of socialization, to include quibbling or the like, is perceived as a waste of time by Scandinavians.

Compared to the Western parent companies, the Chinese place far more emphasis on the expatriates' personal knowledge of China or the Chinese, gained during previous periods as expatriates. To the Chinese, it is essential that expatriates know how to behave in Chinese society. This is in full keeping with the greater emphasis on appearance than in Scandinavian culture. Manners are ascribed greater importance in China than in Scandinavia. This is apparently unknown to a large number of Scandinavian investors. And many not having other firms in the East Asia, they frequently establish themselves in China without having had the opportunity to recruit staff with the desired qualifications. Therefore, Scandinavian firms typically prefer an all-round education enabling the expatriate to do a little of everything. Most expatriates have technical knowledge with some managerial experience. Many Scandinavian managers also mention the importance of a good personal profile, but apart from knowledge of the language they indicate no need for understanding more about the country.

The Chinese are viewed as fairly dishonest and they do not find it wrong to lie. Some respondents, including Chinese, say that the Chinese might sabotage functions in the firm if they disagree with the expatriate about something. Like in other places in the East Asia, the

Chinese tend not to show if they disagree. Instead they do what they find best. Honesty is governed by how loyal they feel to the Scandinavian expatriate and how much they trust him. Apparently, the Chinese aversion to conflict has made them good at improvising to save unpredicted situations.

Feelings of loyalty in China are determined by personalization of relationships. Loyalty is first and foremost tied to the family and other in-groups. Loyalty to the workplace is conditioned by whether it is to the benefit of the family, including themselves or other in-groups. Contrary to the Japanese, the Chinese do not feel particularly tied to their workplace. On the contrary, job hopping is a widespread phenomenon, though it is restricted to people with special skills due to the vast overpopulation. To the extent that the Chinese are loyal to their workplace, their loyalty is directed towards the director or other persons in the firm rather than the firm itself. Thus, Chinese expectations of long-term personalized relationships conflict with the Scandinavian expectations of long-term firm-related relationships where those occupying managerial roles can be exchanged at any time.

Apparently, the negative interpersonal relationships among Chinese have been aggravated by the socialist system. Informing on others, learned and developed during the Cultural Revolution, combined with the emphasis on specific interpersonal relationships, are still deeply rooted in the culture. It will take many years before the Chinese rid themselves of this. In addition, older Chinese are in general suspicious of foreigners, whereas the young tend to admire them. And though the Chinese look up to older people, they recognize that leaders must not be too old to handle the work pressure. The Chinese also ascribe greater importance to status and status symbols than do Scandinavians. They find it difficult to understand that the Scandinavians' position in the firms is not reflected in status symbols and clear hierarchies.

Recommendations

The Chinese personalized attitude makes it is necessary to pretend showing the individual Chinese special consideration. Standard operating procedures are bound to be perceived negatively. Expressions such as 'this is how we do it in other places' are perceived negatively.

It is important to have as much contact as possible with the Chinese just as one must be willing to demonstrate one's ability to adjust equipment or handle other practical situations. To a certain extent, this personal contact should extent beyond working hours.

The Chinese culture is a high context culture, implying that the Chinese need to know people they do business with. Therefore, Scandinavians must be prepared to spend much time and energy in the initial phases, making the Chinese feel they know the Scandinavians well enough to trust them. This socialization process may, as indicated earlier, consist of playing majong with the Chinese or the like. The succes rate of negotiations can be enhanced by a stronger cultural awareness of the Scandinavian negotiators ((see alto Tung, 1989:68).

As the Chinese are not emotionally tied to their workplace, it is important to tie key employees to the firm financially in terms of relatively high bonuses.

Since the Chinese strongly emphasize that expatriates should know something about China and Chinese culture, one must express a certain interest in these issues irrespective of whether or not one is genuinely interested. Expatriates ought to have a basic knowledge of China and Chinese culture prior to working in the country.

It is important to watch out for intrigues among the Chinese and react immediately. The best is to leave these situations to the Chinese vice director if possible. Also, one should be prepared for the considerable amount of time it takes to establish collaboration with a Chinese head of department (see Chapter 6, Internal Firm Relationships).

Expatriates should not take too literally what the Chinese say. In their attempt to sustain harmony, they tell 'white lies'. The Cultural Revolution reinforced Chinese bitterness against the system and hence their rather ruthless pursuit of wealth. In consequence, controlling Chinese performance is hardly avoidable in the lengthy initial period, but should be done as discretely as possible.

It is imperative to establish a relationship of trust with individuals and try to give them an idea of how Westerners think, possibly by letting them stay in Scandinavia for a longer period. It is recommended to the widest possible extent to recruit and train younger people.

In general, a relationship of trust is established by keeping one's word. In effect, the older Chinese will change their attitude and become more positive and collaborative toward foreigners. Therefore, long-term stationing is to be preferred and when expatriates are

exchanged there must be an overlapping period and personal introduction. However, since it is difficult to find competent managers it
will often be necessary to educate and train young Chinese. This takes
time and requires much attention from the expatriate.[7] There are other
benefits to be derived from hiring the young right out of university.
One can recruit them oneself, which is not always the case with
employees allocated by the Chinese partner. Hence, one can choose
the profile that fits best into one's own corporate culture or way of
working. This should be exploited consciously (Maruyama, 1994).

The relative few competent managers available are gradually beginning to demand higher salaries, and since job-hopping is a well known
phenomenon among foreign firms in China, they are difficult to hold
on to. There is no simple solution to this problem, but the more one
can tie a Chinese manager to the firm the better. It would be helpful to
study how companies in other parts of the world tie managers to the
firm by way of bonuses and share options, etc. However, this problem
is hardly resolvable in the short run. Furthermore, one should be attentive to the fact that it may prove difficult just finding people who speak
English. A hotel complained about being merely a training ground for
young interpreters who wanted to further their language careers.
Receptionists left the hotel to be employed by foreign firm as they
became increasingly proficient in English.

In some cases, age of a Chinese is a determining factor in their ability to collaborate with Scandinavian expatriates. Younger Chinese find
it easier to break with tradition than the older ones. On the other hand,
older Chinese feel they should enjoy greater respect due to their age.
In terms of the expatriates, the ability to adapt to Chinese behaviour
seems much dependent on whether or not they have been stationed
abroad earlier. However, this does not mean that the age of the expatriate does not matter. Other things being equal, the Chinese prefer
older people in that it is easier for them to gain respect and respon-
siveness. On the other hand, the Chinese are somewhat afraid of older
expatriates becoming too dominant in relation to the Chinese, indicating an ambiguous attitude towards this issue among Chinese.

Figure 5.1 indicates that the best interpersonal relationships emerge
from collaboration between expatriates of great experience in working
abroad and young Chinese, whereas the poorest combination is older
Chinese collaborating with inexperienced expatriates. Thus, it is recommendable that firms themselves recruit and train young Chinese.

Figure 5.1 Optimalization of Cooperation Between Chinese Managers and Expatriates

	HIGH	POSITIVE	UNCERTAIN
SCANDINAVIAN EXPATRIATES' EXPERIENCE			
	LOW	UNCERTAIN	NEGATIVE
		YOUNG	OLDER
		CHINESE MANAGERS	

In addition, it is important to exploit the Chinese awareness of status by giving them fine titles and large offices to enhance their face and prestige. Offices and other artifacts must reflect their actual position. A way of avoiding problems with status, which cause the Chinese to lose face, is to be attentive to the internal Chinese communication. If one does not understand the language, one can follow their eye movements and become apt at spotting who holds the highest position in the hierarchy.

6. Networking

Introduction

This chapter focuses on the Chinese relationships and networks, *guanxi*, which has gradually become a recognized concept in the West. The Western notion of network is discussed first, since this bears the closest resemblance to the Chinese collection of relationships discussed in this chapter. Comparing the two makes it possible to view the latter from a wider perspective. Second, the concept of *guanxi*, for which no adequate English translation exists, and its characteristic aspects are discussed in detail. Third, expatriate perceptions of and attitudes toward network are addressed as well as Chinese attitudes. Finally, the chapter offers suggestions for how expatriates could and should relate to the Chinese *guanxi*, or personal relationsships and related phenomena.

Western Understanding of Networks

There is a considerable amount of American and European Literature on networks, but Americans tend to stress quantitative studies, and the Europeans qualitative (Hedaa, 1992). Western definitions of network are numerous, and in many cases rather imprecise, probably because networks are viewed as part of a research strategy, i.e., something constructed by the researcher through his/her identification of relationships between entities and people (Gouldner, 1954). Network is a dyadic relationship between two entities, be it people or organizations. It is not confined to a group, but is, in principle, boundless and the number of potential dyadic relationships grows exponentially with the number of actors.

The structure of networks is informal, there are no written laws or contracts[1], making trust decisive. According to Hedaa (1992:179), dyadic networks never reach the point of complete reciprocity. The very essence of network is that mutual exchange is never synchronous and never one-for-all. The glue binding Scandinavian networks may be trust based on friendship, kinship, work, trade, etc.

It is noteworthy that within business research, network seems to be a recent concept gaining increasing ground in the West, whereas in China, it has been an everyday expression for thousands of years. This is inconsistent with evolutionary theory, such as argued by Luhmann[2], claiming that personal trust evolves into systems of trust. Granovetter (1992) refers to networks as weak ties, thus neglecting what Hedaa calls strong ties, such as the family. My approach to networks is in line with Granovetter's, because his understanding is more comparable with the Chinese guanxi. According to Granovetter, the strength of a network relies on a combination of:

1. Time
2. Emotional intensity
3. Intimacy
3. Reciprocal services

These elements do generally apply to a great extent, but the following will show that there are certain cultural specific differences between Scandinavian and Chinese networks. Granovetter (1992:53-85) also mentions that networks, or weak ties, function as bridges between different sub-cultures and thus may provide access to resources not available from persons to whom one is closely related or strongly tied.

The Concept of Guanxi

Guanxi is defined as relationship (connections or networks) cultivated with business associates, officials or others based on mutual interest together with a heavy emphasis on obligations and instrumentalism[3]. *Guanxi*, is probably the best known Chinese word in the West next to tea, and it is often emphasized as a phenomenon which makes Chinese culture distinctive.[4] *Guanxi* is mentioned as one of the three main ideas constituting the basis for understanding the traditional Chinese cultural system. The two others are 'face' and 'doing favours' (renging) (King, 1993). These three concepts are closely interrelated in Chinese culture and tied to a psychological sense of human interdependency. Doing favours, or human obligations, is the norm for interpersonal relationships resting on reciprocity, and *guanxi* is the most important element (King, 1991). Thus, the nature of Chinese relationships is very utilitarian. It is not a matter of behaving like a gentleman, but of establishing relationships for mutual exploitation.

As pointed out by Tung and Yeung (1995:18), *guanxi* is embedded in dyadic relationships between people, not organizational entities. Personal relationships are a characteristic feature of Chinese culture because they ease tensions between the moral requirements of Confucianism and the anti-social attitude in society (Redding, 1990:82). Figure 6.1 illustrates the hierarchical order of the concepts:

Figure 6.1 Phenomena Affected by Personalization

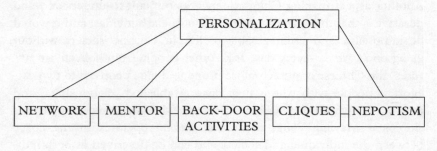

The overall concept is personalization from which Chinese networks and similar phenomena emerge, such as mentors, backstage activities, cliques, and nepotism. These phenomena are also present in Western culture, though not to the same extent as in China.

In his classical study of Chinese culture, Liang Shuming characterizes Chinese society as based on relationships (*guanxi benwei*), as compared to the American society which is based on individuals, and the European which is founded on groups. This indicates how essential 'classical' Chinese sociologists viewed network.[5] Recent research (Redding 1990:83) tends to view personalization as the overall concept, just as I do here. Yet, the Chinese social system is neither characterized by purely individualist nor collectivist tendencies, even though China comes very close to the top of collectivist pole in Hofstede's dimension individualism-collectivism.

The Chinese concept *guanxi*, which literally translated means connections or relationships, differs etymologically from the Western concept of network. First, it is widely used in everyday speech. Second, the Chinese concept of network includes special relationships between individuals who can make unlimited demands on one another, such as

pointed out by Pye (1982). Third, the Chinese people do not view networks as a breach of the social norms of justice and fair treatment,
which would be the case of similar relationships in the West. Thus, no
definition captures the essence of *guanxi*, which is reflected in its different usage in everyday China. Kipnis (1994) gives examples of how
something which is refered to as *guanxi* by some people, will be refut-
ed by others as having no resemblance to the concept.[6]

The social placement of guanxi

Another aspect making Chinese networks difficult to understand and
describe is that they penetrate all kinds of social activities, and it would
be impossible and unimaginable to live in Chinese society without
using one's *guanxi* every day. Like other people from collectivist cultures, the Chinese are much more prone to divide people into two categories: people with whom they have established relationships, and
people with whom they have not (Butterfield, 1982). According to the
sinologist Mayfair Yang, the art of *guanxi* operates in the space
between the individual and society and can be described as both individual-centred and -decentred. The individual attempts to place himself in the centre of any guanxi-network, simultaneously trying to conceal other relationships and how these are utilized, such as whom one
asks about what, which gifts one gives to whom and how, etc. (Yang,
1994).

Individual-centred indicates that one reason for building networks is
because the individual is deficient, making completion through relationships necessary. This is characteristic of collectivist societies.
However, in general, *guanxi* is more person-centred, or individual-centred, than the Japanese *wa* (this means group-centred), which has been
used to explain the relative high frequency of job-hopping in China. If
a relationship is not mutually beneficial, new *guanxi* are formed (Alton,
1989). *Guanxi* connects individuals through exchange of favours, and
if one of the individuals in a *guanxi* refuses to reciprocate a favour, he
lose face. In other words, a person's face (*mianzi*) is conversely related
to the size of debt owed to others. Thus, reciprocal *guanxi* relationships
entail a strong element of moral commitment or trust, since many
Chinese owe favours to a variety of people. Chinese networks may
evolve for a variety of widely different reasons. They often emerge
among people who have been born in the same part of the country,

previous classmates, teachers-pupils, or brothers-in-arms during the revolution.

Relationology

Throughout history, the Chinese have developed their particularistic interpersonal relationships into an exquisite art, or perhaps rather a science (King, 1992:68). The Chinese talk about 'relationology' (*guanxixue*) which, among other things, includes how one establishes and uses personal relationships (*la guanxi*). The latter expression has become widely used in contemporary dynamic China which is confronted with vast bottleneck problems. When asking a Chinese how he will solve a given problem, the standard response is that he will '*la guanxi*', which means that he will draw on his connections. This may imply that he will use existing connections, or try to cultivate new ones through the people in his current network. Relationships which are not used are merely left dormant, to be activated when or if necessary. As *guanxis* are informal, the are never abandoned or terminated formally, but may die out little by little.

The functions of guanxi

In general, *guanxi* relationships are most beneficial to the weaker part of the dyad. Since the two parties are expected to help one another to the best of their abilities, the one in possession of most resources will be rendering most help. As a result, the recipient will end up in a dependency relationship. Thus, networks strengthen interdependency among Chinese. In traditional China, the most important function of *guanxi* was protection in a society characterized by insecurity. No other institutions existed which would resume responsibility for the welfare of the individual. Establishing personal trust among the members of a network reduces the effect of anti-social behaviour in society. But *guanxi* also has its negative side-effects. In traditional China, business people were inclined to conduct business in a different village than from where they lived in order to facilitate the workings of market principles and to avoid the effect of personal relationships on business transactions.[7] The Chinese government has always treated *guanxi* with certain reservations since the ideal typically implied that responsibility to the quanxi took precedence over responsibility toward the state.

Thus, in Imperial China, one could not become a public servant in the same province in which one was born.

The Chinese sometimes use the expression *guanxi-wang* (network of relationships) in a negative context, but generally it refers to something positive. One can get the feeling of being caught up in a web of relationships, since they put one under an obligation to render services. But in general people are proud of having many personal relationships. An often heard Chinese expression is that a person's value is equal to the sum of his relationships. Thus, one can improve one's value by having many relationships.

Kipnis (1994:6) tells of a rural shop owner who denied using *guanxi*, because everybody payed the same price. However, the customers proved to be predominantly people from her own work group, and she attempted to give better service to those whom she knew. In this way, she used her *guanxi* to increase the turnover. In addition, her uncle, a prefect, had helped her get the licence to trade, but being a member of the family she did not perceive this transaction as *guanxi*.

There is a tendency, however, not to involve money directly in *guanxi* transactions in order to make these look more legal, but that does not mean that you do not have to pay back in the future, when you have drawn on a *guanxi*. As stipulated in the definition utilitarian relationships. *Guanxi* is widely used by communist cadres to promote their own interests through mutual services, nepotism, etc. In contemporary China, however, young people tend to place stronger emphasis on relationships than do their elders, whose moral upbringing restrain their usage of *guanxi*. In this context, one should be aware that the younger generation of Chinese are morally ill-bred compared to the older. But nothing seems to indicate that the importance of the concept is declining.

Networks in an historical perspective

Walder (1986) has explained this use of personal relationships as a result of how conditions developed under the reign of Mao Zedong, when people could not choose for themselves where to work or when to change workplaces, and the fact that few rules were written down, which naturally enhanced the importance of being on good terms with the leading cadres of one's unit. This explanation appears to reflect over-politicization, since the Chinese still use personal relationships after having gained more freedom, probably even more, just as they had used *guanxi* even before China was united in 221 B.C. (Yang, 1994:305). Yet, it is probably true that, in certain areas, Confucianism has reinforced a psychological tendency to build personal relationships. Mastering the art of *guanxi* may furnish the actors with a certain political autonomy which many cadres have missed. On the other hand, the Communist's strong moral rearmament, particularly during the first decades of takeover, reduced the use of personal relationships.

Albeit, relationships are vital for surviving in Socialist China, they are not accepted officially since they are part of what the Communist jargon refers to as private (*si*), that is, an organizational form which is not approved by the Communist Party. Nevertheless, networks exist all over China and have been called China's second monetary unit.[8] Western observers had mentioned personal relationships as being one of the causes of the well-functioning planned economy. Despite extensive political turbulence under Mao Zedong, China succeeded in establishing a much higher growth rate than Eastern Europe. Thus, *guanxi* entails maintaining flexible anonymous ties[9] which ensure that there will be the personal relationships necessary to fill gaps in the planned economy. This made it very difficult for the Communists to combat these informal ties if they wanted to.

Middlemen

Middlemen occupy a key position in Chinese society for several reasons, one being that they contribute toward establishing *guanxi* between people who are not interrelated but wish to be so (Tan, 1990:280). Being a commercial middleman in China implies great obligations, with responsibilities that closely resemble those of introducing a young potential couple to one another. If the marriage turns out bad, the middleman is held partly accountable for having introduced the wrong people to one another. Likewise, by introducing two parties to one another, the commercial middleman signals that they can trust each other, and in doing so he also invests something of himself and becomes morally responsible if one party cheats the other. Therefore, Chinese will not introduce people to one another without full consideration of the implications and without thorough knowledge of each party's backgrund. If conflicts do occur later on, the middleman is fully prepared to intervene and attempt to resolve these.[10]

Guanxi in a business context

Although the Chinese tend to personalize all relationships, they pay little attention to general human feelings, such as sympathy. This makes
it difficult to distinguish between the implications of *guanxi* at the personal and professional levels, which the use of *guanxi* demonstrates in
business life. *Guanxi* has considerable influence on financial and managerial conditions. For example, tight networks further the division of
labour between firms, allowing each firm to only play a minor role in
the total production process. As a result, trade occupies a key position
in this society dominated by traditional family patterns, even though
both Confucian and Socialist ideology look down on trade (Redding,
1990:237). Despite these world views, or ideologies, trade has achieved
a preeminent position in Chinese society, demonstrating the strength
of family and personal relationships. Redding (1990:112) mentions
that personal networking in Chinese business life is primarily established in order to reduce uncertainty in three areas of pursuit:

1. Information gathering
2. Stabilizing supply and markets
3. Cementing key relationships in organizations.

The basis of many interfirm agreements is pre-existing personal obligations, and even today agreements are only verbal (Redding,
1990:151). Thus, collaboration between Chinese firms is highly characterized by informal agreements within a network.

Guanxi Compared to Western Networks

Comparing Chinese *guanxi-net* to Western networking reveals num-
rous similarities, but also a great many differences. The most conspicuous dissimilarities are the pervasiveness of Chinese *guanxis* and the
degree of reciprocity. In relation to the three domains mentioned by
Redding, the strong inclination to build networks results in a high
degree of information circulation. In effect, the Chinese know much
more about each other and their environment than is the case normal-
ly in Scandinavia. However, the form does somewhat resemble old-
boys networks in Scandinavia.

Using networks to stabilize supply and markets is a well-known phenomenon in Scandinavia, but there is a greater sense of urgency in Chinese society, having to deal with a variety of bottleneck problems. Compared to Western networks, the Chinese are more binding and come closer to the Western sense of friendship. Thus, the Chinese find friendship which does not include *guanxi* as inconceivable (Pye, 1982:89-91). In the West, we also operate with connections, but there are certain limits for to what extend they can be exploited, which is not quite the case in China. In Scandinavia, networks are often tied to firms, whereas in China they are rather tied to certain persons. That is, in Scandinavia reciprocity exists between firms and are not transferable if one leaves the firm.

Chinese manners differ according to whether they are dealing with members of their network or outsiders, whereas Western manners are more standardized and basically rest on egalitarian principles. *Guanxi* is particularist as opposed to the more universal attitudes in the West. A comparative study on networks in China and the U.S.A. indicating that Chinese networks were twice as substantial as American, and that the Chinese prefer socializing with people of their own age and educational level, whereas they rarely mentioned socializing with kin. However, in China networks are instrumental rather than based on friendship (Nathan, 1993:929). And if compared with Scandinavia, a similar tendency can be observed.

Scandinavians and other foreigners should be aware that when Chinese try to establish friendships and relationships, the relationship is unequal and typically to the benefit of the weaker. Implicitly, friendship means that one uses the other and both use each other's *guanxi* (Pye, 1982:89).

Mentor *(Houtai)*

Parellel with *guanxi*, but less widespread, exists what the Chinese call *'houtai'*, mentor, (*houtai* means backstage). *'Houtai'* denotes one who has connections with high ranking cadres who can offer help or protection in the event one does something wrong, which has been almost unavoidable due to the nature of the system (Chu, 1991:199). This phenomenon makes any relationship with the Chinese inscrutable. In many cases, the apparent formal leader of a delegation is not necessarily the most influential person. One often finds that the person who does not appears to hold a key position in the group has the best contacts further up the hierarchy, which the Chinese refer to as strong *houtai*, meaning this person has influencial backstage connections, making him/her the most influential representative in the delegation. However, during the initial meeting it is almost impossible to see through the interwoven relationships. Only after collaborating over a longer period do foreign firms begin to understand the various actors' backstage connections. Gradually, as the foreign representatives are perceived as part of an in-group, the Chinese open up and explain the nature of their interpersonal relationships.

Backstage Activities *(Houmen)*

What the Chinese refer to as backstage activities range from lobbyism to bribery. Backstage activities are treated separately, since they seem to be tinged with illegitimacy. Literally translated, *houmen* means to use 'the back door', but in reality it implies corruption, bribing someone to achieve something. The general perception among people studying conditions in China is that bribery has become more widespread over the last ten to fifteen years, as the Chinese economy has been facing vast bottleneck problems. The system of two prices, which existed in China from the early eighties to the early nineties, has further reinforced corruption. Bribing cadres in order to purchase goods at government prices, and then reselling these at much higher market prices, yields vast profits. Evidently, the cadres played a key role in this activity, and their behaviour is often mentioned as one of the major causes for the revolt in the summer of 1989.[11] As a result of this situation the Chinese tend to pursue what seems impossible to a foreigner, because in a personalized system everything is possible. As pointed out by Liang, the Chinese are forced to solve their problems themselves, since they cannot rely on society to intervene, as in the West (Liang, 1987:82).

Backstage activity does not always signify bribery. Sometimes it merely implies drawing on one's connections, or attempting to influence decision-makers. In this sense, it resembles lobbyism, which is increasingly used within the European Union. However, it has a more negative connotation than *guanxi*.

Cliques

Like *guanxi*, the tendency toward cliquism is an effect of personalization, but it is also inspired by *guanxi*. However, in general, *guanxi*-networks are more widespread, whereas cliques are minor groups with a higher interaction frequency.[12] Another difference between networks and cliques is that the latter are comprised of a limited number of members, typically less than ten, and are based on mutual interests, such as the game majong. Networks are based on mutual exploitation. Members of a clique usually belong to the same social stratum. Thus, there are cliques of workers, cliques of middle managers, etc. Members of cliques are willing to make special efforts to help one another and to accept greater distance between services and reciprocation.

Nepotism

In China, the connotation of nepotism is not always negative, since it is usually tied to the family. Strong family ties and an autocratic tradition make it is easier for nepotism to exist in China than in Scandinavia. In many cases it is difficult to identify nepotism, partly due to the fact that during certain periods, the government encouraged sons and daughters to take over their parents' work, if possible, in order to reduce unemployment. Also, periodically it has been quite natural to employ children in their parents' work unit, also if this meant that children replaced their parents. Officially, the Chinese authorities are critical of nepotism in the Western sense, favouring kin or friends irrespective of their qualifications when recruiting staff, appointing managers, etc.

Empirical Data

First, we will cover statements by Scandinavian expatriates, followed by comments from their Chinese colleagues. In the following, I distinguish between internal and external conditions to the firm. In general, Scandinavian expatriates are very conscious of the importance of *guanxi*.

External Firm Relationships

A Scandinavian manager states:

> 'In China it is a question of know-who, not know-how. Friends
> and connections are more important than goods and prices. The
> Chinese were shocked both times I turned out a supplier. They
> think that we will never be able to get the goods if we turn out a
> supplier. We know that if A cannot supply the goods, B can.'

The essence of this statement is that Scandinavians and Chinese hold
different attitudes toward connections. Scandinavians attach little
importance to connections, whereas the Chinese consider connections
to be all-important. It is true that Scandinavians attach less significance
to networking than do the Chinese, but the difference is not as cate-
gorical as the statement would indicate. The respondent's interpretation of the Chinese reaction confirms that he, after having lived in
China for three years, still thinks as a Westerner. He has not gained
much insight into, or understanding of, the Chinese way of thinking.
The respondent did not take into consideration that breaking off a connection may create a moral issue.

To begin with, the Chinese first think in terms of personal costs, and
then about whether the goods can be purchased from other suppliers.
What probably made the Chinese uncomfortable was the immoral act
of breaking off a *guanxi* which may become known to other networks
and hence affect other relationships. Plus, the Chinese supplier will
remember having been rejected much longer than would be the case in
Scandinavia, because he loses face, which is of such great importance
in China.

In general, expatriates seem to view networks as having a greater
impact on external than internal firm relationships, which is surprising
from a Western sociological point of view (cf. Granovetter) that networks, or weak ties, grow stronger with increasing intensity and intimacy. Only one respondent claimed the importance of *guanxi* to be
declining. However, having said this he called one of his subordinates
and reminded him of his meeting with Li Ruihuan's son[13], which made
his statement less credible. When I pointed out this inconsistency to
him, he answered that *guanxi* also means to 'help one another'.
Apparently, the respondent tried to find a positive way of interpreting

the Chinese behaviour. Many Scandinavian expatriates tend to view firm external *guanxi*, if not in a positive light, then at least in a tactical light, exploiting the phenomenon whenever possible, which is well in keeping with Scandinavian pragmatism.

Trust

Guanxi and trust are inseparable. Most expatriates recognize the importance of trust in China, but do not associate it with *guanxi*. As one Scandinavian respondent says:

> 'Trust and respect mean more to the Chinese that to us. A pleasant atmosphere is totally decisive.'

Rather than trust and respect, the Chinese would probably say that good connections and keeping face are decisive for creating a good atmosphere. However, expatriates do not associate trust with *guanxi*, or respect with face. Their way of thinking is still determined by their original cultural system resulting in a perception of the Chinese as somewhat sensitive.

Mentor

A manager in Beijing says:

> 'We chose our partners on the basis of their guanxi. They had good connections to Zhu Rongji[14]. Without contacts we will get nowhere, so we are in constant contact with a variety of government agencies, such as the Ministry of Foreign Trade (MOFTEC), the Planning Commission and specific departments.'

This statement demonstrates Scandinavians believe in the importance of having *guanxi*, and even maintaining a mentor who can support their projects. Often the mentor also plays a role in getting a project approved, and in subsequent operations. There are examples of former Chinese government leaders having succeeded in obtaining quotas of foreign currency for certain sectors. The above statement also shows that some Scandinavian firms have succeeded in establishing external *guanxi,* which was a weakness earlier, particularly in relation to firms located in neighbouring countries.

However, it is not only firms that can have a mentor, but also individuals. When negotiating with Chinese delegations, Western business people find it important to get a clear picture of the members' internal hierarchical position, which is the same as trying to identify who has the strongest mentor, or who gets the most support from high ranking cadres. A Scandinavian board member says:

> *'We do not know who is in charge during board meetings. It is a black box. One member of the board never uttered a word, but later on he proved to be the one who made the decisions.'*

This situation was very typical during the 1980s, when Scandinavian business people realized that they could not be certain whether the leader of a delegation would actually have the decisive word if the delegation had internal dissension. On the whole, many Scandinavians were surprised that the Chinese often disagreed internally. Communist propaganda had succeeded in creating an image of the Chinese as party representatives, and not as individuals competing among themselves. What makes it difficult to see through the hierarchy of a delegation is that the Chinese perceive their internal relationships strictly as internal affairs. Furthermore, due to personalization, the power structure can not be determined on the basis of organizational affiliation or position. One must know the group extremely well, or have a Chinese informant to point out whom to keep an eye on. The latter method is the most common.

One expatriate gives an example of different mentors' strengths which had serious overall consequences for a certain project:

> *'Three persons tried to obtain the post of vice-director. Mr. Sun was appointed, but lost the battle because the two rivals managed to cutt off funding. We were also unable to get the premises we had been promised, and other types of cooperation proved impossible.'*[15]

As a result of this conflict at management levels, the joint venture was terminated. This statement indicates the difficulty of identifying the mentors and their relative strength. It took the expatriate several years to figure out the truth of the matter and why so many changes had suddenly occurred.

Backstage activities

Close internal relationships in many cases enable the Chinese to have their way using their interrelationships in situations of conflict. As a Scandinavian respondent says:

> 'If things could be kept at a business level we would have no problems, but issues that are difficult to resolve find their way into the political arena, meaning that the Chinese slip it in the back door, and the political system enables them to have it their way.'

What the respondent is really saying is that the Chinese use their political connections in order to get things their way when two parties to a joint venture have conflicting interests. The above example shows that backstage activities do not always involve bribery, but moreover resemble lobbyism. In this case it was a matter of influencing powerful contacts in the party, not of money or other services. The incomprehensible political system reinforces exploitation of interwoven personal relationships to appease self-interests.

Thus, one of the key problems for expatriates is that Chinese unity, or interrelationship, makes it impossible to control conflicting interests, resulting in the expatriate almost always losing such combats. This contributes to the view that China is a difficult country to work in. One will have to develop matching interests with certain Chinese, if one has hopes of realizing one's desires. On the other hand, the Chinese often disagree internally. Therefore, being attentive to their internal relationships often makes it easier to identify conflicts between Chinese if this is what one wants.

Other types of middlemen are the so-called one-time agents, who claim to know a cadre in a key position, i.e., a mentor. One respondent expresses it this way:

> 'The agent problem is still increasing. People want money for ceding their guanxi. The amount depends on the project, but is typically a couple per cent.'

In many cases someone approaches a foreign firm which is in the process of negotiating a project, saying that he knows, or has good *guanxi* with, the decision maker. The 'agent' is willing to exercise his influence with this person to encourage him to give preference to the given firm over others for a certain commission, either payed in advance or when the project is home and dry. Evidently, the latter is to be preferred, but it is my experience that such agents will argue for the necessity for receiving an advance to buy 'presents' for the decision maker, which indicates an element of corruption. Such arrangements are very problematic. For one thing, it is illegal. It is also difficult to know just what services this middleman, or one-time agent, actually renders, especially since the firm usually stands a chance even without such help. In addition, adding his commission to the price of the project may make the firm's bid more expensive than their competitor's. Therefore, it is important to look into the agent's reputation and demand evidence from him, such as being able to get a hold of the competitor's sales materials, information on the purchasing group's power balance, etc. A representative of a large Scandinavian firm says:

> *'In many case, one has to pay the authorities some percentages.*
> *We often use 'advisers', both local Chinese and others.'*

Apparently, an increasing number of firms trading in China are recognizing that they cannot avoid such 'advisory agents'. In this context, it may prove beneficial to take on a local Chinese partner who can evaluate when to agree to 'percentages'. Also, much seems to indicate firms fully owned by foreigners are more exposed to pressure than joint ventures.

Internal Firm Relationships

Several respondents said that they were not conscious of networking within the firm, but the problem of informal cliques, which is the same, was often mentioned:

> *'Some Chinese protect one another. Sometimes we are presented*
> *with proposals for promotion of completely hopeless individuals.*
> *The reason is that they have too many friends.'*

Cliques play an even more negative role than *guanxi*, being small and relatively interwoven groups working closely together. One expatriate said:

> 'We are also experiencing informal cliques, but our jobs are well-defined and transparent. However, we are constantly attentive to the phenomenon. We are not going to accept small kingdoms in the firm.'

The mentor also exists within internal relationships, as is reflected in the difficulty of removing a given manager. One respondent expressed it this way:

> 'In China everything is very personal. Many people are better qualified than we are, but they will never stand a chance. Everything is kept within the organization. One's connections and friends are decisive'.

If this is true, it demonstrates combinations of the various interpersonal relationships described above: cliques, backstage activities, and the mentor system. These phenomena are often inseparable. In the case of joint ventures, the Chinese party appoints the Chinese managers. Even though these have to be approved by the Scandinavian partners, according to the contract, the result is often dissension if the Scandinavian expatriates cannot collaborate with the Chinese managers. This also applies to the middle manager level. One expatriate explained that it had taken him almost two years to get a Chinese manager replaced, obviously because he seemed to have good connections in the parent firm. Many Chinese compete for managerial positions in joint ventures and those appointed usually have the best relationships with the former managers. Thus, Chinese who perceive their own position as being threatened often try to use their personal mentor to help them maintain their position.

Nepotism

In general, expatriates view everything that resemble nepotism and other types of personal connections very negatively. This is a natural consequence of their Scandinavian upbringing, since this makes

impossible what they consider to be an objective assessment of performance. But in China it is different. One experienced expatriate says:

> *'We often hire spouses of people with connections. Connections*
> *are important in China.'*

One thing that refrains most expatriates from being part of Chinese
personalized relationships is their fear of not being able to remain in
control. The above respondent does not, however, view this as a problem as long as the relationship with the Chinese partners is characterized by trust. The example shows the importance of expatriates learning to think in terms of categories which play an important role in
Chinese society, but which often have strong negative connotations in
Scandinavia. In a society where wages are low and relationships are
important, nepotic appointments often prove rational or to be a sound
investment.

Another study of Chinese managers demonstrated they they, as the
only Far Eastern representatives, found it quite natural to employ several members of the same family (Lasserre & Probert, 1994:19).
Western assessments of performance, which are not characterized by
taking the individual's relationships into consideration, are in most
cases not applicable in collectivist societies. As pointed out by the
above respondent, relationships should be taken into consideration
when employing someone in a collectivist society.

The Chinese on *Guanxi*

The Chinese respondents' general reaction to foreigners' attitudes
toward *guanxi* was that they have no understanding of Chinese connections. A Chinese director explained that the emphasis on *guanxi*,
which he referred to as *guanxi*-nets, is rooted in the extended family:

> *'We attach great importance to family relations (guanxi) and*
> *interpersonal relationships in general. In attaching such great*
> *importance to family relations, we also find social relationships*
> *important. Europeans are quite the opposite. They emphasize*
> *independence. And because they do not attach much importance*
> *to family relations, they also do not view workplace relationships*

as important, which effects their work, management, and managerial style.'

In this quotation, *guanxi* is interpreted to mean 'relations' to make it more comprehensible. The Chine director perceives *guanxi* solely as positive. This illustrates the difference between the official, negative view of *guanxi*, and the actual behind-the-scenes view of *guanxi* as a positive element. However, a few Chinese mentioned that *guanxi* contained both positive and negative aspects. Additionally, it is also remarkable that the Chinese director compares a culture's attitude toward the family with its attitude toward interpersonal relationships in general, which no European would do, even though it seems obvious.

Conclusion

Traditionally, *guanxi* was constructed to reduce uncertainty in an unstable society. Since Chinese society in many ways still lacks stable structures, *guanxi* is still widespread. As it appears from the above, Chinese and Scandinavian attitudes toward *guanxi* differ widely. Expatriates' attitudes are summarized in Figure 6.2.

Figure 6.2 Expatriates' attitudes toward guanxi and related phenomena

Negative attitude	Mentor *Guanxi* among Chinese	Chinese backstage activities
Positive attitude	Nepotism Trust *Guanxi* to Chinese	Trust *Guanxi* to authorities
	Internal	External

Firm relations

Figure 6.2 shows the positive and negative roles of *guanxi*, its role being in general more positive in connection with external relationships than with internal where *guanxi* or cliques are viewed as a threat to control over the firm.

Guanxi among the Chinese makes it difficult for expatriates to get full information, and they are often left with the feeling of being kept in the dark, because they do not know about, or understand, the information circulating among the networks. Even though it is necessary to combat certain connections, expatriates are increasingly recognizing the importance of creating their own networks with selected colleagues in order to strengthen their control.

The Chinese respondents agree that foreigners have no understanding of relationships and they do not seem to think that they can acquire much knowledge about these networks during the three to four years they typically spend in China. Another possibility is that the Chinese simply do not want expatriates to learn much about *guanxi* and other phenomena. Perhaps they are ashamed about the way Chinese society functions. Most Chinese will dissociate themselves from the above mentioned phenomenon except for *guanxi* at an abstract level. But in concrete situations, they will often react pragmatically. In informal talks, the Chinese often blame the political system for the existence of these phenomena, which is not reflected in any of the quotations because I knew none of my Chinese respondents prior to the interviews, and they would never air such opinions to a complete stranger.

Recommendations

Guanxi is a fact of life in Chinese society whether Scandinavian firms and expatriates use them or not, and it would be logical for expatriates to exploit them to their own advantage. Furthermore, overseas Chinese and others use them consciously, which makes it necessary to use *guanxi* in competing with these foreign firms. Another argument for using *guanxi* as an additional safety net is the deficient legal system.

Networks can function as avenues for solving conflict ensuring the firm greater external autonomy, and maintaining internal control. This implies that expatriates must learn to create their own networks, which should not be difficult since networks also exist in the Scandinavian countries and are gaining increasing importance. In addition, most Chinese are interested in having foreign friends. It gives status, in part because foreigners still can help Chinese in a variety of areas. Foreigners still hold certain privileges, such as the ability to buy train tickets and access to means of international communications. They can also help Chinese get abroad. The majority of Chinese still dream about spending time abroad.

However, for two reasons, it is more difficult in practice to create connections with the Chinese than one immediately would anticipate. One is the language. It is difficult to establish personal relationships through a third party, and it is therefore recommended to associate with Chinese who speak English. Second, expatriates will have to adopt a life style resembling the Chinese. Expatriates must feel comfortable and relaxed when being with Chinese. Most Chinese enjoy talking about anything and spend most of their leisure time doing so, whereas Scandinavian expatriates tend to draw a sharp line between work and leisure time, and will confine talk to work-related issues during working horus, which most Chinese do not. Step by step expatriates should adopt a more diffuse life style, where they spend more time chatting with Chinese colleagues informally.

Having lived in China for a certain period, expatriates should seriously attempt to get out of the ghettoes which house only foreigners. In this context, business people can learn something from Western expatriate journalists who solicit contact with selected Chinese informants and often invite them to their homes.

The strength of a network is a function of time, intensity, intimacy and mutual services, as pointed out by Granovetter, and this also applies to *guanxi*. Trust is decisive in the case of *guanxi*. Thus, establishing a relationship of trust to as many Chinese as possible is important, bearing in mind that the relationship will be unequal. There is the risk that it is sometimes difficult to terminate relationships in China, but since most expatriates only spend a few years in China, this is unimportant. On the other hand, foreigners can argue against grease money by claiming that well-established interpersonal relationships already exist. Payment for services is not discussed among friends in China. In China, as in other places, relationships of trust are first and foremost established by honouring an agreement. In China, this includes keeping secrets. The Chinese are experts at leaking information bit by bit at the tactically right moment (see Chapter 9).

Expatriates also have to learn that in China restrictions are usually not absolute. The Chinese are accustomed to solving the most impossible problems by drawing on their connections, an attitude which foreigners should adopt. Being turned down should not make one give up.

One must be attentive to the formation of cliques among the

Chinese, as they are difficult to deal with once they are established, and should be 'nipped in the bud'. Western investors should also bear in mind not only that the Chinese partner should have a strong mentor, but also that this mentor's prestige should be commensurate with the size of the project. If the project is small, the mentor should preferably be insignificant, because significant mentors tend to ignore small projects.

Also, it is recommendable to accept a certain amount of nepotism, if the persons in question can be fitted into the organization. In part, this is a way of establishing relationships with those already employed, and the new recruit will often bring along new *guanxi*. Anyhow, the wage level is still low in China, so one employee more or less does not make much difference.

The most difficult domain within which to offer advice is that involving ethical elements. If possible, one should use backstage activities, since they are fairly safe for foreign firms as long as they resemble lobbyism in Scandinavia. Even if it entails seeking out a high ranking cadre to bring him a box of cigarettes or the like, this is fairly safe for expatriates. Should bribery be mentioned, one should leave this issue to the Chinese, primarily because it is less of an offence receiving grease money from other Chinese than from foreigners. The worst thing to accuse a Chinese cadre of is collaborating with foreign interests against China. Many Chinese have suffered groundless accusations of treason under the Communist regime. In certain competitive situations, one-time agents are inescapable, and again it is primarily the Chinese agents who are punished if the authorities intervene in such arrangements. On the other hand, one should be aware that, even though corruption seems to flourish everywhere, the phenomenon is not more or less accepted by the authorities, as in some African and South Eastern countries. Corruption is still risky business, in particular for the involved Chinese, which is why one should avoid, to the largest extent possible, becoming directly involved. If corruption becomes even more widespread in the future, foreign firms should leave such issues to a Chinese agent.

7. Face

Introduction

This chapter deals with the concept of face in general and culturally determined definitions of face. After a theoretical review, we will take up expatriate reactions to Chinese responses related to face, based on empirical data, and we will cover the Chinese attitude about face. Both Chinese interrelationships and their relationsships to and understanding of foreigners will be examined. Finally, Chinese responses related to face will be treated in terms of the consequences and measures to be considered by expatriates. Some recommendations are given.

Introduction to the Concept of Face

The face is the 'front part' of the head, and thus the first thing noticed when meeting another person. Due to the physiological position of the face, all cultures use face metaphorically to describe a person's status, or lack of same, in those groups with which s/he associates. Face reflects one's relationship with one's social environment which is just as important as the face (Hofstede, 1991:61). In some cultures, such as the Chinese, the metaphorical sense of face is more essential than its physiognomy (Tan, 1990:281).

The linguists Brown and Levinson (1987:13-15 & 61-63) claim the metaphorical sense of face to be universal, which is why language contains universal phrases of politeness. Everybody want others to acknowledge their actions, which contributes to self-esteem. They also want to prevent others from interfering with their actions or to look down on them, which would cause them to 'lose face'.

By nature, face is interpersonal. Any talk of saviing or losing face implies the presence of a second party. One does not lose face to oneself. The decisive difference between face and concepts such as guilt, self-confidence, and self-respect is that the latter are not directly related to other people, although the environment may affect these individualist concepts. Acceptance by others strengthens one's self-confidence. Thus, the real difference lies in how these concepts are interpreted. In very internalized cultures, such as the Scandinavian, one's own interpretation is essential, whereas in externalized cultures, such as the Chinese, the viewpoint of others is more important.

In viewing face as tied to various fundamental cultural values such as honour, virtue, shame, etc., Brown and Levinson (Ibid.) emphasize that the significance of face and its various forms vary between cultures in terms of which behaviours give face, which cause one to lose face, and what kind of people need special face protection, etc. Despite the universal nature of the phenomenon, the import ascribed to face and its role in different cultures vary considerably. These cultural differences imply that, even though everybody wants to avoid losing face, there are no guidelines for behaviour in an intercultural context, so one does not know how to behave in order to avoid causing members of a different culture to lose face.

Differences in the Concept of Culture Between Individualist and Collectivist Cultures

Individualist cultures are in general characterized by individuals with a strong sense of internalization, having an internal locus of control. These cultures are called guilt-cultures. Guilt is something the individual feels and has no direct connection with the environment. One can feel guilty without others knowing. Guilt is particularly predominant in Protestant areas, such as the Scandinavian countries.

Collectivist cultures, on the other hand, are in general characterized by individuals with a strong sense of externalization, meaning their locus of control is external. Therefore these cultures are often referred to as shame-cultures. By nature, shame is social. A person only feels shame if s/he infringes upon the rules of society and others learn about it. Thus, the infringement in itself is not what causes shame but the fact that others know. Like shame, the nature of face is social. The position of face differs from individualist to collectivist cultures. Face plays a more central role in collectivist than in individualist cultures, such as the Scandinavian. However, individualist cultures, preferring direct communication, attach less importance to face than collectivist cultures, which prefer indirect forms of communication and equivocal speech.

Loosing face, particularly in collectivist cultures, means that one is ashamed of other people's perception of oneself and one's immediate family. In effect, the social environment strongly influences one's behaviour.

Definitions of Face

Face is, as mentioned, the individual's evaluation of how others perceive them and thus it is dependent upon public status via-à-vis family, firm, and society. Hofstede (1991:61) mentions that the expression 'losing face' has penetrated into Western languages from Chinese and quotes the Chinese sociologist David Ho: 'Face is lost when the individual, either through his own action or that of people closely related to him, fails to meet essential requirements placed upon him by virtue of the social position he occupies.' This definition seems coloured by its collectivist culture origins emphasizing the family's behaviour and the individual's behaviour as equally important.

The Western sociologist Goffman (1955:213) describes face as self-representation. 'Face is an image of self delineated in terms of approved social attributes.'. In Western, individualist cultures face is used to achieve self-esteem based on the individual's own actions, and actions by family members are less important. Furthermore, it is typical of these definitions that they do not consider what is here referred to as the ethical aspect of face.

Hofstede's Discussion of Face

Even though Hofstede and other scholars view shame and face as closely related, shame and protection of face are opposites when considering long-term versus short-term life perspective, all of which Hofstede originally referred to as Confucian dynamism in his decentralized studies of Chinese values in Asian countries (Hofstede & Bond, 1988:5-21). Hofstede explains this distinction stating that the sense of shame supports reciprocal relationships where one pays attention to one's own social contacts, which is why shame enhances one's sensitivity to keeping commitments. Thus, according to Hofstede (1991:177), guilt points forward. However, if this inclination becomes too dominant, refered to by Hofstede as 'exaggerated protection of face', it may lead to a reserved attitude or passivity in social situations.

Hofstede's thesis is that protection of face is greatest or most exaggerated in more stable societies, whereas shame is dominant in dynamic societies, pointing towards the significance of face declining in conjunction with societies becoming increasingly dynamic, such as the Chinese. Hofstede's definition is sublime since it is difficult to distinguish between face protection and shame, which is why he adds 'exaggerated' or 'passive' to face protection.

As I have suggested, I assume this vague definition to be the result of these scholars not having been aware of the fact that the Chinese language has two words for face. If this assumption is right, it indicates that shame is pointing forward and is dynamic, whereas guilt and ethics contain elements pointing backward, as they easily lead to the conclusion that conditions are determined by faith.

The Concept of Face in China

One of China's most famous writers, Lu Xun, wrote of face: 'It is all very well if you do not stop to think, but the more you think the more confused you grow. There seems to be many kinds: each class in society has a different face.'[1] There is no doubt that face is a predominant concept among the Chinese. Redding (1993) goes so far as to say that it is the most important factor in understanding interpersonal behaviour among Chinese.

According to a study conducted by Redding and Ng (Ibid.:195), 98% claim to develop a sense of shame, apprehension, anxiety, and tension if they lose face. Only a minority expressed physiological effects, such as loss of appetite (33%) and insomnia (21%). At the psychological level, gaining face is just as important as losing it. The results of gaining face are usually satisfaction, proudness, and self-assuredness.

Due to the importance of face in China, the Chinese use face as a point of reference for evaluating behaviour in a far more sophisticated and developed manner than people in, for example, the Scandinavian counties. The Chinese use two words for face, *'lian'* and *'mianzi'*. Even though they do not always distinguish between the two colloquially, 'mianzi' most resembles the Western concept of face, whereas 'lian' refers to the 'depth' of face, to the more abstract ethical aspects.

'Lian'

'Lian' is the ethical aspect of one's personal behaviour, and one must behave as a decent human being. To lose one's 'lian' means that one has committed something shameful and is thus without integrity. It is the most severe social condemnation to which an individual can be subjected.[2] Everybody starts out having 'lian', but can lose it depending on one's ethical qualities. Even the poorest can show proper ethical behaviour and thus possess 'lian', but may not be able to achieve much 'mianzi' (Oxfeld, 1993:7-8). Thus, one can only lose 'lian', it cannot be given by others. Lost 'lian' is difficult to restore, which is not the case of 'mianzi'.[3] On the other hand, one can refer to face ('lian') as thick or thin, depending on how much one emphasises ethics or proper behaviour (Silin, 1976:44-45). However, one cannot talk about 'lian' in terms of great or small as is the case with 'mianzi', which has no girth.

A person, family, clan or other groups can lose 'lian'. This emphasises that in most cases the concept is not to be understood as pertaining to the individual but rather to the collectivity. The family's behaviour may affect a person's face. The same applies to 'mianzi'.

'Lian' is the ethical basis for trust, which is the precondition for giving less priority to contracts and formal agreements. Otherwise, 'lian' is not much mentioned in connection with commercial transactions. If mentioned, it is typically in reference to a person of 'thick face' (shud), meaning that he pays little attention to the moral rules of the game and is thus dangerous to do business with.

'Mianzi'

Literally translated, 'mianzi' means 'surface', and concerns one's reputation based on one's social position and prestige. It is good to have but not decisive for one's life. Not to have 'mianzi' means that one's performance or business has not been successful (Redding & Ng, 1983:100). Thus, 'mianzi' is much more transferable than 'lian'. Others can give or take one's 'mianzi' at discretion.

'Mianzi' plays a part in everyday business transactions, and it contributes toward regulating interaction between commercial actors because one party's aggressive behaviour will deprive the other party, or parties, of face. This is in keeping with the Confucian principle of controlling one's emotions and avoid conflict (Chen, 1992:89-90). Thus, the positive regulatory function of face in the Chinese society is significant (Redding & Ng, 1983:95).

In an attempt to illustrate the concept of face to Westerners, 'mianzi' has been compared to a credit card. It is important to maintain a certain balance in reciprocity. Like a credit card, 'mianzi' can be overdrawn if one does not give as much 'mianzi' as one receives (De Mente, 1989:61-62). To maintain equilibrium, the Chinese are, in general, willing to compromise and let everybody appear to be the winner in a given situation. Similar to other phenomena in the Chinese culture, 'mianzi' forms part of hierarchical relationships. A high-status person can give a great deal of face to a person at a lower hierarchical level by contacting him himself instead of letting others do it (Tan, 1990:22). Similarly, the Chinese hunt for 'mianzi', or prestige, is a significant dynamic force. To obtain greater 'mianzi', they will always try to outdo one another (Oxfeld, 1993:263).

An often-cited example of the importance of face stems from two Americans teaching management in China. A group of Chinese management students all began arguing each vying to be ranked lowest in the group, which would make the poorest 'win' in the end, and thus avoid losing face (Lindsey & Dempsey, 1985:75). Undoubtedly the event took place, but the interpretation is American. To the Chinese, it is natural verbally to let oneself appear to be the inferior, but it is naive to think that the one who won, or lost, felt that he himself had won.

The Chinese are incredibly experienced in distinguishing between manners and essence, and one should bear in mind that 'mianzi', or saving face, refers to manners.

Since Chinese do not want to lose face, they are reluctant to refuse something openly, or to say something that others may not wish to hear, which would cause the other party to lose face. This is one of the reasons for the extensive use of middlemen in Chinese society. Now, the size of one's 'mianzi' is something one constructs to be used later, making it possible in a conflict involving two other parties to draw on one's own face in relation to A, enabling him to apologize for B's mistake. This takes a middleman capable of evaluating the value or size of his own face (Bond, 1991:58). A third person is often involved as middleman in restoring a person's lost face. In this way, the Chinese use 'mianzi' to strengthen not only their external interrelationships, but also their internal relationships (quanxi), referred to as front stage behaviour, as opposed to back stage behaviour which should not be exposed publicly (Bond & Hwang, 1986:245). Thus, when business people phone someone to invite him for a seminar, for example, they will often say 'give me face by attending' which is a polite way of indicating that the one invited has greater face than the one inviting. If the person, whom one wants to invite, is even more important, one will call on him in person to invite him hoping that he will give one face by attending (Redding, 1990:65).

Traditionally, the Chinese are willing to accept much to save one another's face. Smith (1986:17-18) mentions examples from old China where servants, who had been caught stealing, had been given the chance to return the stolen goods, thus enabling them not to lose face. His story indicates that, in some situations, 'mianzi' is more important than the ethical 'lian' (to steal), which is unusual viewed from the perspective of Western culture. This is not always the case. But both concepts are ascribed great importance in China, and most Chinese will not be able to explain the difference. Often one hears Chinese say that the two concepts cover the same. Incidently, Smith's story is from Shanghai, which is known today for harbouring the most conscientious Chinese. This applies regardless of whether they still live in Shanghai or have moved to other places in China.

The examples indicate the subtlety between the two concepts and how difficult it is for a Scandinavian to interpret them. One way of understanding the difference is to compare 'mianzi' to reputation and 'lian' to self-esteem, but this analogy is only approximately true. The Chinese fear of losing face, or causing others to lose face, tends to make them sustain superficial harmony in their interrelationships (Tan, 1990:280). This superficial harmony often hides profound internal conflicts that are rarely brought out in the open and resolved. The Chinese can fight 'harmoniously', behaving politely towards one another but, fighting indirectly using every possible means.

The positive aspect of saving face is that the Chinese often tend to compromise. Just remember that a compromise can be both sincere and insincere. Insincere compromises are often constructed in order to prevent conflicts. The expatriate will not discover immediately whether or not a compromise is sincere, not until the decisions resulting from the compromise are implemented.

Nevertheless, 'mianzi' is relative. The same person can have great 'mianzi' in relation to subordinates and little 'mianzi' in relation to intellectuals.[4] To enjoy big face means to enjoy high prestige in the eyes of others. Little face is the opposite.

According to Hu's (1944:22-44) classic study (quoted by Redding in Bond (ed.), 1986:246), the six most important categories of face in China are:

1. Enhancing one's own face
2. Enhancing other's face
3. Losing one's own face
4. Hurting other's face
5. Saving one's own face
6. Compensation (restore, retaliate, self-defense).

Bond and Lee have argued that face is particularly important when (1) the same people meet over and over; (2) when members achieve identity through group activities rather than through individual activities; (3) in authoritarian societies in which criticism of superiors may threaten the social order. [5] Thus, in China, face is not necessarily tied to one person but often to a collectivity such as the family, working group, etc. (Bond & Hwang, 1986:247). One can actually make references to a family's face.

In a small empirical study among overseas Chinese business people, Redding and Ng (1983:113) found giving and receiving face to be most important. Of secondary importance was giving face to achieve other ends.

This shows that face is just as important as the principle of reciprocity. Thus the Chinese attitude toward face is pragmatic. Linguistically, the difference between the Chinese and the Scandinavian use of face is the usage of two different words in Chinese for face and the importance to Chinese not only of losing face, but of giving, getting, harming, wanting, enhancing or striving for face ('mianzi'). Also, the Chinese often refer to the size of one's face, which can be both big and small (Lin, 1989:187), just as one can enjoy high or low prestige in the Western world. Thus, albeit face is more widely used in China than in the Scandinavian countries, it is partly a question of different words and concepts. As indicated, well-known Scandinavian concepts such as ethics, prestige, reputation, self-esteem, and original sin can approximately replace the Chinese concept of face.

The most important differences in weighing the Scandinavian and Chinese concepts of face against one another are illustrated in Figure 7.1.

Figure 7.1 Differences in Scandinavian and Chinese concepts of face

	The Scandinavian countries	China
Face ('mianzi')	Shame (less important	The respect of others (important)
Face ('lian')	Guilt (important)	Self-esteem (important)

The figure illustrates the Chinese division of the concept of face. Both 'mianzi' and 'lian' are important in both cultures, but their value differs. Shame is relatively less important in the Scandinavian countries than in China, whereas guilt is more important. It may come as a surprise that self-esteem is important in China, but the reason is that both concepts of face are relational. Self-esteem is achieved by exhibiting high moral standards and living up to other's expectations. When 'lian' is translated as 'moral', it refers to externalized morals, not internalized, as in the Scandinavian countries.

Empirical Review

Empirical data will be categorized as face from the perspective of Scandinavian expatriates working in China, and from the perspective of their Chinese colleagues. However, the main purpose is to establish an understanding of the concept of face viewed from the perspective of Scandinavian expatriates. The empirical discussion also focuses on the concept of 'mianzi', whereas 'lian' is not discussed in connection with the interviews. As most of the Scandinavian expatriates did not speak Chinese, they did not consciously distinguish between the two concepts. What they in most cases referred to as 'face' corresponded to 'mianzi'. The Chinese respondents consistently used 'mianzi' and not 'lian'. However, the Scandinavians can use 'lian' to appeal to the Chinese sense of morals, even if one speaks English and refers to both concepts as face, although this makes the usage more complicated.

Scandinavian Expatriates Working in China

Scandinavian expatriates tend to find face more important for the Chinese than for themselves. One respondent initially stated that face was equally important anywhere, but later said that the expatriates could stand losing face eight hundred times whereas the Chinese could not stand losing face once. Another respondent felt that the Chinese usage of the term was purely for improving their own tactical situation. Yet another said that face was primarily important among the Chinese. Most of the interviewees referred to examples of situations in which they had caused the Chinese to feel they lost face. Naturally, the causes in each instance varied widely.

Firms dealing with external face clashes, as viewed from a Scandinavian perspective

It was primarily those respondents managing Scandinavian fully owned or near fully owned firms who most strongly experienced face as a problem in external relations, probably because they were attending to more external relations than joint venture partners. One manager told that the Chinese salesmen felt they had lost face because he, as a purchaser, had brought along a completed contract leaving them no option to negotiate. The Scandinavian manager did not view it as having been a question of prices or other kinds of influence, but rather as a matter of not having followed the rituals properly. The next opportunity he had, he would not bring along a contract, but would negotiate it. This example also says something about the Chinese haggling mentality.

A Scandinavian manager in Beijing tells about a more direct and visible reaction to losing face:

> *'The Chinese are very conscientious. Once we misplaced a high-ranking cadre at a banquet, resulting in his leaving. Later on we had to figure out a way to restore his face.'*

From my experience, this reaction was extreme, and quite unusual for the Chinese in relation to foreigners, as the Chinese are not prone to start an open conflict. Either the offended had no other way of showing his frustration, or he was being temperamental. A more typical Chinese reaction would have been to swallow the offence but remember it. Given that the Scandinavian firms referred to here are experienced and employ many Chinese, this example shows that one must constantly be aware of such potental mistakes which are relatively easy to avoid. If one does not know in advance who the leader is, it is usually apparent from they way the Chinese look at each other. If it is suggested to the 'wrong' person to occupy the seat of honour, he will look at the person who ought to occupy this seat. Preferably, one should know their ranking in advance.

According to the respondents, problems of external face are in general of less importance and easier to resolve than internal, involving daily contact and thus the possibility of accumulating insults. External contacts are often short, limiting the importance of face which is why the offended Chinese will often excuse mistakes committed by foreigners. This is in line with Bond and Lee's argument that face is most important in connection with continual contact between human beings.

Clashes internal to a firm, from a Scandinavian perspective

Viewed from the perspective of the Scandinavian expatriates, the greatest problem involving internal firm relationships is that the Chinese are extremely closed, either because they have lost face or because they are afraid of doing so. In the words of a Finnish manager:

> *'If you pick on someone's responsibility domain at a management meeting, he will never again tell you anything or ask you about anything in the future. No news is good news.'*

Many of the respondents mentioned that the Chinese will not say if they do not know how to solve a problem. Instead of asking for help, they try themselves to fix the problem or leave it unresolved until the Scandinavian discovers it for himself. The typical story is that several days or weeks may pass before the Scandinavian discovers that a machine has broken down. Often it only happens when he discovers that orders have not been satisfied.

> *'When we had received three new compressors, the Chinese said*
> *everything was all right. Later on they said that two gaskets*
> *were missing. Subsequently, I discovered that two of the com-*
> *pressors had not been working for half a year. Nobody had ever*
> *said anything.'*

Because of situations like this, the Chinese are often perceived as
unwilling to collaborate, or even as devious, apart from being very
closed in general. Nearly all respondents felt inadequately informed by
the Chinese, but their interpretation as to why differed widely.
Whether the respondents attributed negative motives to the Chinese or
interpreted their behaviour as fear of losing face, they found that the
Chinese gave the firm's interests a low priority. Respondents seldom
mentioned that perhaps the Chinese did not bring up problems fearing
that this could be interpreted as deficient qualifications which might
result in getting fired. It probably never dawned on the Scandinavians
that this could be the case.

> *'The Chinese are difficult to interpret. They never say what you*
> *do not want to hear. This we interpret as if they are for and not*
> *against. Later on, they do something different which we inter-*
> *pret as an infringement of the agreement. We get angry and*
> *show it, but the Chinese do not (show it).'*

The Chinese try to save the foreigners' face, but when foreigners express
anger, the Chinese interpret it as an assault to their face. Even though
the respondents emphasized the importance of being conscious of face
when working with the Chinese, in concrete situations they tend to react
spontaneously, with reactions rooted in their own culture. There is no
doubt that foreigners are often hurting face unconsciously, which shows
their inadequate understanding of the Chinese concept of face.

Some foreigners ascribe positive motives to the Chinese, such as fear
of disappointing foreigners or upsetting them by telling them a
machine does not work. Obviously, no matter what the Chinese
motives are, the motives ascribed to the Chinese by foreigners affect
interaction. Those who see positive motives contribute to improving
the climate, which leads to the Chinese demonstrating greater open-
ness. And in the case of losing face, the respondents felt that the
Chinese either shut themselves up or swallowed the shame, causing a

series of problems. The typical reaction is for the Chinese to shut themselves up and avoid the foreigner, or say as little as possible to him. In itself this is an important element in creating the negative image that many foreigners working in China hold of Chinese colleagues.

Conscious manipulation of the foreigner's face

If face is used at all consciously in Scandinavian firms, it is mainly in a negative way when foreigners do not know how else to handle the Chinese. They trap the Chinese leaving him no way out.

> 'We had a Chinese vice-director who leaked information to the competitor that had helped him getting his son to Germany. To get rid of him, I chose to present the documentation to the board and the vice-director at once, and he left. Offending a Chinese is easy, he is very vain.'

The importance of keeping face is often interpreted as vanity by Westerners. This example is most telling of how foreigners deliberately use their knowledge about face to place a Chinese colleague, whom they have abandoned as hopeless, in an impossible situation.

Many respondents did not believe in the positive use of giving face.

> 'If I feel they try, I support them, but if you praise a Chinese too much, he'll be happy for a week and then repeat the same mistakes.'

Such relapses are a recurrent theme in several contexts and I shall later return to this phenomenon. A relapse originates in the Chinese adapting to the foreigners' demands without feeling convinced about their validity.

Even though the above quotation originates from a foreigner who has been working in China for a couple of years, it can hardly be said that it is in vain trying to build up face. Just keep in mind that building up face is a continual process. And remember that the process is situational, that different types of praise are not equally important.

According to the traditional understanding of face in China, as discussed earlier, the perception of face is fairly consistent, indicated by

the long memory of having lost face. Foreigners, who have been working in the Far East for many years, tend to ascribe greater importance
to face and be more attentive to the phenomenon. Their experience
makes them attempt to understand the Chinese more deeply, and they
put a stronger emphasis on giving face. They tend to view their contacts with Chinese as a 'positive' opening process. As an expatriate,
who earlier worked Malaysia, says:

> *'In the beginning, the Chinese are very closed, but gradually
> they open up and tell about their problems. They find it difficult
> to say things plainly but it applies to Chinese as to others: if you
> like me, I like you.'*

The experienced expatriates have a positive attitude towards the
Chinese. They are often fully aware that they can only work in countries where they can establish a positive attitude with the native
employees with whom they must collaborate. Thus, they create a more
informal relationship with the Chinese by expressing themselves positively, making it easier for the Chinese to forgive them if they hurt their
face unintentionally.

Chinese Leaders and Face

In the following, the Chinese attitude toward the expatriates and the
Chinese attitude about interrelational face are discussed.

Chinese managers on expatriates' understanding of face

In general, the Chinese respondents attached great importance to
expatriate attitudes toward China. Even though expatriate managers
come to China to supply firms with knowledge of management and
technology, the Chinese find expatriate knowledge of the country just
as desirable as their expertise. In the words of a cadre from the economic zone:

> *'The expatriates must understand the concept of face (mianzi).
> The Chinese attach such great importance to face that they view
> it as a question of whether or not the expatriates possess feelings*

(dong qing). The Chinese are used to being master in their own house and will not accept if the expatriates exclusively treat the Chinese as employees (bei guyong), and they (the Chinese) can be very imaginative as to ways of sabotaging the firm, such a tampering with the machines, etc. Management ought to integrate the concept of face. If the expatriates exclusively play by strict rules, then he will not get anywhere. Showing the employees respect is decisive.'

This example illustrates something general about the Chinese attitude towards expatriates and is not aimed at people from the Scandinavian countries in particular. The respondent indicates that expatriates in general ascribe too little importance to the employees' face in particular, and to treating the Chinese employees fairly, which is the same as saying expatriates treat the Chinese degradingly.

Emotions, or (interpersonal) competence (qing), is a key concept in Chinese tradition and language, often used in connection with a negation, such as callous or ruthless. The above quotation illustrates a recurrent theme in Chinese culture. They are a proud people, particularly in North China, interpreting everything very personally. In such a culture it is extremely important to be sensitive to how others react. The worst one can do in this type of culture is to treat everybody as equals (referring to the previous discussion of universalism versus particularism.) The Chinese prefer particularist manners, treating each individual separately.

In South China being viewed as an employee does not have the same negative connotations, since many employees come from poor rural districts. A Chinese manager says:

'Face is important for collaboration with an expatriate manager. If a Chinese manager at a large meeting advances opinions to which the expatriate manager disagrees and the latter repudiates these, pointing to several misinterpretations and spelling out the right interpretation, the Chinese manager will feel incapable of escaping the situation honourably due to the presence of many subordinates. First of all, this has to do with the way in which the expatriate manager expresses himself. You do not always have to agree with the Chinese, but you should not just cut them off like that. The expatriate may say that in his opinion the sit-

*uation should be interpreted in this or that way, allowing the
Chinese manager to preserve his face.'*

This quotation illustrates the extent to which it is more important how
a message is communicated, rather than focusing on the contents of
the message itself. It is imperative to say things the right way, and in
Chinese culture, the more positively one expresses oneself the greater
the effect. This is probably the case anywhere in the world.

Chinese managers on the attitudes of Chinese about face

Most Chinese managers emphasized the importance of face among
themselves:

> *'If a senior manager issues an order to which one disagrees, we
> still will not allow him to lose face. Maybe we will not follow his
> advice, but we will never oppose him directly. After the meeting
> we may discuss things with him. Sometimes we will think, let
> him have his way, we do as we see fit. The end justifies the
> means as you say.'*

This quote indicates that maintaining a superficial harmony is more
important than subsequent dispositions. This attitude is almost a logical consequence of the strong awareness of face.

Several Chinese managers mentioned that Chinese actually attache
great importance to the 'superficial' (biaomian), such as face and similar social conventions, which indicates that it is more significant in
China than in the Western world.

The Scandinavian countries have no tradition for distinguishing
between what one says and does. On the contrary, preferably these are
identical. What this therefore means is that expatriates must acquire a
knowledge of new social conventions when arriving in China. In particular, they must understand that, whereas it is indeed unethical to say
one thing and do the opposite, in situations as described above, to do
so is showing the senior manager respect by not criticizing him openly.
To agree openly does not imply that one has to adopt his ideas. If this
was the case, the result would be a conservative stagnating society.

Even this Chinese manager, who denies that face is of any importance, would not allow his subordinates to lose face:

'Face does not mean that much in China. We have our methods for criticizing others and ourselves. Perhaps it is more important to the young Chinese. I am pretty straight forward, but if I am to criticize a production manager, I will never do it in front of his subordinates.'

The Chinese in particular, though also the expatriates, indicated face to be more important to young Chinese than to the old. The expatriates emphasized that the young ones thought they could handle everything, and if rebuked, reacted vehemently, whereas Chinese over forty tended to mentioned that they had been criticized during the cultural revolution and thus were used to criticism. The latter is undoubtedly true, and keep in mind that many will remember those who criticized them during the cultural resolution. Also, it is hard to decide the effect of meetings involving ritual criticism and self-criticism, but it is probably true that young Chinese attache great importance to face.

Conclusion

Metaphorically, face always involves a person's evaluation of others and is thus oriented towards relationships. It is more important in China than in Scandinavia, and the Chinese have two words for face, one referring to the degree of moral integrity, the other to social status or prestige, both viewed from the eyes of others. This conclusion addresses both expatriate and Chinese attitudes toward face.

A firm's external problems with face tend to be fairly easy to resolve, because interaction in most cases is of short duration. However, a firm's internal interactions are typically more constant, with a higher frequency of contact. Expatriates often face problems in such situations. They find the Chinese difficult to understand or socialize with because expatriates are often incapable of determining the threshold of face.

Expatriate reactions to face were categorized as negative, ignoring or positive. Applying negative face manipulation, the expatriates deliberately try to harm face, usually to get rid of Chinese. Expatriates choosing to ignore the sensitivity to face treat Chinese on a par with their own fellow countrymen.

Expatriates involving themselves in the process and trying to enhance face are typically more experienced people, who have worked in other Asian countries before. They are also those who do best in China and hence feel most comfortable. It is evident that a positive attitude has a reinforcing effect.

In general, the Chinese perceive foreigners as showing too little consideration for face, which is why more attention should be given to this aspect. The Chinese attitude toward their colleagues is that, under any circumstance, it is most important to keep superficial harmony, no matter how they actually act. According to the expatriates, this attitude not only prevails among the Chinese, but also affects their relationships with foreigners. Finally, it should be noted that the expatriates were unfamiliar with having to distinguish between what is said and what is done.

Recommendations

Based on both the literature reviews and the empirical examples, expatriates can take various measures, enabling them to avoid harming face unintentionally and to use their knowledge of face constructively. Some of the following recommendations are based on my personal observations during interviews with representatives from Scandinavian firms. These cannot be deduced directly from the previous citations but are generated on the basis of my overall impression from the interviews.

However, before addressing the more concrete circumstances, it should be mentioned that building up face, if it is done in the right way, costs nothing, whereas hurting face unintentionally often costs something, such as breakdown of information flow, resulting in unaddressed deficiencies in a firm's operation. Face is one issues that expatriates, without risking anything, can attempt to understand and use with potential positive effects if they are willing, at least to a certain extent, to adapt to Chinese social conventions. However, willingness to understand the Chinese perception of face is not enough. It also takes skill. In most cases, expatriates have not learned anything about behaviour prior to being stationed in a foreign country. It is a knowledge they have to acquired along the way.

The following addresses the most appropriate behaviour in relation to the Chinese attitude toward face. Attempts to change Chinese attitudes are not discussed as this is hardly possible during the span of a few years.

Compared to the Scandinavian countries, it is imperative in China to comply with formalities and rituals. Appearance, or facade, is more consequencial in a collectivist society, such as the Chinese. First, rituals in China differ from those in the Scandinavian countries that we follow intrinsicly, and second, the Chinese always distinguish between outward appearance and actual essence, whereas Europeans tend to combine the two. The appearance of phenomena is more salient and pervasive in China than in the West.

Chinese face consciousness requires a build up and enhancement of face by continuously emphasizing virtuous aspects of performance. Although this may sound like useless idle talk to our ears, one must continually point out positive aspects despite the fact that one finds the Chinese failing or relapsing into an earlier phase of the process. Sometimes, Scandinavian expatriates will feel uncomfortable either praising the Chinese or being themselves praised to the skies by the Chinese, as they are quite unfamiliar with such behaviour, preferring things more straight forward. However, it is recommended to do it, since it is very important to the Chinese.

Expatriates should be attentive to the fact that enhancement of face is not only a matter of verbal behaviour, even though this is the most relevant aspect. Non-verbal behaviour is also significant, such as visiting an ill colleague, as the Chinese love to feel they are receiving special treatment. But a line must be drawn between face enhancement that is intended to show true appreciation for extraordinary performances, and that which aims to establish a better and more trustful climate in the firm. Correspondingly, one must not commit oneself to more than one can answer for, as the Chinese are very quick to take foreigners at their word.

Face consciousness means that the Chinese employ indirect communication extensively, being afraid of losing face or causing the newcomer to lose face. Indirect communication implies that the actual purpose of the communication is not verbalized explicitly but is to be read between the lines, or perhaps expressed in terms of a 'white lie'. To avoid the situation in which it is felt that the Chinese withhold information, it is recommendable to concentrate on establishing trust with a limited number of people, and hence to focus on a small number of areas of concern, at least in the beginning.

It is important to bear in mind that one can give face to people of a lower ranking than oneself, but this type of giving face should be employed primarily in external relations, or in important situations internally, as the expatriates might risk losing status in the eyes of their Chinese employees. Giving face should not be mistaken for a friendly atmosphere in the firm, indicating that everybody is equal. The Chinese want their leaders to act as leaders, otherwise they cannot give them face. As mentioned earlier, the Chinese understanding of relationships is more hierarchical than the Scandinavian.

If the Chinese feel they have lost face, they rarely express it directly, which is why vicious circles easily occur, caused by expatriates robbing the Chinese of face unintentionally resulting in the Chinese becoming increasingly closed. Having selected an inner circle of people to whom one wants to establish trust, it is decisive that the expatriates do not harm face unintentionally which is the precondition for the Chinese gradually becoming more open and trustful. Therefore, one must be very careful in how one contacts the Chinese, as one may find it difficult to control oneself when the Chinese, to keep face, resort to what in the Scandinavian countries is perceived as unfair methods. If one loses control of oneself, one can easily say something which the Chinese interpret as an assault to their face. In addition, this behaviour will make one lose face in the eyes of the Chinese and hence also lose some of the respect which one may have established.

As the Chinese threshold of face differs from the Scandinavian, the issues at stake are often of such nature that Scandinavians will not pay any attention to them. They may not even concern the person with whom one communicates but, for example, his or her family, causing a person to lose face. If one is inexperienced in socializing with the Chinese, it takes a long time to acquire sufficient insight into Chinese life to be able to predict how they will react to a foreigner's behaviour. Face only functions if one is socialized to understand this concept, which is why it cannot be transferred to expatriates. Therefore, violating one another's thresholds of face is almost unavoidable, but expatriates can develop an increasing understanding of the Chinese pattern of reaction. This understanding is decisive, and those who do not learn the lesson may easily take unexpected reactions to heart. Almost all expatriates who react in this way end up going home.

Not taking Chinese reactions to heart makes it easier to construct a positive, or at least sensible, explanation of face keeping reactions, which inspires greater trust in the expatriates and hence makes the Chinese more open, further facilitating a positive attitude. It is essential to bear in mind that the Chinese remember loss of face for a long time, and it may take a long time to restore face. It is important for expatriates to not corner the Chinese, making them unable to escape. Therefore, one must express oneself with sufficient ambiguity. In general, it serves no purpose to rob a Chinese of face in order to get rid of him, as was suggested by one respondent. Firing him would have the same effect, referring to him as over-qualified, thus avoiding the creation of an enemy in the system who may routinely obstruct plans. Most Chinese who are laid off return to the very state owned firm that has invested in the joint venture.

8. Perception of Time

Introduction

This chapter addresses both attitudes towards time and the consequences of different time perceptions. Also, different views of materialism and economy are discussed, because they are linked up with Hofstede's dimension of time orientation. Thus, the major issue is perception of time, not what managers in China spend their time on. Others have studied how Chinese managers spend their time (Child, 1994:Cp. 5).

The two cultural attitudes towards time is mainly analyzed by applying two different theoretical approaches which simultaneously describe different aspects of the concept of time. The two approaches are Hofstede's dimension long versus short time orientation, and Hall's distinction between monochronic and polychronic perceptions of time. The analysis starts with differences in time specific to the Scandinavian and the Chinese cultures based on empirical data and secondary literature.

Differences in the Perception of Time

On a series of dimensions, the two cultures differ widely, inclusive of monochronic and polychronic perceptions of time, which is illustrated in Figure 8.1.

Thus, China and Scandinavia differ on both dimensions. As stated earlier (Chapter 4) Scandinavian time orientation is medium-long compared to Chinese, which is extremely long. Also, such dimensions are only applicable to country specific analyses. The object of such dimensions may differ in various cultures represented on a given dimension.

The Chinese Perception of Time

The Chinese never developed the same abstract perception of time as the Westerners. Time is tied to concrete events, and traditionally the Chinese have not viewed time in a continual perspective, such as the

Figure 8.1 Different perceptions of time between Scandinavian and Chinese cultures

	Long-term perception of time	Medium-long time orientation
Monochron		**Scandinavia**
Polychron	**China**	

West has done for 2,000 years. According to Chinese tradition, time only moves in one direction, and Needham (1988:167) emphasizes that the Chinese have never perceived time as cyclical, such as the Indians, even though this perception of time was introduced in Chinese society with Buddhism. The Chinese have organized time according to the year of establishment of the reigning regime, or in periods of sixty years, which has tempted many to interpret their perception of time as circular (Shapiro et al., 1991:94). However, assuming that Needham is right, their perception of time should be viewed as a spiral since it contains both direction and cyclic traits.

Holding Deadlines

According to Hall, polychronic perception of time results in greater emphasis being placed on responsibility for outcome, rather than meeting deadlines. Contrary to this, the Scandinavian monochronic perception of time makes it imperative to maintain deadlines. Much empirical data and literature support this observation.

In 1890, the Englishman A. Smith (1986:44) wrote from Shanghai:

> *'How many of those who have had the pleasure of building a house in China, with Chinese contractors and workmen, thirst to do it again?'*

Even though the British place considerably less emphasis on precision than Scandinavians, Smith felt that the Chinese cared even less about meeting deadlines than the British. In the same year and the same spirit, the sinologist Ball (1992:662) published a comprehensive work in London.

'Fix a time for an engagement with a Chinese, and he comes half-an-hour late, or even two or three hours late without the faintest idea that he has done anything wrong'.

In contemporary China, meetings tend to start more or less on time. However, Scandinavians, who have tried to make more informal engagements with Chinese, can probably relate to Ball's example. The Chinese arrive late and never explain why, and as far as they are concerned, there is no need to discuss their late arrival. Wasting other people's time does not seem to represent a problem to the Chinese, being used to a less linear perception of time. In fact, due to their polychronic perception of time, they conduct several activities simultaneously, which is why a fixed appointment means less. However, with some satisfaction, Ball notes that when hiring a rickshaw, the coolie will wait outside all day long gratis for the opportunity to take you back.

A Swedish board member of a joint venture in China says:

'Time schedules never hold in China. If you ask, they deny that they will not be able to keep the schedule. When they are behind schedule, their explanations are multiple. Patience and patient expatriates are a must in China.'

Furthermore, the Chinese are disinclined to admit that deadlines cannot be met, which may have something to do with their protection of face. Scandinavian expatriates, who are unfamiliar with Chinese culture, often react to such situations by feeling cheated. Therefore, patience is a decisive quality. Several expatriates stressed that patience was the most important thing they had learned during their stay in China.

One expatriated recalls similar experiences:

'You often end up in situations telling the Chinese that something has to be finished in two weeks. »Yes«, the Chinese answers, but when he has not finished the work after two weeks, he explains the situation by stating that others are behind schedule, which is why he cannot do anything about it. In the West, we view the totality of the situation. In China, you receive an answer for what you ask about, no more.'

It is worth noting that a Chinese tends only to feel responsible for his own domain, which makes it easy for him to blame others whom he does not feel compelled to contact if they do not keep their word. In general, the Chinese seem to blame others when things go wrong. This attitude confirms the previous discussion of the distinction between in-group and others in a collectivist society such as the Chinese.

In connection with delivery of local raw materials, a Scandinavian respondents says:

> *'The Chinese do not share our attitude toward fulfilling contracts. Our suppliers are often delivering goods three months late, which makes it necessary to have a large stock of raw materials in China. Just-in-time management does not function here.'*

Knowing this, one can take such phenomena into consideration, but establishing oneself in China requires considerably more available funds than most would anticipate.

Decision-making in a Temporal Perspective

One Scandinavian respondent says:

> *'The Chinese are probably afraid of approaching their state-owned »big brother« [parent firm] to say that they have made a blunder. The Chinese would rather hold off making a decision for two or three weeks to make sure that it is carefully prepared. They never say: we were wrong, let's get on.'*

The last part of this quotation is typical of Scandinavian culture, where decision-making power is often delegated, making it forgivable to make mistakes. Mistakes are frequently viewed as being caused by misunderstandings, which is why there is no reason to hide them (Fivelsdal & Schramm-Nielsen, 1993:29). Contrary to this, mistakes in China will usually be viewed as reflecting personal inadequacy, since they are so inclined to personalize relationships. Thus, mistakes are perceived as deliberate which is why persons making mistakes are subject to criticism or relatively severe punishment in China.

The above quotation indicates that the respondent finds the slow Chinese decision-making process to be caused primarily by the political system. No doubt the political system has reinforced slow decision-making with the Communist system causing people to avoid responsibility. This contributes toward a slower decision-making process in China itself than in overseas Chinese societies. People want to play it safe. And the Chinese respondents were not disinclined to place some of the blame on bureaucracy, stating that it often takes too long to obtain approvals from administrative bureaus. However, they emphasize that the slow decision-making process is culturally determined, and that it also exists in neighbouring countries. Thus, a Chinese respondent says:

> 'China has a long history, which is why the Chinese are inclined to view things in a long-term perspective. Europeans prefer quick decisions. In this, the Chinese and Japanese are similar. A decision-making proposal has to pass through the entire system, from employees to section managers, and further on to the department manager and the managing director.'

The Chinese director finds the decision-making process slow in China as well as Japan, but he draws no line between the protracted decision-making process and the slow development at industry or social levels, whereas Scandinavians do. However, it should be emphasized that in the case of Japan, the two levels are not necessarily related, since Japan has experienced rapid social development, but decision-making processes reamin long-winded. The comparison with Japan only applies to large firms, which is relevant in this context, because firms collaborating with foreigners are large in general.

It is far from true that decision-making processes are always long and drawn-out in Chinese firms, many of which are small and patriarchal. These types of firms, often run by overseas Chinese, or to an increasing extent by private Chinese entrepreneurs, are known to be very flexible, indicating rapid decision-making. This also seems to be the logical consequence of small family run Chinese firms, since the patriarch can make quick decisions without consulting others, and he will seldom encounter problems with the implementation. Flexibility and rapid product adaptation are characteristics of overseas firms, and the same seems to apply to small firms in China.

Meetings Viewed in the Perspective of Time

In general, Western expatriates find it important to meet with Chinese managers in order to make these feel committed. Traditionally, the purpose of Communist meetings has been to spread propaganda or information about politics. This may indicate a different attitude about meetings held by the two cultures. However, in both people meet for the purpose of making decisions and informing one another, though they place a different emphasis on these aspects, and in China most decisions are made by the highest ranking cadre involved in the given situation.

A Scandinavian respondent says:

> *'We always take minutes to enable us to see where we are. It provides us with the framework for our operations. The flow of paper is one-way – top-down. Much time is wasted on meetings in China. The Chinese think that the longer a meeting lasts, the better it is. A meeting of six hours is a good meeting.'*

The respondent probably stresses the use of minutes from meetings because it is unusual in China. This indicates that decisions, if any, must be implemented by the chairman personally, and the next meeting does not start with a summary of the previous meeting (Child, 1994:153). This is probably one of the reasons why the respondent finds meetings a waste of time. Another reason is that, in most cases, meetings are organized in order to inform party members about the latest central political decision. However, the last part of the quotation probably should not be taken literally. Most likely, the expatriate is struck by the fact that meetings last longer in China than in Scandinavia.

A Chinese respondent says:

> *'I tell him [the Scandinavian director] when we have meetings of our party cell. If production does not run to schedule, we encourage the party members to set a good example and encourage other workers to make an extra effort. The Scandinavian director only sees the immediate result, and if he cannot see any result, he says meetings are a waste of time since no concrete problems are being resolved.'*

This statement is a good illustration of why the Chinese have meetings, that is to convey information and not for the purpose of making decisions. However, it should be emphasized that not all party meetings are held with the purpose of improving production. The statement also indicates something about the expatriate, who after two years in China still feels that meetings are only necessary when having to make decisions. Meetings of the nature described by the Chinese joint venture respondent are actually advantageous to the operation of the joint venture, which is not the case of all party meetings, since the purpose of some of these is quite the opposite: to strengthen the interests of the Chinese party.

Contract Negotiations

It takes more time to negotiate contracts in China than in Scandinavia. However, many Scandinavian negotiators find the Chinese to often use up time consciously. As a Scandinavian diplomat says:

> *'They love to protract negotiations, often right until one has to leave for the airport. Then they say: if you agree to this and that point, we can sign here and now. One feels very tempted to do so after having waited for this moment for three weeks, the family is waiting at home, and the manager has called several times to ask when one planned to return. On this point, they are very professional.'*

It is a common belief among Scandinavian expatriates that the Chinese are not only slow, but also tactical and, many will add, good negotiators. Such statements contain an element of conflict between high and low context (see Chapter 4). Scandinavia is a low context area, where one thing is finished at a time. The Chinese, instead, have several issues running at once, and they are not as conscious about time as the Westerners, taking the low wage level into consideration. Situations like the one described above primarily occur during the first phase of negotiations to establish a firm or sell a project. For logical reasons, expatriates living in China react differently than foreigners coming to Chine with the sole purpose of negotiating a contract. The former are not subject to the same time pressure.

Material Wealth and Frugality

Material wealth and frugality are, in a different way, related to the above discussion based on Hall's distinction between polychronic and monochronic perceptions of time. The aspects discussed below are based on Hofstede's time dimensions in which economy of resources is one of the elements determining whether or not a country has a long-term pole orientation towards time. Thriftiness and material wealth are closely interrelated.

Expatriates perceive the Chinese as very materialistic, which is understandable in view of their low wages. However, this does not mean that the need for materialism disappears once their living standard raises (referring to the development of Hong Kong). A Scandinavian board member says:

> 'Motivating the Chinese is quite easy if the means is money.'

Chinese materialism shows in the importance they attach to money and material things. Wages and in particular bonuses are much more important means of motivation in China than in Scandinavia. The Chinese are also perceived as frugal which can be viewed as an effect of materialism. Expatriates often view this thriftiness as irrational. One expatriate says:

> 'They think everything I have bought abroad, has been too expensive. If they can save 500 yuan on a spare part, they will leave a machine capable of producing for 2,000 yuan a day to sit idle for a whole month. They do not combine money and production.'

Many expatriates have similar experiences. Part of the reason is that the Chinese are acting under internal instructions to buy locally whenever possible, a situation which expatriates not always are aware of. However, the major reason is probably that most Chinese are not accustomed to balancing time and money, or combining the two. This has been the case both prior to and under Communism. Many Chinese have been unable to influence the size of their incomes, which is why there has been no incentive to combine the two. Thus, if comparing the two aspects, material wealth is more important than time.

A Scandinavian respondent in Beijing says:

> *'Our summer excursions consisted of a trip to McDonalds. I would order a bus to take us there, but the Chinese considered this too expensive and suggested we took our bikes.'*

Such events indicate that the Chinese are not always thinking only of themselves, but inherently think in terms of economizing. Having lived in poverty for centuries, frugality has become internalized to the extent that they cannot suddenly change their behaviour.

Envy

According to the Scandinavian respondents, the Chinese need for material wealth often results in envy. One respondent says about the Chinese:

> *'Envy is one of the worst things about the Chinese. It is often trivial things, which one does not think about, that cause problems among the Chinese: »He gets five yuan more than me, but I produce more than him.« The Chinese are very selfish. It is all a matter of price.'*

Material gain and poverty among the Chinese, combined with the Socialist system, which divides power and responsibility, have contributed toward creating a general negative attitude among the population. In their study, Lasserre and Probert (1994:17) demonstrated that the Chinese are more prone to send each other poison pen letters than are other populations in the East Asia. In general, interpersonal trust is low in China, and the atmosphere has apparently deteriorated even further under Communism. Such letters come addressed to the manager describing colleagues' erroneous dispositions, inadequate knowledge or the like. These letters are mailed without the knowledge of the victimized. An expatriate managing director in Beijing describes the phenomenon:

> *'Our accountant was transferred back to the parent firm. So I recruited a new one myself. Well, the second in command in the*

book-keeping department constantly looks out for mistakes he might commit. She is spreading the rumour that he is unqualified, which she has also told the Chinese members of the board. I'm going to ask an external consultant to evaluate the book-keeping, but I'm certain there are no problems. If my assumption proves right, the second in command will be fired. She creates ill-feelings.'

This is an example of how Chinese express their envy or jealousy indirectly. Simultaneously, dismissing the female book-keeping may lead to a vicious spiral, because she can exploit her connections in the parent firm. Expatriates must be careful when dealing with staff issues and should consult their Chinese colleagues in the management. Finally, the example shows that joint venture firms are better off recruiting staff themselves, rather than borrowing staff from the Chinese parent firm for a contractual number of years. Chinese managers admit that it is difficult to avoid a negative atmosphere arising among the employees. One Chinese respondent says:

'Negative relationships sometimes occur among the employees which I have to solve. Naturally, it is unavoidable when these conflicts sometimes become apparent in front of him [the expatriate], but he cannot do anything himself to solve the problems. At most, he can assist in resolving them.'

Envy and jealousy are a great problem in Scandinavian and other firms in China, and are often tied to pecuniary issues, which is why it takes much empathy from expatriates to reduce such problems. In this context, one should be particularly careful to thoroughly explaining the wage and bonus systems (Tretiak & Holzmann, 1993:115).

Haggling Mentality

What is here referred to as haggling mentality is derived directly from Chinese frugality. One way of saving is to persuade the other party to reduce his price or to buy less. A Scandinavian manager of a joint venture says:

'China is the land of compromises. When I need 100 irons, I suggest buying 200, we end up buying 120, and the Chinese think they have been good at making the foreigner reduce his needs. We have had several discussions, and the Chinese have always succeeded in getting it their way. Had I said 100, they would have said 50.'

The Chinese haggling mentality, which they do not themselves refute, is in part caused by their eagerness to demonstrate results to their superiors, thus getting more face or praise. I have witnessed Chinese reminding foreign business people to be sure to add 10% to the price, so that they can accept a price reduction. Also, according to the same respondent, the Chinese are typically willing to compromise. Earlier studies have emphasized that the Chinese understanding of compromise differs from the Western (Kirkbridge & Tang, 1990:3).

Westerners view a compromise as a sub-optimal solution, whereas the Chinese view what they call compromise as situations in which the parties reach optimal solutions by combining mutual interests. I myself have experienced on numerous occasions how the Chinese praise the Japanese for being 'good' at reducing prices. In this context, it means meeting the Chinese half-way, i.e., compromising. The Chinese are fully aware of the fact that the Japanese deliberately start out with a higher price.

In traditional Chinese societies and in privately owned firms one can usually get a price reduction, and the same applies to a great extent to the national export sector, where they know that overseas Chinese expect price reductions. Treating each purchaser individually is an effect of personalization. It corresponds to what was previously referred to as a particularist attitude, and to some extent explains the Chinese tendency for haggling.

The same respondent later says:

'When we meet to discuss various issues of the firm, I sometimes feel as if the situation is one of two firms negotiating a contract.'

Both statements confirm desire to test the limits, and some respondents call the Chinese childish, referring to this phenomenon.

Conclusion

The Scandinavian perception of time tends to be linear, whereas the Chinese view time as developing in a spiral. Likewise, the two cultural attitudes differ on the importance of keeping deadlines. Chinese place less emphasis on keeping time schedules than do Scandinavians. In particular it seems to annoy expatriates when Chinese frequently refuse to decide on anything until the time schedule has been exceeded. This makes it difficult to predict when things are actually going to be accomplished. Due to vast unemployment, it is not difficult to make workers arrive on time. The problem is primarily with management, who often allows fixed time schedules to lapse.

In the People's Republic of China, decision-making is in general protracted, in part because the Communist bureaucracy gives cadres unlimited decision-making powers, and in part because negative incentives have stronger weight than positive. The same does not apply to privately owned Chinese firms inside and outside China, in which the autocratic owner himself makes and implements decisions without having to take into consideration any other interested parties except for the Communist bureaucracy. Party meetings, the contents of which are concealed from foreigners, are in general viewed as a waste of time. However, a few consider these meetings as a threat to their firm.

The Chinese are materialistic, and the Scandinavians find them easy to motivate with money. Frugality is internalized to the extent that it is not always rational viewed from a financial standpoint, because the Chinese often do not reflect on the value of time or lost earning possibilities. Combined with the drawbacks of the socialist system, the lack of a positive social attitude toward people outside their in-group has developed a high degree of envy and jealousy among the Chinese. This envy is often expressed indirectly and often in poisonous ways.

The Chinese attempt to influence decision-making processes in ways that resemble a constant negotiation process. They will haggle about anything. The Chinese deliberately use time to gain financial or other advantages when negotiating with foreigners, because they know that foreigners view time as money.

Recommendations

Conditions in China are such that Scandinavian business people must allocate more time to doing business in China than they are used to, something which many Scandinavians have not yet learned, as the above statements have demonstrated. A Chinese may be monochronic in relation to work, but polychronic in other contexts, such as his private life. Therefore, it is decisive for expatriates to seek out some essential areas within which they can attempt to make the Chinese monochronic. Also, there probably are business situations where a polychronic approach is just as efficient as a monochronic.

It is important to make sure that Chinese party members, to the widest possible extent, inform expatriates about the reasons for party meetings. It is also important for expatriates to keep in mind that such meetings are not necessarily bad for foreign interests. Thus it is recommended that expatriates pay attention to party politics. Much of the information spread through the party apparatus, is also published in a more formal version in China Daily and other English-language newspapers and journals.

One should be prepared for the Chinese inability to meet deadlines, and it is recommendable not to attempt to push the process, in particular the slow Chinese decision-making process. It is much better simply to add accrued costs to the price. If one tries to force the Chinese to make a decision, negotiations may reach a deadlock and the Chinese will give no indication of their position.

Desire for material wealth combined with envy, makes it necessary to construct material incentives very carefully to avoid conflicts between Chinese workers, conflicts which they find difficult to forget. The Chinese are easily encouraged to demonstrate thrift on behalf of the firm, but this too requires a certain amount of supervision and training, since their traditional perception of frugality is not always profitable under new circumstances.

Expatriates must be prepared for Chinese attempts to influence decisions. Therefore, it is recommendable to attempt to get the Chinese to present their own proposals, even though this process is time consuming. It is also important that expatriates leave room for compromise when presenting proposals.

Involving the initial negotiations to establish or sell projects, one must never attempt to push the Chinese into making a decision. The extra costs of protracted negotiations must be 'invoiced' to the Chinese in another way. When selling projects, this is usually not problematic since the competitor, if any, suffers the same costs. When negotiating the establishment of a firm, it is decisive for the parent firm and its management to know that the initial phase will be longer and more costly than in most other countries. But since the undertaking usually runs for several years, these initial costs are fairly small in comparison.

9. Selected Managerial Processes in Scandinavian Firms in China

This chapter and Chapter 10 deal with a series of cultural issues affecting organizational processes and structures in Scandinavian firms operating in China. The distinction between structure and process is subtle. Further, most of the phenomena discussed here, perhaps all of them, can be viewed as both processes and structures, such as power. Nevertheless, I have chosen to distinguish between process and structure because some of the phenomena are more process based than others.

This chapter builds on empirical data and the interpersonal relationships described earlier, which are the basis for the organizational processes discussed.

The Planning Process

Planning concerns future actions and is, as such, inseparable from the perception of time, since one's attitude toward the future will always affect one's attitude toward planning. The respondents widely agreed that the Chinese are »today's people«, as one of them expressed it. The Chinese have a long-term perception of time regarding building up the family's prosperity and the like, but in terms of business planning, their time perspective is very short. To the extent that the Chinese make business plans, these are characterized by personal intuition rather than strategic thinking (Redding, 1990:77). A Scandinavian expatriate says:

> 'The Chinese have an incredible short-term perspective. This applies to management, too. If this year is good, they think the next will be good, as well. Sometimes we put on the long-term glasses, whereas the Chinese look a year ahead at the most, which they find to be very far. When I say we must be prepared for declining demands in two years, the Chinese say it is no good looking ahead for trouble, we will solve the problems, we did last time.'

During planned economy, all planning took place above the factory level, which is why Chinese managers have never been accustomed to caring about planning, and not been trained to undertake this activity. Several Western respondents blamed the Chinese inclination to ignore planning on the state owned units, which assumed responsibility for everything and were omnipresent. A Scandinavian expatriate expresses it this way:

> *'The Chinese are not good at consequence analysis. When we make a decision in the West, we are prepared to make the next decision, if something happens, but the Chinese do not consider the next step.'*

However, this tendency is also identifiable outside Communist China, where overseas Chinese primarily pursue fast profits and flexibility, and as a result are capable of adapting fast to market changes, but they rarely enter into industries which require long-term investments, such as the car industry (Redding, 1990:173; 1994:101). Overseas Chinese place a relatively strong emphasis on strategic planning, but they do it in an incremental way (Lasserre & Schütte, 1995:135). Another Scandinavian respondent elaborates on the above:

> *'It has been difficult to conduct analytical discussions with the Chinese. They do not think in terms of consequences, but in terms of »right and wrong«. They are not used to thinking in terms of scenarios.'*

For many years, the Communists have divided phenomena into right and wrong, which may explain this attitude to some extent, but cognitive differences cannot be excluded either. The above statement can also be interpreted as an expression of the Chinese being accustomed to viewing things holistically, whereas Westerners are more prone to divide functions into analyzable units.

It may seem immediately surprising that a country like China, which is viewed as operating with a long-term time perspective, in reality places such little emphasis on long-term planning. There is no unequivocal explanation for this phenomenon, but it may be that the Chinese family orientation excludes tight ties with firms which they do not own. What is most important to the Chinese is to demonstrate success in improving the family's prosperity. Another, or supplemental, explanation may be that, because of their tendency to believe in faith and practical thinking, the Chinese do not really believe they can plan anything. Planning requires belief in the predictability of phenomena and belief in being capable of controlling certain sub-phenomena. It should be borne in mind that, according to Taoist thinking, the future is unpredictable. Finally, culturally the Chinese are oriented toward the past, and such cultures in general place very little emphasis on planning. Their aim is to restore the glory of the past and not to design new projects. Hoon-Halbauer (1994:325) mentions that the Chinese today tend only to think about the present because they have no faith in the future of the political system.

Another factor, as Child (1994:253) claims, is that due to the foreigners' wish to control, the Chinese are not being permitted to participate in strategic processes since the foreign partner is afraid of too great Chinese influence.[1] However, this was not my impression from interviewing both Scandinavian and Chinese managers, even though some Chinese managers mentioned that they could manage more tasks. Expatriates, who are used to placing great emphasis on planning, must be prepared to assume responsibility for planning, as most Chinese are inexperienced in this activity and have a very short-term time perspective. Finally, it should be mentioned that planning is difficult in a country where one only has limited knowledge and where the political future is more uncertain than in Scandinavian countries'.

A specific aspect related to planning is the importance of producing fast yields. A Scandinavian respondent says:

> *'The Chinese are world champions in profit. But their way of making profits differs from our's. When we [the Scandinavian party] could not guarantee a certain yield after only two years, the Chinese suggested that we closed down the firm. How were we to guarantee the profit of our joint venture?'*

This example is extreme, but several respondents say that the Chinese place strong emphasis on fast yields, and continual deficits often cause tension between the parties. Another Scandinavian respondent says:

> *'Profit is the key to unity. We always argued when we came out*
> *in the red. That changed with the black bottom line. Projects*
> *must yield profit.'*

Placing great importance on profits is in keeping with the Chinese
materialistic attitude and the party's interest in procuring more capital.
It also illustrates that some business affairs have a stronger impact on
interpersonal relationships in joint ventures in China than in
Scandinavia, albeit the phenomenon is not unknown in Scandinavia.
When poverty comes in the door, love flies out the window. However,
there are example of both parties having agreed on profit not being the
most important aspect of the joint venture, but rather to ensure both
parties orders.

The above indicates that, in general, each partner's purpose for the
joint venture differs, which is also often mentioned as the direct cause
of inadequate cooperation. Several, both Chinese and foreign respondents, illustrate this by quoting an old Chinese proverb: 'same bed, different dreams' (*Tong chuang yi meng*).

Information

Flow and exchange of information are central to managing a modern
firm. How does the expatriate ensure that the Chinese provide him
with the necessary information and how is information spread to the
Chinese employees?

In China, information is viewed as having an exchange value to a
larger extent than in Scandinavia, which is why Chinese employees
tend to give bits and pieces of information when they find it tactical to
do so. This is an expression of the Chinese managers' didactic managerial style (see Chapter 2 and Silin, 1976:60).

Collecting information

Most expatriates feel they get too little information from their Chinese
colleagues, who are typically selected by each party in the case of joint
venture. This means that even though they have to approve of each
other's candidates, the expatriates have no influence on which qualifications their colleagues possess.

One reason for the lack of information is undoubtedly that expatriates do not speak Chinese, and many Chinese managers do not speak English. Since a relatively large amount of information is informal, the spoken language is important. A Scandinavian managing vice-director says:

> *'I have fine relationships with my managing director, but I have to come to him. Even though his office is next to mine, he never comes in here.'*

Without saying it directly, it is evident that the expatriate feels he gets too little information. Other managers say directly that they get too little information and too much gossip. Thus, the expatriate must, to the widest possible extent, try to formalize the information flow. A Scandinavian managers expresses it this way:

> *'The Chinese said the bonus system between the departments was unfair, so we designed a new one. But perhaps the problem was not the bonus system. You can never be sure. Much happens behind your back. All the Chinese know everything, but we know nothing. Foreigners talk too little with one another.'*

This statement raises two problems. First of all, the Chinese provide too little information, or the foreigner does not understand the Chinese signals, and many foreigners also object to not being informed about existing regulations. Second, even though there is a high concentration of foreigners in Beijing, their intercommunication is sparse. Several Scandinavian respondents often referred to these problems, the latter being a kind of self-criticism. They admit that they could form a Scandinavian club, but do not do it, referring to being afraid of revealing that they have problems in their firms in China. Unlike the Westerners, the Japanese spend much time together outside working hours, both formally and informally, and are by the way also more open about the problems related to operating in China than Westeners.

Firm relevant meetings

In Scandinavia, meetings are used to spread and collect information. One effect of the great power distance in China is that meetings cannot be conducted like in Scandinavia. Expatriate managers typically participate in two types of meetings, management meetings and meetings with subordinates, and the managing director also participates in board meetings. Regarding meetings with subordinates, a Swedish expatriate says:

> *'For two years I have said that we should discuss the problems. This is the first time they have presented anything [a new bonus system]. The Chinese way of rationalizing is that if one does not say anything, one also can not say anything wrong.'*

Western expatriates in general stress that the Chinese remain quiet during meetings, being afraid of saying something that may disturb the harmony. This is problematic, since the Chinese employees do have an opinion on issues concerning the firm. This is then either expressed only through Chinese interrelationships, or in their behaviours. That is, they tend to do what they find best regardless of what they have been told to do, and then hope the foreigner will not discover it, which evidently causes numerous problems for the expatriates.

In Scandinavia, decision making at meetings requires everybody to feel as equals, and they are in fact relatively equal, which is not the case in a hierarchical society, and therefore meetings have a different function. In general, the Scandinavians respect the person who dares to raise his voice and go against the manager. In China, this will be perceived as a personal attack on the manager's face. The result of this is that communication in management meetings is top-down. Inherent in the concept of face is that conflicts must be avoided. One effect of the Chinese face awareness it that critical discussions are prevented or limited.

In a hierarchical society like the Chinese, the major purpose of meetings is to present top-down information. Therefore, it will probably take a long time to discover how to use meetings for making decisions, if this is possible at all in a country like China. Decisions are typically made through informal consultations, which a Scandinavian top manager confirms, who has been a member of several boards in China:

> *'Problems can never be solved at the table. You have to break off discussions for half a day, after which the Chinese will return. The Chinese always have to consult with their hinter-*

*land. They are not autonomous decision makers. You do not
have a local partner in China, all of China is your partner,
which is why nobody dares to make decisions.'*

Other board members give the impression that there have been some
improvements in this area during the 1990s (the above respondent's
experiences primarily date back to the 1980s). However, improvements do not mean that there are not still firms and regions acting on
the old principles. Nor does it mean that one can expect the same efficiency at board meetings as in Denmark, far from it. A representative
of a Scandinavian firm, which no longer has a Chinese partner, says:

*'When we had Chinese members on the board, a board meeting
took two full days. Now it takes two hours.'*

This also indicates that Chinese members of the board not only lack
autonomy, but also professionalism in a Western sense.

The Decision-making Process

The level at which decisions are made says something about the degree
of centralization in a firm. This aspect will be addressed in the following chapter. Here, the specific cultural aspects of the decision making
process are discussed.

In Scandinavia it is taken for granted that those in power and those
responsible are identical, but this is not the case in China.
Scandinavian expatriates feel that the Chinese go too far in separating
power and responsibility. A Scandinavian respondent says:

*'The Chinese want power, but not responsibility. The Chinese
cadres do not assume responsibility but use power to lay hands
on as much as possible. When they have power, they use it to
place people in front of themselves. It is always the one in front
of him who falls. Manager guidelines are blurred.'*

The respondent finds it to be a general trait that the Chinese separate
power and responsibility, thinking primarily of cadres in those bodies
which stipulate the guidelines for what joint ventures are allowed and

not allowed to do. Blurred guidelines is a way to avoid being held responsible, which in connection with personalization reinforces the difficulties of control by rules in China.

Traditionally, the Chinese have had a much clearer picture of power than of responsibility, and there are many classical Chinese works on power, both political and military, and these principle are widely transferred to commercial activities, including management.[2] Another reason for the Chinese fear of responsibility is the many shifts in political direction which the Communist Party has been through since it came to power in 1949.

The discussed organizational dependence is also an important reason for Chinese employees, including managers, being reluctant to assume responsibility, which might result in one ending up in opposition to the manager. In the Chinese tradition, it is safest to refrain from involving oneself too much.

A Scandinavian respondent says:

> *'My main task is to integrate the heads of departments. I do much to provoke them, to make them talk about the problems in the firm.*
>
> *The Chinese would prefer me to make all the decisions, but I refuse. So the function managers and the Chinese vice-director eventually do make the decisions. I forced him to choose between A and B. He was to suggest his solution.*
>
> *Chinese, who have to make a decision, usually come for advice. I'm here to help them. I say to the Chinese: »You are the expert«, but they find it very hard to accept. Sometimes there are too many problems, then I have to interfere. It is a process of discovery and learning in which one tries to involve them in management, but it is difficult. Personalization hampers the process, but I'm sure I will succeed.'*

The Scandinavian respondents often emphasize the difficulty of forcing the Chinese to make decisions, and because they are unaccustomed to making decisions, they cannot reach a consensus or choose a leader who has the decisive word. Often, the Chinese will attempt to get the expatriate leader to sanction or, even better, to sign the final decision.[3] That the Chinese consult the expatriates in the beginning is understandable, since it takes a long time to gain experience with how expatriates want things done. They are not in a position to know because of their experiences in the planned economy. It is a process during which the Chinese gradually acquire knowledge about Western business management and fit it into their own cultural and political framework. Therefore, it is a discover and learn process, not only for the Chinese, but also for the expatriates. However, both parties would benefit strongly if they made this more clear to one another than is the case today.

Consensus in decision making

As a result of the Chinese priority for harmony, and both parties' emphasis on control, most joint venture contracts stipulate consensus in decision making. However, expatriates are of the impression that the Chinese place more weight on consensus decisions. A Scandinavian board member says:

> *'It is stated in our joint venture contract that all decisions made by the board must be consensus decisions. This demand for consensus is a great problem. It means that we cannot make decisions.'*

This applies especially to old joint ventures entered into in the mideighties. At that time, 50/50 joint ventures were much more common in China than they are in the 1990s. But even if it is not mentioned explicitly in the contract, the Chinese prefer reaching a consensus, according to most expatriates. This also applies to management (Tretiak & Holzman, 1993:108). Based on their cultural tendencies, it is very likely that the Chinese place greater value on consensus. Their bent for holistic thinking points in the same direction, but they are also used to everybody supporting a decision once it is made.

Contracts and agreements on cooperation should clearly state which questions require consensus in order to limit the number of topics requiring consensus. But expatriates should be aware that reaching consensus on key issues furthers mutual trust.

Passivity

As indicated above, Scandinavian expatriates in general perceive the Chinese as passive and lacking initiative. A Scandinavian expatriate expresses it this way:

> *'The Chinese lack initiative, which also applies to their own domain. The Chinese will do no more than what he is told in order not to do anything wrong. Often you think, why did not he do that? But »it is better not to do anything, then nothing will happen to me«. This is probably a legacy from the state own firms.*
>
> *Especially people of the of age of 35-40 or above, who have lived through the cultural revolution, lack initiative. They represent 30-40% of the employees in this firm, and they are bitter because they never got the chance at education, among other things, during the cultural revolution. Your can divide the Chinese into those who can remember the cultural revolution, and those who have been brought up after that period.'*

Passivity among employees is, in part, rooted in their traditional fatalism, reflected in an unwillingness to act, such as by putting paper in the fax machine when the tray is empty. The Communist reign has reinforced fatalism with people, by and large, being unable to influence their own situation. People above the age of 35-40 are perceived as much more passive than younger people, who in turn are often perceived as presumptuous to the extent that they find it very difficult to accept criticism.

One should be aware that the Chinese way of conducting business differs from the Western. A socialist firm could be compared to a production unit in a Scandinavian firm in which all decisions, other than the physical organizing of production, were made outside the firm. However, expatriates widely agreed that young Chinese are both willing to and apt at learning, especially within the exact sciences. But it takes time to master Western management methods, because they require a radical new way of thinking, which can only be acquired during the process and not over night. Expatriates, at least, do not find the young ones passive in questions concerning their own lives. Many firms have problems with job-hopping, especially because many young Chinese often change jobs depending on who offers the best wages and working conditions. The older generation's passivity is primarily rooted in that they have only ever been used to negative motivation from the state owned firms.

> *'The Chinese are passive. They must know exactly what to do and how before they do anything. Doing something wrong is perceived as very negative. Punishment is emphasized all the time [in China], whereas we emphasize the positive aspects. Do it better next time. That is the difference. Therefore, they are very cautious.'*

Others emphasize the difficulty of getting the Chinese to implement decisions made by the board of the management, until the administrative layer has received these in writing. They only feel it safe to implement decisions made by their superiors if they can later prove, should anything go wrong, that orders came from the top (Child, 1994:256).

The influence of Socialism is often blamed for the Chinese passivity, and thus seems to be the major cause. Lasserre and Probert (1994:13) thus found that managers in China stood out from Chinese managers in Taiwan, Hong Kong, and Singapore in terms of lacking initiative, responsibility, and need for control and guidance. Their study did not distinguish between different age groups, but indicated a difference between Chinese who remembered the cultural revolution and those who did not. However, being flexible, the Chinese tend to adapt fast, which especially applies to the young and managers with experience from abroad.

Control

In this context, control can be divided into two aspects. One pertaining to which of the parties entering into a joint venture has or should have the greatest influence. This is a structural issue which will be addressed separately in Chapter 10. The other aspect, which is addressed below, concerns how the firm's top management make sure that middle managers, executives, and workers perform the tasks they are expected to undertake. Being passive does not mean that the

Chinese merely do what they are expected to do. According to Western expatriates, they tend to 'take the easy way out' which the Chinese refer to as being flexible.

A Swedish respondent says:

> *'One must personally control everything in China. Our Swedish vice-chairman of the board once said to me that after a few years the Chinese would be able to run the factory themselves. I laughed. If I'm gone for two weeks, the quality of our products starts deteriorating.'*

This statement, along with earlier quotations, demonstrates, that the Chinese do what they are told when monitored. However, their way of performing tasks has not been internalized, which is why they start to perform operations in their own way if not monitored directly. Another Scandinavian respondent expresses it this way:

> *'Control in China is very informal, but it is there. The Chinese write everything down. I control much and walk around asking if this or that has been done. Formal control, i.e., walking around and talking to people, is necessary.*
>
> *Although I tried to make the organization as flat as possible, I still have to exert much control to make sure that we are heading in the same direction, because there are numerous short-cuts, and these are utilized if the Chinese are given the opportunity to do so. »Should we do it properly or merely fix it the way we usually do?«.'*

What the respondent talks about is a kind of direct control where the manager is walking around inspecting the individual employee, pretending to talk with them, which corresponds to what here is referred to as informal control, since the procedure is not formalized. This procedure requires that the expatriate speaks Chinese, which is the case with only a few Scandinavian representatives. Alternatively, expatriates will have to content themselves with looking interested, and then interfere if something is done in the wrong manner.

This quotation indicates that expatriates find direct control necessary, and that the Chinese only follow the rules if they know they are being watched. Therefore, viewed from the perspective of the Scandinavian investor, expatriates must be familiar with equipment and production.

The Firm's Relationship With External Authorities

Typically, a schism arises between internal and external relationships. To a certain extent, internal relationships can be made efficient, whereas external are totally controlled by the environment. A Scandinavian respondent says:

> *'I only interfere in the contact with the authorities if it involves money. In general, the authorities function poorly. I have attended meetings at the bank, with the tax authorities and with MOFERT. In the presence of a foreigner, the authorities cannot fabricate as many excuses for why nothing happens.'*

As the quotation illustrates, expatriates leave it to the Chinese to negotiate with the authorities as much as possible. However, the general impression is that if expatriates turn up occasionally, this may speed things up.

Conclusion

In relation to planning firm activities, the Chinese are very myopic, perhaps due to their general consideration for the family and other groups with no direct relationship to the firm and its future. The Chinese are not accustomed to undertaking planning activities in relation to the firm, which probably contributes to their inclination to let personal intuition take precedence over strategic thinking. It is typically the foreign party who presents proposals for strategic planning.

In the beginning, decision making in Scandinavian firms in China will probably be fairly informal and authoritarian. But expatriates do try to encourage the Chinese to make co-dicisions, this being a way of tying leading Chinese employees closer to the firm. This may be of crucial importance in situations such as the current, where there is a vast need for proficient Chinese managers.

In general, the Scandinavians are dissatisfied with Chinese demands for consensus, and try to minimize those areas which require consensus. It is thus important to increase horizontal collaboration among Chinese department managers with which they are unfamiliar, since the communists have always advised against horizontal communication.

The purpose of meetings is different in China and Scandinavia. In Scandinavia, meetings are primarily organized to reach decisions through discussions, decisions that everyone can accept and therefore are willing to implement, whereas in China the purpose is often to spread information which is perceived as valuable and to be used economically, being distributed in small portions. Management and staff meetings tend to function as media of information diffusion, since the Chinese are reluctant to say anything at meetings due to the great separation of power combined with their fear of losing face. Formal meetings, during which decisions are made based on mutual analysis and discussion are difficult, if not impossible, to carry through. Board meetings take considerably longer than in Scandinavia, since the authority of many Chinese board members is still restricted.

Especially older Chinese, who have lived through the cultural revolution, are perceived as passive by Scandinavian expatriates, which other studies confirm. The young ones, on the other hand, are very open to the Western line of thought. They also possess some aptitude, even though some refer to them as being presumptuous. Thus, it is difficult to find qualified managers, because Chinese above 35 to 40 years are tainted by their experiences during the cultural revolution.

Scandinavian expatriates find it necessary to personally control Chinese employees as these will only follow rules if subject to direct surveillance.

Chinese managers and middle managers prefer to receive written orders to ensure themselves against being held responsible for having implemented decisions which later might be invalidated.

Finally, long periods of training and learning are required, which is hardly surprising, since the Chinese avoid conflict, pretending to accept conditions with which they do not agree. The centralized socialist system has further cured people from taking initiatives, and has reduced their knowledge of operating a firm under a market economy.

Recommendations

The Chinese are accustomed to thinking tactically, but not strategically. In the context of a firm, it is the expatriate's responsibility to train the Chinese to think strategically rather than tactically. The expatriate must be prepared for the Chinese bent for tactical thinking, which is often directed toward obtaining advantages at the expense of the Scandinavian partner.

The expatriate must be prepared for having to do the planning himself, since most Chinese have no experience in this domain, and their perspective is very short-term. In general, one should be prepared for the Chinese tendency to opt for immediate yields. And be aware that long-term deficits often cause tension between the partners.

Management meetings and other formal ways of gathering information tend to be more difficult in China than in Scandinavia, making it necessary to collect informally a great deal of information. Also, one should be aware that Chinese board members are not autonomous decision makers, which is why board meetings take so long.

It should be stated clearly in any contract and agreement for collaboration, where the board and the management should reach internal consensus, that such situations should be limited to only a few specific kinds of decisions. Under normal circumstances one should, to the widest possible extent, reach consensus among the partners through negotiations, even though the process is time-consuming.

Despite the fact that the Chinese accept hierarchies, in the beginning they will only follow the hierarchical communication channels if subjected to direct surveillance. Therefore, the Scandinavian investor should be prepared for the necessity of letting expatriates stay for a long time, and the need for expatriates possessing technical expertise. The process of involving the Chinese in the firm and making them follow general impersonal guidelines is a long and very time-consuming process. The successful outcome of such efforts are especially dependent on being able to construct positive incentive systems, which make the Chinese feel it pays to take initiatives, since they are inclined to focus on potential negative sanctions rather than positive material and face building measures.

It is vital to be open to a discover-and-learn process, as the transition to more market oriented firms affects both political and cultural conditions. The more explicitly the expatriate explains to the Chinese the importance of discover-and-learn experiments the better, again to help reinforce the positive, rather than the negative. Here, it is important to emphasize that for the expatriate as well, who is not as familiar with Chinese conditions as the Chinese, the process is one of discovery and learning.

Decisions and consultations with the Chinese primarily have to take place in the shape of informal contact with Chinese colleagues in order to make them feel that they have a say in the decision making process. The aspect of responsibility should be soft-pedalled in the beginning, and remuneration should be linked to achieved results. Possible miscalculations should not be sanctioned negatively, but at first simply explained away and corrected. It is important to engage Chinese managers in the running of the firm and make them feel secure in making decisions themselves. In the long-term, responsibility and decision making competence should be combined, but not until the Chinese is capable of taking over the management of his domain.

It seems relevant to leave most of the communication with the authorities to the Chinese, using the expatriate as a trump card in difficult situations. And the firm's external face and reputation (*mianzi*) can be enhanced by giving presents to the local community, proving the firm's good morals *(lian)* and demonstrating that it can afford and is willing to contribute.

10. Aspects of Management and Organizational Structures

There is no sharp distinction between interpersonal relationships and managerial functions, as individuals from the two cultures interact when performing managerial functions. This chapter addresses a series of issues more directly related to the structures of management and organization. The basis for discussing organizational structures is the distinction between centralization, complexity, and formalization (Robbins, 1991:285 cont.).

Centralization

Low personal trust contributes toward creating centralized organizations (Tayeb, 1988:46). Compared to firms in countries with relatively small power distance, such as the Scandinavians, firms in countries like China, which are characterized by relatively great power distance, are more centralized. A Danish expatriate says:

> *'The Danes would call our organization »enlightened despotism«*
> *if they compared it with a Danish organization. This is how a*
> *Dane would feel if he entered this pyramid. Management is*
> *extremely top-down.'*

In general, Scandinavian firms in China are more centralized than the parent firm, which the Scandinavian managers usually accept in the beginning, but then they gradually attempt to decentralize the organizational structure. The Dane continues:

> *'I try to decentralize. This is one of the most important things I*
> *do. Decisions must be made, and I am not making all the deci-*
> *sions. Anything that can be allocated will be allocated. The*
> *Chinese do not like decentralization.'*

Allocation is perceived as synonymous with delegation. These statements illustrate the conflict between the Chinese tradition for leaving it to others to make decisions for them, and the Scandinavian tradition where decisions are delegated as much as possible, viewing it as an advantage to divide various functions into smaller domains for which specific employees assume responsibility and manage. This is the background for the implicit, and sometimes explicit, confrontations between the two attitudes. Similarly, Child (1994:269) found decision making in joint ventures to be concentrated around the managing director, and no others at or below the department level participated in decision making. Even though the Scandinavians are used to decentralized organizations, it is surprising that none of them point to the positive aspects of centralization. A centralized organization run by a Scandinavian managing director increases the Scandinavian partner's possibilities for control. However, other conditions point toward a somewhat different direction than strong centralization. The managing director of a fully owned Danish firm says:

> 'When I, as the manager of a joint venture, suggested that we delegate the responsibility for wage systems and the planning of working hours to the foremen, the Chinese director's response was that such ideas were not viable in China. But when we took over the factory, the idea was implemented and the foremen were satisfied. They got a »lift«, and responsibility.'

This indicates that it is the Chinese managers, or their superiors, who are against decentralization, and their resentment is, at least partially, rooted in the political environment. Thus, top-level management seems to be more conservative than middle managers. The above example also indicates that those referred to in general as middle managers want more influence and are not afraid of the accompanying responsibility, which confirms previous statements about only being delegated responsibility and not influence. This could indicate that the possibility for decentralizing is much greater in fully owned foreign firms than in joint ventures.

Complexity

The typical Chinese reaction to decentralization is to expand the number of hierarchical levels. Later in the interview, this Scandinavian respondent says:

'The more middle managers they can squeeze in, the better. Then there are more to talk with on the way up, and more to make decisions and sign.

Middle managers have no power. So I remove hierarchical levels. Often the Chinese come and ask for more departments, but I refuse! They love to construct boxes. One department for cords, one for low-voltage, and one for high-voltage. Then we must have four supervisors, a senior supervisor, and a head of department. The more desks and tea cups the better.'

This Chinese reaction of constructing a more complex organization is, in part, a way of protecting themselves. Traditionally, the incentive structure in state owned firms has been predominantly negative, which is why the Chinese are accustomed to shirking responsibility to the widest possible extent. It is remarkable that the respondent mentions that middle managers have no power. This indicates the separation of power and responsibility, since these middle managers must have some kind of responsibility or there would be no reason to appoint them. Separating power and responsibility is very alien to Scandinavian expatriates, which means that, in practice, they attempt to combine the two internally.

Steep Hierarchy

The relatively great power distance in China, compared to Scandinavia, implies that Chinese tend to prefer hierarchical institutions and firms, but this does not mean that they always follow hierarchical channels in their actual behaviours. Quite the contrary, it is in general difficult to implement standardized procedures in China, because there is no tradition for formalization in the Western sense of the word.

A Danish respondent describes it this way:

'In the beginning they came here all the time, but I do not have the energy to listen to them. If they have problems, they must learn to go to their department manager and then he must come to me. And we take the same route back. Otherwise I could not

> *do anything else but listen to stories about their sick mothers and* *sisters.*
>
> *We have a hierarchical system with which they must comply. The Chinese is not fired the first time [he comes into my office], it also depends a great deal on what he has to say. In most cases it is something about the wage.'*

Since the Chinese, at least in the beginning, perceive expatriate managers as absolute monarchs, just as the directors of the state owned firms, they attempt to make him endorse some personal wish by contacting him directly. Among expatriates, this has left a picture of Chinese as behaving fairly anarchistic toward rules. A Finnish respondent says:

> *'The Chinese want to be free as a bird. The best is if no rules exist at all. The Chinese are individualists, and their behaviour in traffic is a good example. There are rules, but the Chinese act according to their own rules and interests and »do not give a damn« about these rules.'*

Several Western respondents use this anarchistic behaviour in traffic to illustrate the Chinese attitude toward rules. The above quotation indicates that Chinese reactions are often not internalized, they only follow those rules which they are forced to, or follow the interpersonal face rule to which they are committed. This implies that, if they cannot spot anybody with whom they have a relationship, which is often the case in traffic, they will violate the rules. Violating the rules is not perceived as a question of morals as in Scandinavia. Another respondent says it more precisely:

> *'The rules are that there are no rules. The legal system was broken down during the cultural revolution. Only a few older jurists remain.'*

The respondent agrees there is a lack of respect for rules in China, but blames the political system which, in breaking down the legal system, has contributed toward externalizing respect for the law, meaning that the Chinese will feel obliged to follow the rules only if they are under direct surveillance from others. However, Scandinavian expatriates themselves do not follow the hierarchical channels in their external relationships. An expatriate says:

> '*We are in a country where everything is decided top-down. We have recognized that the top manager is the boss. One has to aim directly for the top if one wants a little flexibility.*'

Flexibility is a nice euphemism for getting one's wishes through. Like other quotations, this indicates that top cadres actually make decisions, which they can do unchallenged since nobody dares to go against them. No matter what the reason is, it is useful to distinguish between highly and lowly educated people, since highly educated Chinese must be supposed to be less anarchistic than people with only elementary schooling. The latter dominate the traffic, and are the majority working in firms, but not among the high ranking cadres who make decisions. Stating this, it should also be stressed that those of less education are more simple minded and hence find it easier to accept certain conditions as fated, whereas those who have an education tend to refute conditions which they do not find flattering. However, as demonstrated below, not all educated Chinese refute their culturally determined tendency to have an attitude toward rules different from that of Westerners. The above quotation shows that expatriates adapt to the way of doing things in Chinese society, although they do not accept the same procedures in their own firms in China. Expatriates are more likely to use the privileges connected with being a foreigner to evade hierarchical channels.

Formalization

By formalization, Child (1994:266) means written, standardized reports submitted at fixed deadlines. In general, Scandinavian firms have a high degree of formalization, whereas Chinese firms have a very low degree or no formalization. In addition, formalization is difficult to carry into effect due to the Chinese disinclination to control by rules. From the present data it is not possible to say anything about the degree of formalization in Scandinavian joint ventures. But in the twelve European joint ventures studied by Child, six were found to have a low degree of formalization, and six medium high. None of them had a high degree of formalization. However, a few, with investors from other parts of the world, were indeed characterized by a high degree of formalization. This indicates that, within certain industries, a high degree of formalization is possible (Ibid.). The low degree of formalization adds to the difficulty of decentralizing and transferring managerial functions to the Chinese, as there are no fixed rules for managing the firm. A Chinese manager explains the Chinese attitude in this way:

> *'If you Scandinavians receive an order, you follow it blindly and do not question whether or not it is sensible, whereas the Chinese will always think: »Perhaps I can produce the same result in an easier way.« We focus on the outcome rather than the way in which it is produced.'*

This confirms that the Chinese attitude toward rules is much more pragmatic than the Western. It is characteristic of countries with a relatively great uncertainty avoidance, such as China, to have many rules, but they do not necessarily feel obliged to follow them. In a country like China, it is difficult to construct rule systems in the firms, when the majority of the employees hold the above attitude. The Scandinavians, who live in open countries with a small power distance and little control, tend to take it for granted that employees comply with the rules. The Chinese are much more used to direct control, which could be explained culturally by their externalization or external control. This means that their attitudes toward rules of the firm and the means for achieving objectives in general are less internalized. As a result of this different perception, the Chinese often find Scandinavians simple minded, because they follow rules without question. On the other hand, the Scandinavian with his cultural background, often finds that the Chinese think only of their own comfort, rather than of what is in the interest of the firm. This different attitude toward rules result in that Scandinavians, often against their will, resorting to direct personal control and, to whatever extent possible, constant surveillance, since they do not feel the Chinese can be trusted to follow the rules.

However, one should be aware that Chinese managers of joint ventures are often subject to pressure from external Chinese organizations to meet general political goals which are not always in keeping with those of the joint venture. Furthermore, some are expected to submit weekly reports to the authorities in order to enable these to keep informed about foreigner activities (Pearson, 1994:23). An example from the 1980s was the government's demand that international joint ventures yielded fast profits in order to attract foreign capital to China. However, this has played a minor role in the 1990s.[1]

Power Versus Dependence

Dependence is the opposite of power, according to Western thinking.[2] Combined with the lack of rules, Chinese managers' great power over their employees in centralized state owned firms means that employees are very dependent on whether their relationships with their managers are positive or negative, since they can seldom refer to rules. Even if they can, they will often have difficulties in enforcing their rights because managers at various levels protect one another, and China has no well-developed legal system. The sociologist Walder (1986:25) has used the concept of organized dependence to describe the Chinese situation in relationship to the workplace and the authorities, because these organizations can make decisions which affect employees' lives in almost all areas, including those employees who, prior to being employed in Scandinavian firms, had been employed in state owned firms. A Scandinavian respondent says:'

> '»*Please you manager*«, *this is a key principle in China.* »*As long as the manager is well, we are all well. As long as the boss does it, we must do the same*«. *This attitude no doubt stems from the state owned firms.* '

This quotation illustrates that feelings of dependence upon managers exist in Scandinavian firms, but much more for Chinese subordinates than for managers of joint ventures. The latter have relatively great freedom compared with their colleagues in the state owned sector (Pearson, 1992b:57-77). In addition, they hold a fairly strong position due to the lack of qualified managers in China, and their personal networks.

This feeling of dependence creates a kind of fixation towards the manager, and results in Chinese employees spending too much energy on trying to satisfy their superiors. Sometimes, the Chinese go a step further and invite the manager home for dinner or the like, with the purpose of placing him in a situation of reciprocity. With Scandinavian managers, this strategy often fails, because Scandinavians do not understand the situation in the same way as the Chinese, which creates a basis for distrusting the Scandinavians. Likewise, in order to avoid getting into conflict with their superiors, the Chinese demonstrate submissive behaviour. They do it verbally by expressing great respect for directors and others in managerial positions, such as always using their titles and family names when addressing them. It is not unusual for Chinese employees to use titles when addressing one another, irrespective of for how long they have known each other. Contrary to this, Scandinavians prefer initiative and the courage to air one's opinions, if it is not directed at the director personally.

Personnel Policy

This subject is comprehensive, but only a few important aspects will be addressed below. Personnel policy is one of the issues on which it is most difficult to reach consensus, because it deals with human beings, and hence is strongly governed by cultural and political conditions. Therefore, in most of the firms visited, the personnel manager was a Chinese, but not in one of the fully owned Scandinavian firms. Here, the managing director was also personnel manager, indicating the Chinese unwillingness to cede this position. They would rather cede the position as managing director to the foreign partner than that of personnel manager. In personnel management, Scandinavians are used to standardized norms for performance assessment and discipline, because they view employees as performing roles. However, an effect of Chinese personalization is that standardized norms are often impossible to implement.

Personnel orientation

Due to continual face giving, the attitude toward personnel is more individually oriented than in Scandinavia. But where to draw the line is in part left to the individual manager, and in part determined regionally. The North Chinese are more averse to being viewed as employees, i.e., being treated universally, than the South Chinese. In addition, people from Shanghai are especially concerned about face. In general, Chinese managers are people oriented, whereas Scandinavian managers are task oriented.[3]

Performance assessments

Performance assessment and other personal issues do not function in China unless they emphasize the positive aspects. However, conducting such assessments is almost impossible, if they involve criticism without taking into consideration the possibility of loss of face.[4] Therefore, job reviews are not feasible, but it may have a positive effect to single out individual persons each month, since the Chinese will start competing for the opportunity. Therefore, all employees should be singled out gradually to ensure that none of them lose face. The danger of internal tension is greater than the danger of losing the effectiveness of the reward with every one ending up being mentioned anyhow. However, most of the firms I visited refrained from such performance assessments.

At the top managerial level, Chinese fear responsibility, which makes it is difficult to get them to accept promotion, especially if it means having to supervise previous colleagues (Child, 1994:259).

Motivation

As mentioned earlier, it is a general attitude among expatriates that, due to their obsession for material gain, Chinese workers are not difficult to motivate with money, which is quite understandable with the current unemployment rate in China. The only aspect that surprised expatriates in the beginning was the Chinese disinterest in group bonuses. A Scandinavian manager says:

> *'In the beginning, I tried to design group bonuses, but the Chinese did not like it. They prefer to make the entire product themselves and receive a bonus based on how many units the individual produces. The Chinese are very jealous of one another, but apart from that we have no labour problems.'*

The Chinese are known for their collectivist tendencies which makes many Western managers think they prefer to work in groups. They are surprised when they learn that, in this context, the Chinese are more individualistic than Westerners. The reason is that Chinese workers do not perceive their colleagues as part of their in-group, causing the previously mentioned antisocial attitude to become active. The Chinese materialism and bent for jealousy makes it expedient to pay a relative large proportion of the wages in term of bonuses. Also in relation to managers, individual pecuniary motivation effects their performance significantly, and many Chinese joint venture managers have a bonus system tied to the operating result. None of the Western respondents mentioned using non-material motivation, such as appealing to their sense of morals when they had done something wrong, which is surprising since this sentiment is widespread among the Chinese.

Disciplining

One of the areas within which the differing attitudes between Scandinavia and China toward face plays a significant role is discipline, or other ways of rebuking or training employees. Since expatriates will never know as well as the Chinese, just how sensitive they are about face, it is a good idea to leave as much discipline and rebuke as possible to the Chinese managers, thus reducing essential contact to a few Chinese managers. If it is necessary to air one's dissatisfaction, it must be done face-to-face or indirectly, such as removing favours, which the Chinese immediately perceive as a sanction. Publich exhibition of punishment only leads to attempts at revenge. In general, it is difficult to tackle conflicts in a society where face plays a decisive role, since the Chinese do everything possible to avoid conflicts, and the Western methods for resolving conflicts cannot be succesfully applied in China.

Distribution of managerial positions in general

Since all expatriate respondents except two were working in joint ventures, control over managerial functions was important because the management of the joint ventures studied had both Scandinavians and Chinese. In 1990, a research group in Beijing[5] found that key managerial positions were not distributed according to investment in international joint ventures in China. This does not immediately seem surprising, since one of the purposes of the Chinese allowing the establishment of joint ventures was to learn foreign management. Thus, encouraged by the Chinese, most joint ventures operate with a parallel structure. That is, Chinese occupy all posts, while the foreign party is allowed to occupy as many post as they wish, provided there is a Chinese vice managing director if the foreign party wants to hold directorship. If the Scandinavian parent firm wishes to maintain a certain amount of direct control over the firm, which in most cases is recommendable, introducing the parallel system is not efficient. In general, the managing directorship is filled in parallel. Often this post is held by the foreign investor in return for a Chinese vice managing director. Other managerial positions are not necessarily filled by both a Chinese and a foreigner.

Even though the managing director comes from the parent firm, the Chinese are capable of creating a purely Chinese management which a foreigner is incapable of controlling if all posts are filled by Chinese vice-directors. This system causes many problems, because the Chinese often create a system within the system. A representative of a large Scandinavian firm says:

> 'We do not want an organization with a Chinese vice manager at all levels. We have a Chinese managing vice director, but of the eight heads of department, two to three are Chinese, the remaining expatriates.'

This firms is one of the few Scandinavian firms which finds it important to ensure that not all posts are occupied by Chinese vice directors, fearing that if this were the case, they would be incapable of controlling the firm. The most adequate control is established if at least one of the directorships is occupied by a foreigner only. Thus, the above statement is not typical, but shows how it is possible to avoid the problems of control mentioned by most other firms.

Another reason for dividing directorships is that, in many areas, Chinese authorities demand that the Chinese vice director receives a certain percentage of the expatriate manager's salary.[6] However, the Chinese manager does not himself receive the money; it is allocated to the Chinese parent firm. Obviously, the purpose of this rule is to demonstrate that, compared to his foreign colleague, the Chinese does not receive much less for the same work. However, the result is that both parties are dissatisfied. The Chinese managers are dissatisfied with not receiving the money themselves, and the foreign party is dissatisfied with having to pay the Chinese parent firm. Often, the foreign partner does not know how much the Chinese director actually receives (Child, 1994:270).

Distribution of the managing director post

Most Western partners in joint ventures want the post as managing director, and they usually get it, but a Chinese managing director of a joint venture said:

> *'Originally, we had a foreign manager. But the Finnish partner found management in China had much to do with human beings, such as contact with employees and authorities, banks, and tax authorities. After a period, the Finnish partner suggested that we [the Chinese] take over the post as managing director. The Finnish partner now holds the post as vice managing director. I do not find that it matters who holds the post. What matters is that the two parties can collaborate.'*

This statement is representative of many Chinese managers, but most expatriates do not like to have a Chinese director above them. It is decisive that the two parties can collaborate. If this is the case, it does not matter who holds the post. In any case, the Chinese will be undertaking most of the internal and external contact since they know how to resolve problems. If a foreigner occupies the post, it is primarily to be able to interfere should the Chinese make arrangements which he does not agree with.

The expatriates' domains

No matter which post the expatriate holds in the joint venture, there are certain functions which he must count on having to supervise. First and foremost, seeing that all necessary functions in the firm are attended to in order to keep the firm going. In this context, it is important to isolate a control function responsible for intervening actively in various functions. Since expatriates only have a limited knowledge of how the Chinese systems function, it is important that this person concentrates on a few key aspects, which he is in a position to govern. In many cases, the expatriate attempts to influence all processes at once. This typically results in conflicts with the Chinese managers because expatriates, intentionally or unintentionally, collide with Chinese cultural or political attitudes. It differs from one firm to the other which tasks expatriates should prioritize, but it pays to leave tasks having to do with staff, plus external relationships, to the Chinese colleagues. One exception is dismissals. Here, Chinese managers are most likely to be reluctant. Other typical functions to be undertaken by expatriates are planning and marketing, especially in the case of exports.

Transfer of Western Management Principles

Albeit the official Chinese policy is that the population should learn technology and management from the foreign partners, most Chinese managers feel they do not need to learn much about management. Quite the contrary, the Chinese often say that they have learned about Western management, but it is useless in China. In addition, it is in general difficult for the proud Chinese to accept as adults the role of pupils, something which is reinforced by the 'teachers' being foreigners. A Scandinavian board members says:

> *'The Chinese still find themselves to be superior culturally. They do not recognize that they have to learn. At least not those on the board.'*

This statement indicates some limits as to what Chinese managers want to learn from foreigners, at least in the short-term. Chinese managers feel that they have primarily something to learn about technology and production, and in some cases accounting. The latter because presentation of accounts differs in state owned firms from joint ventures. In addition, in China there is resistance to teaching aspects of management tied to values, such as organizational behaviour, human resource development, and strategy (Borgonjon & Vanhanacker, 1993:8).

It also varies in terms of what foreign firms want to transfer. Early on, Scandinavian investors thought they could merely move the firm to China. Today, they are much more inclined to compromise and adapt to certain aspects of the Chinese culture and forms of organizing. This does not mean that all aspects are adaptable. Products for export must be of a certain quality.

Conclusion

As it appears from the above, Scandinavian firms in China are more centralized than their parent firms. Decentralization seems difficult, but over time the tendency seems to be toward decision making at lower levels and delegation of decision making competence, even though this is contrary to Chinese culture. Chinese managers attempt to avoid decentralization or, failing this, to establish more complex organizations by adding more middle managers to assume some of the responsibility. But according to Scandinavian respondents, these are not allocated any significant influence which corresponds to other observations.

The Chinese prefer hierarchical organizations, but they do not follow formal hierarchical channels of communication, feeling that if the manager has made a decision, the middle managers neither can nor will go against it, which is why going directly to the top manager is expedient. Hierarchical organizations also make it easier to change or improve certain aspects, such as quality control, which has caused many problems in Scandinavia and other joint ventures of centralized organizational structures.

Rules are not as internalized among Chinese as among expatriates. This has given many expatriates the impression that the Chinese are almost anarchistic in their attitudes toward rules. The lack of control by rules makes the employees feel personally dependent on the managers, which is why they are so fixed on sustaining a good relationship with their manager. In consequence, they corroborate anything he says, no matter what they themselves think.

Chinese managers tend to separate power and responsibility through issuing guidelines which are deliberately formulated vaguely, making them open to multiple interpretations. This is in keeping with the Chinese tradition and has been strongly reinforced by the volatile Communist political line. Separating power and responsibility implies to not involve oneself seriously in the firm, and if Chinese managers are forced to make decisions, they prefer to do it collectively, and consult one of the expatriates afterwards.

A number of personnel issues differ between China and Scandinavia. Job interviews and individual performance assessments easily cause loss of face, which is why such issues are avoided in most Scandinavian joint ventures.

Somewhat surprising to Scandinavian expatriates, the Chinese prefer individual bonuses, being afraid of having to work for one another, which they do not like. On the other hand, the increasing importance of money means that bonus systems, which are perceived as just, are strongly motivating in China. In most cases, disciplining is left to the Chinese managers, who are also primarily attending to the firm's relationships with external authorities.

Most joint ventures operate with a so-called parallel system, i.e., managerial post are filled with both Chinese and foreigners. In reality, the majority of posts are occupied by Chinese, since it is too expensive for most joint ventures to have more than one or two expatriates. Therefore, the Chinese have an intact managerial system, which is not the case with the foreign investor. In consequence, the Chinese have greater possibilities for exerting control than the foreign partner.

The Chinese proudness and their fear of being criticized politically for being too Western-like and oriented toward capitalism result in strange limitations to transferring management principles. The so-called soft aspects of management, such as strategy, organizational behaviour, and human resource development, especially cause resistance.

Recommendations

In effect of the great power distance in China, Scandinavian expatriates should take into consideration that a relatively centralized organization will be more efficient than a decentralized one, at least to start with. Gradually, expatriates can attempt to implement more decentralized decision making, but they must be prepared for being consulted in almost all decision making situations.

Also, Scandinavian expatriates should be prepared for Chinese attempts to resist lowering decision making levels by constructing complex organizations, which spread and make responsibility invisible, because the individual does not like to appear responsible. Therefore, expatriates must watch out for organizational gemmation.

It is important to increase the formalization of meetings in China in order to ensure continual progress from one meeting to the next, which the Chinese with their personalized style are not used to. One approach is to take minutes of all meetings and to start the following meeting summarizing and approving minutes from the previous meeting. In general written instructions are recommendable in the beginning as they reduce the Chinese cadres fear of subsequent criticism from Chinese superiors.[7]

Because the Chinese feel dependent upon the manager, the expatriate must be aware of the type of manners he establishes when addressing different employees. If it is evident that he prefers some to others, this will often arouse envy among the Chinese. Expatriates should also be aware that the Chinese will often try to place them in situations of gratitude so that the Chinese will feel entitled to demand a work related quid pro quo. If this is not satisfied, the Chinese will feel offended, which may cause negative reactions against the expatriates and the firm. On the basis of this, expatriates should not accept gifts. If receiving an invitation for dinner or the like, expatriates must evaluate the situation. When accepting such invitations, the Chinese will often expect future gratitudes in return. On the other hand, one should not refuse an invitation from a colleague with whom one expects to be collaborating for a number of years.

Performance assessments must, if required, only emphasize the positive aspects. Pointing out anything negative should, if possible, be left to the Chinese managers. And extensive usage of middlemen is recommendable in order to avoid direct face confrontation. The obligations inherent in the role of middlemen makes it more likely for these to gain both parties' trust. Expatriates should also attempt to influence the recruitment of staff, avoid borrowing executives from the Chinese parent firm. In addition, motivation and disciplining can be left in most cases to the Chinese managers who are often better at handling such issues in keeping with the Chinese tradition. Expatriates should, however, acquaint themselves with these issues. In connection with dismissals, the expatriate must assist his Chinese colleagues.

The parallel managerial structure of joint ventures, implying that all posts are filled with Chinese, should be avoided. Apart from the position as managing director, which both parties demand, dual manning is usually not required. Most joint ventures in China are relatively small.

Western managerial principles which are transferred must be presented as value free and universal, which reduces the Chinese managers' fear of being criticized for being capitalist oriented.

For all aspects of managerial transfer, training is vital, but it must take into consideration Chinese pride and manners. Therefore, role playing and the like will be unsuitable. And finally, expatriates must be prepared to adapt their organization to the Chinese tradition and values, aspects which were discussed in the previous chapters.

11. Conclusion

China is the world's most densely populated country and is currently witnessing rapid economic growth. It is also the oldest country in the world and has never been totally occupied by a Western power. Therefore, the population has developed its own traditions for interrelationships reinforced by the fact that for long periods, such as from 1949 to 1978, the country has been relatively isolated from the West. By contrast, Scandinavia consists of small countries with small populations, and countries which have always been dependent upon communication with other countries and their populations.

Since China opened up to foreigners, approximately 100,000 expatriates have worked in China. Although the percentage of Scandinavians is limited, the extent and frequency of contact between Scandinavians and Chinese have nevertheless increased exponentially during the first part of the 1990s, and this tendency is expected to continue into the next millennium.

This study has demonstrated vast and multiple differences between Chinese and Scandinavian behaviours, traditions, and values. Differences in behaviours and traditions can largely be explained by different values between the two cultures.[1] Even after long-term contact mixing representatives of the two cultures, nothing seems to indicate that their values change, even though their behaviours may change in the short-term. That the Chinese behaviour does not change is reflected in their 'relapses' into traditional way of performing, if they are not under close surveillance.

This study has demonstrated that general cultural dimensions do not suffice to describe actual cultures. An example of this is, as mentioned, that different collectivist cultures hold different objects of collectivism. In some places the total workplace is perceived as an in-group, in others, such as in China, only a few of one's colleagues are counted as members of one's in-group. Therefore, general cultural dimensions are insufficient for giving insight into a specific culture. Also, difference in the degree of collectivism and the dimension of power distance may constitute a basis for insight into many dissimilarities between two cultures, but this requires specific descriptions of the cultures studied.

Personalization and Roles

In interpersonal relationships the Chinese distinguish between family affairs, personalized relationships with their in-group, and negative attitudes toward people outside their in-group. In effect, they attempt to construct trust based networks with a number of people in the environment. These trust based relationships give the feeling of security in a society which is otherwise dominated by little general interpersonal trust. Low interpersonal trust combined with the lack of a clear rule system creates dependence on people in powerful positions, such as managers. This feeling of dependence enhances indirect communication and potential exposure to shame. Mannerisms come to occupy a key role in the Chinese perception of other people.

The Scandinavians, who are more individualistic, view work related interpersonal relationships as relationships between role owners who, to whatever extent possible, are to receive and give universal treatment. Relationships are determined by rules, and the individual is entitled and committed to expressing his/her opinions. The Scandinavians are governed by guilt, which is not related to other people's perceptions. This is why direct communication is acceptable. Individual behaviour is internalized and other people are perceived positively or at least neutrally.

The Chinese family-like personalization resembles in many ways the attitudes in the Scandinavian agricultural societies, at least in the countryside until the Second World War, even though Scandinavian culture has never placed as much emphasis on behaviour as the Chinese culture. At that time, the family in Scandinavia occupied the role in society which the social system occupies today, and the extended family was bound together for financial reasons. Today, the Scandinavian family is based on emotions, but the family unit has, on the other hand, diminished. The Scandinavians do not find it necessary to spend time on getting to know commercial partners. Time is strictly organized in the Scandinavian countries. The Chinese are more polychronic than the Scandinavians, which is why they are often managing several activities at once. After working hours, the Chinese manager will often visit his contacts or employees, whereas the Scandinavian goes home to his family. Scandinavians more so than Chinese tend to separate private life and work.

From the above summary of the most important cultural differences between the Chinese and the Scandinavians, certain internal connections between the aspects of the two cultures become apparent. The most appropriate basis for understanding the contrast between the two cultures is the disparity in importance ascribed to personalization and roles. The Chinese personalization can be traced back to the Confucian tradition, which emphasizes particularistic interdependence between father and son, teacher and pupil, etc. Breaking these relationships implies shame in relation to those persons involved. Thus, the feeling of shame increases the focus on specific persons, and hence personalization.

The Scandinavian culture's emphasis on roles can be traced back to Protestantism and its internalization of religious tenets. Internalization combined with individualism results in less particularistic and more universal behaviour. Universal behaviour tend to divide people into broad categories such as roles.

Optimization of the Intercultural Interaction

Smooth communication and positive feelings between the managers of international joint ventures are imperative for constructive cooperation between the Chinese and the Scandinavian management. This is particularly true due to the organizational structure common in Sino-Scandinavian joint ventures, where the top level management typically is exercised by a team of a general manager from the Scandinavian area and a deputy general manager from China. Many of the problems mentioned can be overcome by creating particularistic trust-based relationships with Chinese colleagues, but the question is how to do this? Essentially, trust-based relationships are established in China as anywhere else, that is, by keeping one's promises, but in addition (superficial) harmony is more important in China than in Scandinavia.

But appearances, or expressing human feelings (renqing) are relatively more important to Chinese than to Westerners. If this is correct, then the opposite is also correct logically, that is, essence (specific management measures) are relatively more important to Scandinavians than to Chinese. This relativity should be emphasized, as I am not contending that essence is not important to the Chinese. Appearance includes giving face and adapting communication styles to Chinese norms, such as showing respect for the Chinese. Although the concept mainly contains verbal communication, it also comprises certain actions, such as gift-giving, visiting Chinese employees, caring for employees' well-being, and other aspects covered by the Chinese word *renqing*, which is best translated into human obligations rather than the more direct translation human feelings. In the Chinese tradition, feelings (qing) are perceived as social contrary to the Western tradition which considers feelings personal.

Essence is the basic way of conducting business and running a company according to Western tradition but making the necessary adaptations to the Chinese tradition. Figure 11.1 shows that when a particularistic and a universal culture have to cooperate, the best way would be to combine a particularistic appearance with a universal essence. However, the model should not be misinterpreted to mean that Westerners can do as they please as long as they satisfy the Chinese verbally. Instead, the conclusion is that many problems could be avoided, if the Western expatriate was more sensitive to the traditional Chinese ways of communication, such as face-giving, showing respect for elder Chinese, building trust-based personalized relationships with the Chinese staff. For example, in the case (Chapter 7) of the Chinese

Figure 11.1 Optimization of contact between Scandinavians and Chinese

		Particulartistic		Universal	
Scandinavian and Chinese perception of interpersonal relationships	Appearances	YES	YES	YES	YES
	Essence	NO	YES	NO	YES

Scandinavian and Chinese satisfaction with the four situations	Scandinavian satisfaction	OK(viewed as surface personal-	Low(acts immorally)	Fairly Low (Cheats, lies)	Very high (idealized)
	Chinese satisfaction	High(face important)	Very High (idealized)	Fairly Low (hidden personalization)	Low (uninteresting)

Best choice   Worst choice
for   for
Scandinavians   Scandinavians

manager who was criticized at a management meeting, it would have been better to handle this situation face-to-face, also stressing his positive contributions. Had the criticism been presented in this way, the situation may not have turned out as troublesome as it did. Naturally, the Chinese criticize one another, but they do it more subtly than Westerners. However, it should be mentioned that there are certain business methods which Westerners find difficult or impossible to accept ethically, such as corruptive practices, which are apparently also penetrating Sino-Western joint ventures (Stone, 1994).

On the other hand, it is unrealistic to believe that Scandinavians can make the Chinese demonstrate universal behaviours which is why the ideal situation for the Scandinavians is not viable, i.e., a situation in which both parties in appearances and in essence behave universally. If expatriates acquire the ability of particularist behaviour, they will routinely give the Chinese face by praising them verbally or in other ways making them feel special. These particularist appearances are acquirable through training, and do not directly affect actual dispositions, but the Scandinavians will be satisfied with universal dispositions. The outlined constellation implies a schism between word and action, which the Scandinavians are not used to and do not like, but it is the best alternative.

It should be emphasized that even though the above approach will create problems, it is easier to change appearances than realities. Therefore, if the Scandinavians succeed in changing Chinese appearances, this has also to do with their wish to please the Scandinavians, which is why they must be prepared for the Chinese relapsing into traditional ways of acting, if they are not subject to direct surveillance.

Even though the chance of changing Chinese values are very limited, the opportunities for influencing the selection of Chinese managers are increasing (this is another aspect discussed in this chapter). Like many other counties, China harbours different personalities or epistemological types. Maruyama (1994:169) argues that more than half the world can be divided into four epistemological types, and combinations of these (H.I.S.G). The distribution of the four types differs from one country to another, which is why it is recommendable to increase one's influence on and awareness of the selection procedure. In those cases where the foreign partner actually has influence on selection, the expatriate can choose a Chinese colleague of an epistemology resembling the Scandinavian. Apart form this, young Chinese working together with experienced expatriates is a good combination. Somewhat surprising, the Chinese do not necessarily prefer older expatriates, finding that these think they know everything and therefore are unwilling to listen to and cooperate with the Chinese. Older Chinese especially still carry the fear of being 'colonialized'. Thus, younger expatriates with experience in other parts of East Asia are ideal.

Finally, it should be mentioned that the firms' ways of functioning have repercussions on interpersonal relationships. According to several respondents, interpersonal relationships between Chinese and Scandinavians are better in firms that yield profits than those operating with a deficit for many years. Again, good interpersonal relationships help make the Chinese more willing to try Scandinavian managerial methods.

Pragmatism

Another characteristic of the Chinese is their extreme pragmatism, which is partly reflected in 'white lies' and attempts to make the best of any situation, persisting until they succeed. The aim is more important than the means which, combined with personalization, means that loyalty, honesty, etc., are conditioned. The Chinese are thus pragmatic as to content but not form.

The Scandinavians, on the other hand, are characterized by a high degree of pragmatism regarding form, but only to a limited extent concerning content. The result is flexibility, and in many situations they are willing to compromise on their principles for interpersonal and firm related issues. Pragmatism is probably the Scandinavians' most constructive cultural trait in connection with being stationed in China. Pragmatism reminds the Chinese of their own attitudes, which is why the Scandinavians do not appear as 'herrenvolk' that want to change everything.

Consequences for Preparation

Scandinavian managers must be prepared to invest more in behavioural aspects than they are used to. Expatriates must be mindful of entering into and developing individual personalized relationships with a number of Chinese holding key positions in and outside the firm in order to gain their loyalty and honesty. Also, in terms of appearance, they will have to adapt themselves to Chinese personalization, networking, face protection, etc., since these characteristics cannot be expected to change in the foreseeable future. They have existed for more than 2,000 years.

My study has underlined the hypothesis that the more expatriates understand about Chinese culture, the greater the possibility for predicting their behaviours. Empirical findings show that some expatriates are capable of predicting a Chinese reaction to the extent that they can take it into consideration a priori.

Therefore, courses in Chinese culture and behaviour for future expatriates are recommendable. Similarly, courses for Chinese managers in Scandinavian culture are equally relevant, but it is more difficult to persuade the Chinese to participate in such activities. For established firms, it would be ideal to organize common management courses for representatives of both cultures. They should be the basis for discussing each other's blind spots.[2] In addition, such courses could lead to open discussions about observed differences, which are typically not addressed during busy working hours. It is my experience that the Chinese have nothing against discussing their culture, but the design of such courses must be different from the outline used in Scandinavia, including role playing and the like.

Apart from deficient knowledge about Chinese culture, another reason for the widespread negative attitude among expatriates toward Chinese managers is probably that the majority of expatriates work in small firms in China with only one expatriate. Most of them have limited contact with other Scandinavians, which is why it is difficult for them to absorb and process their experiences with the foreign culture, being unable to share their experiences with others in the same situation. If this assumption is true, it is to be anticipated that developments in the late part of the nineties will head toward more insight into each other's cultures, which might constitute a basis for more positive attitudes and more constructive intercultural relationships. This is due to, in part, the length of the period expatriates spend in China and, in part, to an increasing number of large Scandinavian firms establishing themselves in China. Each of these employs a larger number of expatriates, often people who have worked in other places outside Scandinavia prior to working in China. The latter category do better than first time expatriates.

Finally, it should be mentioned that older Chinese are much more opposed to Western traditions and behaviours than the young ones. Even though eating biscuits does not change one's values, the young generation's positive attitude toward the West, or at least the upper layers of its culture, means that the superficial layers of Chinese culture change. Over time, this change will penetrate further down into Chinese culture. This would indicate a gradual improvement in interpersonal relationships between the two cultures.

On the other hand, the values of Chinese culture will undoubtedly undergo a renaissance as China becomes stronger financially and more modernized than today. The effect may be that the Chinese place a greater emphasis on their cultural values. This could lead to greater difficulties in intercultural communication. Also, China's growing role in the global economy points in the same direction. The latter is already reflected in the ever increasing political conflicts on the global political scene between the Western countries and China. Thus, in the long run, improvements in intercultural relations between the West and China would appear to be on the horizon. In the short run, the measures outlined may improve this contact.

Managerial Structure

Scandinavian firms in China are typically more centralized than in Scandinavia, and the degree of formalization is in general lower in China. Apart from being conditioned by the culture and individual skills, the latter is also related to technology. A high technological level implies a higher degree of formalization, which also applies to China. Large firma have a higher degree of formalization than small. The point is that, if comparing firms of equal size and product, the degree of formalization will be higher in Scandinavia than in China. Very formalized Scandinavian firms will thus find it more difficult to collaborate with unformalized Chinese firms, than Scandinavian firms with a flexible structure, because Chinese managers are incapable of meeting the high degree of formalization required by some Scandinavian firms. Similarly, very decentralized firms will find it more difficult to collaborate with Chinese firms that are more centralized. However, as indicated earlier, it is easier to go from decentralization to centralization than the other way around. The same applies to formalization, which indicates that degrees of formalization represent a greater barrier than degrees of centralization for Scandinavian firms establishing themselves in China.

Chinese managers are perceived as passive and risk averse by Scandinavian expatriates, who therefore try to force their Chinese colleagues to make decisions. But the Chinese reaction is to construct more complex organizations. The decision making process is informal and best conducted face-to-face. However, language barriers impede the possibility of this type of decision making.

Recommendations on Managerial Structure and Strategy

When selecting managers, having two managing directors who speak a mutual language should be given higher priority, since most communication in China is informal. Therefore, it should be stated in the contract between the parties entering into joint ventures that the board is responsible for recruiting the managing directors. Today, this is primarily done by each investor suggesting one or several from his organization, which often implies that they have no mutual language.

The Scandinavians perceive the Chinese as having a short-term perspective in relation to the firm. It is typically the expatriate who takes initiatives, which he often has difficulties getting the more conservative Chinese to accept. If he succeeds, it usually involves protracted discussions with the Chinese partners. At the same time, the expatriate must ensure that the firm is kept running by surveilling virtually all processes, since Chinese managers are passive and in no way have any knowledge about management and operations in a market economy. Even though the expatriate must monitor diverse processes, he should avoid interfering actively, because he is not sufficiently familiar with the series of specific local conditions connected to these processes to be able to control them. The typical approach is to leave as many activities as possible to the Chinese, and then concentrate on the most immediate problems, such as planning, product quality, new technology, and marketing. But the problems differ from one firm to the next. The expatriate should thus be prepared for a certain division of labour, where he can typically concentrate on the more abstract functions, such as planning and marketing.

Many of the firms' relationships to the authorities are best handled
by the Chinese themselves. This also means that the expatriate can be
involved in cases where it is necessary to underline the seriousness of a
problem. Expatriates and foreigners in general hold a special status in
the eyes of the Chinese. This should be exploited consciously, with
expatriates interfering only when external processes come to a stand-
still or reach a deadlock.

Training is a decisive precondition for the optimal functioning of a
joint venture, not only in terms of expatriates learning more about
China, but with training the Chinese in how to keep a firm going in a
market economy where the firm operates very autonomously compared
with the state owned Chinese firms. Many Chinese managers still lack
understanding of the basic conditions of a market economy.

The primary intercultural clash takes place at the top management
level. Scandinavian expatriates in general have good relationships with
middle managers and workers, and possible conflicts are easily
resolved. Not so with joint ventures in China. Clashes or conflicts must
be resolved in a way that is acceptable to both parties as the Chinese,
through their networks, can sabotage decisions with which they disagree.[3] Therefore, constructing situations which are acceptable to both
parties is imperative. It is better to compromise one's preferences than
to construct a situation which is quite unacceptable to the Chinese
partner. A certain amount of Western control can be secured by not
filling all managerial posts with Chinese managers or vice managers.
Such measures prevent the Chinese from running the firm without
consulting the expatriates, since they do not possess all the necessary
information.

Strategic considerations

Based on a cultural analysis, the vast differences in values should cause
Scandinavian investors to consider one of two strategies where this is
possible. If choosing to enter into a joint venture with an active
Chinese investor, this partner must have similar or complementary
strategic objectives. This means a long period of intensive preparation
uncovering the Chinese firm's real motives. If one cannot reach consensus on vital issues, one should avoid joint venture, even though this
offers the advantages of a local firm, such as local knowledge and
access to local networks. The choice of Chinese partner is extremely

important.[4] Within most industries, getting a partner (preferably good) will be better than no partner.

The second strategy for Scandinavian investors is to avoid joint ventures, or enter into cooperation with a passive investor in China. A fully owned Scandinavian firm in China usually experiences few cultural clashes at the top management level. This goes especially for Scandinavian firms with a high level of technology and hence a high degree of formalization, which should opt for establishing fully owned firms in China. However, it should be stressed that even in fully owned Scandinavian firms, the manager will be perceived as a father or teacher figure who is expected to educate and inspire the other employees, but most Scandinavians will find it easy to accept this role. Expatriates should preferably stay for at least three years as it takes time to become familiar with Chinese society's way of functioning. In addition, the Chinese personalization makes replacements difficult. Finally, Child (1994:273) points out that it has become easier to establish firms as the Chinese gain more international experience. My empirical findings disclose nothing to this end, but having travelled much in China, I am inclined to support Child's impression.

Limitations of this Study

One limitation of the applicability of results from this study is that it has not been possible to experiment with these on an actual project. The applicability of results can ultimately be confirmed or disconfirmed only by being applied to the establishment of a firm. Another limitation seems to be that the study contrasts two viewpoints rather than presenting the interplay. This is in part caused by the study design, but also the empirical fact that Scandinavian managers are especially preoccupied with those conditions which cause frustrations and clashes than those causing no tensions. In effect, they are more inclined to talk primarily about the former. In addition comparative analyses focusing on differences tend to exaggerate difference at the expense of similarities in order to clarify the former. This is an almost inherent element in the research strategy which also applies to this study.

In the normative sections on recommendations and in this chapter, attempts have been made to reduce this weakness, partly by listing conditions for the most constructive interpersonal relationships, and partly by discussing to what extent transfer of management and organizational structure from Scandinavia to China is possible and desirable.

Focusing on cultural differences always carries the danger of producing stereotyped pictures. This criticism could probably also be raised against the present study, but I have attempted to incorporate the Chinese respondents' viewpoints whenever possible. Nevertheless, it should be emphasized that the aim has not been to present specific Chinese viewpoints, but to demonstrate certain overall cultural tendencies. As already implied, there are naturally Chinese who do not fit into the pattern outlined here. Some Chinese managers want to assume responsibility, and others do not find superficial behaviours important, etc. However, they do not represent how Scandinavians perceive of Chinese in general. In defence of focusing on differences, it is a precondition for getting the involved parties, both actors and researchers, to learn about the cultural differences, as well as the other party's perceptions of them.

A third limitation is the lack of focus on industries, size of firms and other situational factors. Cultural values have a general affect, whereas organizational processes and managerial structure are influenced by a series of other factors. In addition, a relatively large number of the Scandinavian firms, which established themselves early in China, were relatively small and had little international experience, which is why their expatriates were often poorly equipped for the task. This intensified cultural clashes, but the situation has changed since the mid-nineties. Those firms currently investing in China are large Scandinavian concerns that, in many cases, are able to draw on expatriates from other parts of East Asia.

Final Comments

The dynamic nature of the Chinese economy cannot be emphasized strongly enough. How economic development will affect cultural differences is currently being discussed, but one thing is certain: it is easier to establish oneself in China in the late nineties than it was ten years ago due to economic and infrastructural development. The vast exposure to foreigners has also resulted in certain Chinese business people, in particular cadres, having become more critical of the traditional ways of doing things, and many old habits, even behaviours, are changing. However, this hardly means that Chinese values will change, but adapting certain superficial traits of their culture to international standards will probably suffice. Any idea of changing Chinese values toward Western values is futile in the foreseeable future.

One implication of the above is that expatriates must be prepared for the Chinese relapsing into old habits if not subject to direct control for a longer period. Therefore, new investors must count on having a larger number of expatriates stationed in China for a longer period than in other third-world countries, such as India. I hope that my project has served as a reminder of the influence of cultural values, no matter which subjects become dominant in the coming years, when foreign firms establish themselves in China. During the years I have been working with this project, China has become a pin on the world map in almost all boardrooms. Economic development in China means that we will have to learn to live with 1,2 billion Chinese, for better or for worse. Development has belied the old proverb that East and West shall never meet. They already have, cross-cultural behavioural patterns have just not been determined yet. Hopefully, this project has helped clarify just how such patterns of behaviour could be organized.

Notes

Chapter 1

1. Worm, 1995 and 1995 nian guomin jingji he shehui fazhan de tongji gongbu (1995 Statistical Communiqué of Economic and Social Development of the PRC, *Renmin Ribao* (People's Daily). Overseas edition, March 7, 1996.
2. It should be noted that form, extent and meaning of face-to-face communication is determined culturally, which may cause misunderstandings and cultural clashes.
3. Child operates with three main factors affecting organizations: culture, economic system and situational factors. Child, J. (1981 Culture Contingency and Capitalism in the Cross-national Study of Organizations. *Research in Organizational Behavior*. Vol. 3:303-356.
4. The description of the five dimension is based on Hofstede (1991).
5. Adler (1983:40) points to how cross-cultural management studies should clarify if nation replaces culture, and whether the population of a country is culturally homogeneous or heterogeneous. I agree with this point, which is why the two issues are briefly discussed here.
6. Han is the name of ethnic Chinese. Apart from these, there are 55 minority groups of which the most important, according to population, are zhuang, hui, uigur, yi, miao, manchuer, Tibetans and Mongols. Brødsgaard, K.E. (1990) *The Game about China*. Copenhagen: Mellemfolkeligt Samvirke, p. 102 cont. (in Danish).
7. Only four had been there for a short period, which is indicative of expatriates. Either one goes back almost immediately, or ons stays in China for a long time.

Chapter 2

1. This review is based on Tu Wei-Ming (1984) *Confucian Ethics Today*. Singapore, and Pye, L. (1991) *China - An Introduction*. New York: Harper Collins. (Chapters 1 & 3).
2. One of the sources relating most directly to Confucius is Lun Yu (the conversations), see Legge, 1994:2).

3. See e.g. Liu, Yunbo (1990) *Zhongguo Rujia Guanli Sixiang* (Confucian Administrative Thought in China). Shanghai: Peoples Publishing House.

4. For a more comprehensive discussion see Tu, Wei-ming, 1984:110-12.

5. They are: humanity (ren), justice (yi), decency (li), wisdom (zhi), and reliability (xin). Having mentioned these, Pye continues: 'Confucian scholarship was an endless process of discussing all possible meanings and connotations of these and other words. (Pye 1991:44).

6. F. Mote says that Li is the only concept specific to the Chinese culture. Mote, F. (1971) *Intellectual Foundations of China*. New York: Alfred Knops, p. 4748.

7. Staying in China for a few days one is bound to hear the expression: 'Zhengfu you zhengce, women you duice', but you are only attentive to it if speaking Chinese. Interpretors rarely translate that kind of expressions.

8. For a discussion of 'yuan', see Yau, O. (1994) *Consumer Behaviour in China. Customer Satisfaction and Cultural Values*. London: Routledge.

9. During the 1990s the two have been combined to a certain extent in that today one almost has to have a higher education to become a member of the party, which is the autocratic party's way of attracting the intelligentsia. However, being rich in today's China also yields high status.

10. Kahn, H. (1979) *World Economic Development. 1979 and Beyond*. Boulder, p. 121. The expression that has gained ground is post-Confucianism, neo-Confucianism is a school of the philosophical Confucianism developed in the 12th century.

11. Redding's study only includes Chinese firms outside the People's Republic of China.

12. Both expressions stem from Redding, 1990:131-132. The expression 'didactic' originally stems from Silin, R. (1976) *Leadership and Values. The Organization of Large-Scale Taiwanese Enteprises*. Cambridge: Harvard University Press, p. 60.

13. See e.g. RSVP, and please bring a Cheque. *The Economist*. July 17th, 1993:58-59.

14. Similarly, Lin, Yutang characterizes the Chinese as 'not social minded (1988:164).

15. Chu (1991: Chapter 1) provides a very good review of the popular use of tactics. She uses the term strategy.
16. See e.g. Li, S., X. Yang & J. Qin (1990) *Sun Wu's Art of War and the Art of Business Management*. Hong Kong. (Sunzi og Sun Wu are two different names for the same person).
17. There are many translations of this book. For example *The Taoist I Ching*, translated by T. Cleary. Kuala Lumpur: Estern Dragon Books. 1991.
18. This process is described in e.g., White, G. (1993) *Riding the Tiger*. Stanford: Stanford University Press.
19. See Decision of the CPC Central Committee on Reform of the Economic Structure. Adopted Oct. 29, 1984. In *Major Documents of the People's Republic of China*. Beijing, 1991:415 cont.
20. For a discussion of the hybrid forms, see Nee, V. (1992) Organizational Dynamics of Market Transition: Hybrid Forms, Property Rights, and Mixed Economy in China. *Administrative Science Quarterly*. 37:1-27.
21. The figures are from the People's Republic of China Year Book 1991/92. Beijing, 1991:183-185.
22. Ibid.
23. Zhongguo Tongji Nianjian (China's statistical year-book) 1994. Beijing: Tongji Chubanshe.
24. I am deliberately using the word 'quota' rather than objective since it involved volumes that had to be met. During the 1970s the authorities gradually started to distinguish between normative and compulsory quotas.
25. China's Financial Fix. *The Economist*. July 10th, 1993:66. The high evaluation of 80% stems from the usually well-informed Qi Xin. 'Li Peng jiaochu jingjiquan, Jiang Zhu fuze shou lantanzi' (Li Peng hands over economic power, Jiang and Zhu take over responsibility for the mess. *Jiushi Niandai* (The Nineties) July, 1993:32.
26. China's Financial Fix. *The Economist*, July 10, 1993:65-66.
27. Ibid.
28. See for example Byrd, W. & G. Tidrick (1987) Factor Allocation and Enterprise Incentives. In Byrd, W. & G. Tidrick (eds.) *China's Industrial Reform*. Oxford, p. 62ff.
29. The regulations were printed in the People's Daily, September 10, 1986 and were effective October 1, 1986. However, as far back as

February 1983, the Government had encouraged experimentation with contract systems, and in effect 3.5 million people were already employed on a contract basis when the system was introduced formally.

30. More than 93% found that many problems could have been avoided had it been possible to speed up decision making. Adler et al., 1989:64.

Chapter 3

1. This section builds on Lindkvist, L. (1991) *A Passionate Search for Nordic Management*. Copenhagen: Samfundslitteratur, p. 11 cont.
2. This section of Protestantism is based on Schramm-Nielsen, 1993:62 cont.
3. See Schramm-Nielsen (1993). Section 9.3 My section on educational policy is based on Schramm-Nielsen, who only discusses Danish educational policy.
4. This is a postulate based on my own observations of Chinese in Denmark.
5. Lessem, R. & F. Neubauer (1994) *European Management Systems. Towards Unity Out of Cultural Diversity*. London: McGraw Hill Book Company, p. 89. As the title indicates, this book isn't particularly about the North, but it is noteworthy that Part III is devoted to pragmatism.
6. Most cultures have similar expressions, but rarely as developed and detailed as the 'Jante Law'. The Chinese say: 'The pigs are afraid of growing fat, and people are afraid of becoming known.' When a pig gains a certain weight it is often killed.
7. Bliss McFate, P. (1984) To See Everything in Another Light. *Daedalus*. Vol. 113, No. 1. (Quoted in Lindkvist, 1991:29.)
8. Skandinavisk ledelsesstil en stopklods i udlandet. *Børsen*. 01.12.1994.
9. Laine-Sveiby quoted in Selmer, 1993:125.
10. Ibid.
11. Specific as opposed to diffuse, see section 4.15.2.

Chapter 4

1. For a similar discussion, see G. Hofstede (1983) Cultural Pitfalls for Dutch Expatriates in Indonesia: Lessons for Europeans in Asia. *Euro-Asia Business Review*. Vol. 2, No. 1:42.

Chapter 5

1. The concept of personalization is applied in the same broad sense as what Redding refers to as 'personalism'.
2. Immediately it may seem paradoxical that people in a collectivist culture individualize or personalize their contact with others, whereas people in individualist cultures standardize or collectivize these. Hopefully, it will become evident to the reader that this is a logical consequence of the two sets of values.
3. Similarly, Child found the Chinese didn't think expatriates understood properly the Chinese system of state owned enterprises and Chinese cultural values. Child, 1994:276.
4. See e.g. Usunier, J. (1994) Oral Pleasure and Expatriate Satisfaction: An Empirical Approach. Paper presented at EIASM workshop on *Cross Cultural Perspectives: Comparative Management and Organisation*. November 11-13. Henley Management College.
5. Here cited from Yau 1994:71. The word pragmatism about the Chinese was originally used by F. Hsu (1963) *Clan, Caste, and Club*. New York: Van Nostrand Co.
6. De Bettignies, H. (1991) Management in Asis: An Overview. In Putti, J. (ed.) *Management: Asian Context*. Singapore: McGraw-Hill, pp. 255-56, offers a good discussion of the ethics and dilemma.
7. Correspondingly, Wagner found in a survey of approx. 200 American joint venture managers in China that the greatest problem was the lack of competent Chinese managers (89%). Wagner, C. (1990) A Survey of Sino-American Joint Ventures: Problems and Outlook for Solutions. *East Asian Executive Reports*. March:8.

Chapter 6

1. A network of suppliers may involve contracts, but these will never govern the network.
2. Here quoted from Wong Siu-lun (1991) Chinese Entrepreneurs and Business Trust. In Hamilton, I.G. (ed.) *Business Networks and*

Economic Development in East and Southeast Asia. Centre of Asian Studies, University of Hong Kong, p. 14.

3. Slightly paraphrasing a definition formulated by professor Rosalie Rung, Simon Fraser University, Vancouver, Canada.

4. A Nathan (1993:928) writes: 'One of the most common hermeneutic findings about the distinctiveness of Chinese culture is that it lays greater stress than other cultures upon the use of *guanxi...* the Chinese term for certain kinds of particularistic ties between pairs of people.'

5. Lians Shuming (1987) *Zhongguo Wenhua de Yaoyi* (The Essential Meanings of Chinese Culture). Hong Kong: Joint Publishing Company, p. 83. The work was originally published in Chengdu in 1949 but, has never been translated into English. The prominent Chinese sociologist Fei Xiaotong touches upon the same idea in *From the Soil. The Foundation of Chinese Society, a Translation of Fei Xiaotong's Xiangtu Zhongguo.* Introduction and Epilogue, G. Hamilton & Wang Zheng. Berkeley, 1992:24. Originally published in Peking in 1947.

6. In this context, Kipnis talks about 'shifting referentiality'.

7. This historical description of the functions of *guanxi* stems from Redding, 1990.

8. Wall, J. (1990) Managers in the People's Republic of China. *Academy of Management Executive.* Vol. 4, No. 2:23. Strictly speaking, these concepts have not been invented by the Communists, but merely taken over from the traditional political system. See, Strand, D. (1993) Civil Society and Pubic Sphere in Modern Chinese History, in Des Forges, Luo Ning & Y. Wu (eds.) *Chinese Democracy and the Crisis in 1989).* New York: State University of New York Press, p. 55.

9. Chinese networks were anonymous to the third party, in this case the central planning authorities controlled by the Communist Party.

10. For a good description of middlemen and an introduction to the concept, see Engholm, Chr. *Doing Business in Asia's Booming 'China Triangle'.* London: Prentice Hall Int., p. 129.

11. This phenomenon is described in a series of works on the reform process. Here cited from Wang Xiaodong (1993) A Review of China's Economic Problems: The Industrial Sector, in *Chinese Democracy and the Crisis of 1989,* p. 154.

12. The discussion of cliques is based on Silin, 1976:Chapter 5.
13. Li Ruihuan is a member of the Polit Bureau's Standing Committee.
14. Zhu Rongji is a member of the Chinese Communist Party Polit Bureau's Standing Committee, and Vice Prime Minister responsible for financial affairs.
15. The Chinese name is fictitious, but otherwise the story is true.

Chapter 7

1. Here quoted from Lockett, 1988:488.
2. One of the most severe accusations one can witness in Chinese society is: 'I try to preserve (actually give you) your face but you will not have it.' (Chinese: 'Gei ni lian, ni bu yao lian.').
3. Yau (1994:74-75) has a good discussion of the difference between 'lian' and 'mianzi'.
4. The examples are from Yau, 194:74.
5. Bond, M. & P. Lee: Face Saving in Chinese Culture. Quoted in Redding & Ng, 1983:113.

Chapter 9

1. Child emphasizes that this is much more the case with American joint ventures than with others, but the European attitude is not far from the American (Child, 1994:253).
2. One of the best academic works in English within this field is Hou, Sheang & Hidajat (1991) *Sun Tzu: War and Management. Application to Strategic Management and Thinking*. Singapore: Addison-Wesley Pub. Company. A more popular example is Gao Yuan (1991) *Lure the Tiger Out of the Mountains. Timeless Tactics from the East for Today's Successful Manager*. London: Piatkus. For a general review of the use of military thinking in commercial situations, see Chu, Chin-Ning (1991) *The Asian Mind Game*. New York: Rawson Associates.
3. Björkman found the same tendency. Björkman, I. (1992) *A Preliminary Framework for Analysing Role Perception and Behaviour among Chinese Managers in Sino-Western Joint Ventures*. Paper presented at the Conference on Current Development in Joint Ventures in the PRC. June 16-18. University of Hong Kong.

Chapter 10

1. A respondent found this to be the main reason for dissolving the joint venture, where he had been the managing director.
2. Emerson, R. quoted in Thompson, J. (1967) Organizations in Action. New York: Mc Graw-Hil, p. 30.
3. The same difference is found in joint ventures between German and Chinese firms. Domsch, M. & Lichterberger (1990) In Search of Appropriate Management Transfer: Leadership Style of West German Expatriate Managers in the People's Republic of China. The Journal of Human Resource Management. Vol. 1, No. 1:78.
4. Child found that individual performance assessments were not viable in China but states the reason to be that the employees had three-year contracts. Child, 1994:259.
5. The Management of Equity Joint Ventures in China, 1990:100.
6. In Tianjin's Technological and Developmental Zone the rate is 80%.
7.   J. Ireland says that the Chinese are disinclined to follow orders until they have received them in writing. Ireland, J. (1991) Finding the Management Approach. The China Business Review. Vol. 18, No. 1:14.

Chapter 11

1. Even though most of the sources used in this book confirm this conclusion, few do not. Thus, in a survey of Canadian and American firms Punnett & Yu found cultural differences to be of little importance with long-term contact. Punnett, B. & P. Yu (1991) Attitudes toward Doing Business with PRC. In O. Shenkar (ed.) *Organization and Management in China 1979-1990*. New York: M.E. Sharpe. Armonk., p. 152. Americans are possibly more prone to refute that culture plays a role in the business. Also, when asked directly if culture has an impact, people tend to deny the importance of this abstract factor.
2. The concept is borrowed from J. Schramm-Nielsen who describes blind spots as cultural traits which others point to as being characteristic of the given culture, but which members of the culture never refer to when characterizing their own culture. J. Schramm-

Nielsen (1993) Dansk-Fransk samarbejde i erhvervsvirksomheder [Danish-French Business Collaboration]. Copenhagen:The Copenhagen Business School Press. Part 3:44.

3. The Management of Equity Joint Ventures in China. CEMI, 1990, Beijing, p. 30.
4. There are many suggestions about what to require from a Chinese partner. See for example Tretiak, D. & K. Holzmann (1993) Operating Joint Ventures in China. *The Economist Intelligence Unit.* Hong Kong, Chapter 1.

Bibliography

Adler, N. (1983): A Typology of Management Studies Involving Culture. *Journal of International Business Studies*. Fall, 1983:29-47.

Adler, N., Campbell, N & Laurent, A. (1989): In Search of Appropriate Methodology: From Outside The People's Republic of China Looking In. *Journal of International Business Studies*. Spring, 1989:61-74.

Alton, P. (1989): Wa, Guanxi and Inhwa: Managerial Principles in Japan, China, and Korea. *Business Horizons*. March-April.

Andersen, H. (1995): Kina kræver folk med speciel psyke. *Børsen*. January 13. Copenhagen.

Andersen, V & Gamstrup, P. (1994): Om Problemformulering og projektarbejde, in Andersen, H. (ed.): *Videnskabsteori & metodelære*. Copenhagen: Samfundslitteratur.

Ball, J. D. (1992): *Things Chinese*. Oxford: Oxford University Press. Originally published in London in 1892.

Bettignies, H.D. (1991): Management in Asia: An Overview, in Putti, J. (ed.): *Management: Asian Context*. Singapore: McGraw-Hill.

Björkman, I. (1992): »A Preliminary Framework for Analyzing Role Perception and Behaviour among Chinese Managers in Sino-Western Joint Ventures«. Paper presented at the Conference on Current Development in Joint Ventures in the PRC. Hong Kong, June 16-18.

Boisot, M. & Xing Guo Liang (1992): The Nature of Managerial Work in the Chinese Enterprise Reforms: A study of Six Directors. *Organizational Studies*. Vol. 13, No. 2:161-184.

Bond, M. (1991): *Beyond the Chinese Face*. Oxford: Oxford University Press.

Bond, M. & Hwang, K. (1986): The Social Psychology of Chinese People, in Bond, M. (ed.): *The Psychology of the Chinese People*. Oxford: Oxford University Press.

Borgonjon, J. & Vanhanacker, W. (1993): Management Training and Education in the People's Republic of China. *Euro-Asia Centre Research Series* 18.

Brown, P. & Levinson, S. (1987): *Politeness. Some Universals in Language Usage*. Cambridge: Cambridge University Press.

Brødsgaard, K. E. (1990): *Spillet om Kina*. Copenhagen: Mellemfolkeligt Samvirke.

Byrd, W. & Tidrick, G. (1987): Factor Allocation and Enterprise Incentives, in Chen, Jiyuan & Tidrick, G. (eds.): *China's Industrial Reform*. New York: Oxford University Press.

Campbell, N. (1986): *China Strategies. The Inside Story*. Hong Kong & Manchester: University of Manchester/University of Hong Kong.

Campbell, N. (1987): Entreprise Autonomy in the Beijing Municipality, in Warner, M. (ed.): *Management Reforms in China*. London: Frances Pinter Publishers.

Chan, P. & Justis, R. (1990): Franchise management in East Asia. *Academy of Management Executive*. Vol. 4, No. 2.

Chen, C. (1991): Confucian Style of Management in Taiwan in Putti, J. (ed.): *Management – Asian Context*. Singapore: McGraw-Hill.

Chen, Min. (1992): Socialism and Confucianism: Problems of Chinese Management. *The Journal of Contemporary China*. Vol. 1, No. 1:86-98.

Child, J. (1981): Culture, Contingency and Capitalism in the Cross-national Study of Organizations. *Research in Organizational Behavior*. Vol. 3:303-356.

Child, J. (1994): *Management in China During the Age of Reform*. Cambridge: Cambridge University Press.

Chu, Chin-Ning (1991): *The Asian Mind Game*. New York: Rawson Associates.

Cohen, M. (1991): Being Chinese: The Peripheralization of Traditional Identity. *Dædalus*. Vol. 120, No. 2.

Cragin, J. (1990): Management Technology Absorption in China, in Clegg, Dunphy & Redding (eds.): *The Enterprise and Management in East Asia*. Hong Kong: University of Hong Kong Press.

Czarniawska-Joerges, B. (1993): Sweden. A Modern Project, a Postmodern Implementation, in Hickson, D. (ed.): *Management in Western Europe*. Berlin: Walter de Gruyter.

Davidson, H. (1987): Creating and Managing Joint Ventures in China. *California Management Review*. Vol. 29.

De Mente, B. (1989): *Chinese Etiquette & Ethics in Business*. Lincolnwood: NTC Business Books.

Decision of the CPC Central Committee on Reform of the Economic Structure. Adopted Oct.20,1984. In *Major Documents of the People's Republic of China*. Beijing, 1991.

Domsch, M. & Lichterberger, B. (1990): In Search of Appropriate Management Transfer: Leadership Style of West German Expatriate Managers in the People's Republic of China. *The Journal of Human Resource Management.* Vol. 1, No. 1.

Eberhard, W. (1967): *A History of China.* London: Routledge & Kegan.

Engholm, Ch. (1994): *Doing Business in Asia's Booming »China Triangle«.* Englewood Cliffs: Prentice Hall.

Feng, Zongxian (1992): Industrial Concentration in China and its International Comparison. *Advances in Chinese Industrial Studies.* Vol. 3:113-123. London: Jai Press.

Fievelsdal, E. & Schramm-Nielsen, J. (1993): Egalitarianism at Work: Management in Denmark, in Hickson, D. (ed.): *Management in Western Europe.* New York: Walter De Gruyter.

From the Soil. The Foundation of Chinese Society, a Translation of Fei Xiaotong's Xiangtu Zhongguo (1992). Introduction and Epilogue by Hamilton, G. & Wang Zheng. Berkeley. *Xiangtu Zhongguo* was first published in Beijing in 1947.

Fung, Yu-Lan (1966): *A Short History of Chinese Philosophy.* London: MacMillan.

Gao, Yuan (1991): *Lure the Tiger Out of the Moutains. Timeless Tactics from the East for Today's Successful Manager.* London: Piatkus.

Goffman, E. (1955): On Face-Work: An Analysis of Ritual Elements in Social Interaction. *Psychiatry.* Vol. 18.

Gouldner, A. (1954): *Pattern of Industrial Bureaucracy.* Glencoe, Il.: Free Press.

Granovetter, M. (1992): Economic Action and Social Structure: The Problem of Embeddedness, in Grannovetter, M. & Swedberg, R. (eds.): *The Sociology of Economic Life.* Boulder: Westview Press.

Gullestrup, H. (1992): *Kultur, kulturanalyse og kulturetik.* Copenhagen: Akademisk Forlag.

Hall, E. & M. (1990): *Understanding Cultural Differences.* New York: Intercultural Press Inc.

Hamilton, G. (1984): Patriarchalism in Imperial China and Western Europe. *Theory and Society* 13.

Hedaa, L. (1992): *Organisationer i netværk.* Copenhagen: Inst. for Erhvervsøkonomi og Ledelse, Copenhagen Business School.

Henley, J. & Nyaw, M. (1990): Developments in Managerial Decision Making in Chinese Industrial Enterprises, in Clegg, Dunphy &

Redding (eds.): *The Enterprise and Management in East Asia.* Hong Kong: University of Hong Kong Press.

Hicks, G.L. & Redding, S.G. (1983): The Story of the East Asian 'Economic Miracle': The Culture Connection. *Euro-Asia Business Review.* Vol. 2, No. 4:18-22.

Hjort, K., Løngreen, H. & Søderberg, A. (1993): *Interkulturel kommunikation. Spændingsfeltet mellem det globale og det lokale.* Copenhagen: Samfundslitteratur.

Hofstede, G. (1984): *Culture's Consequences.* Abridged edition. London: Sage.

Hofstede, G. (1982a): Cultural Pitfalls for Dutch Expatriates in Indonesia: Lessons for Europeans in Asia (Part 1). *Euro-Asia Business Review.* Vol. 1, No. 1:37-41.

Hofstede, G. (1983): Cultural Pitfalls for Dutch Expatriates in Indonesia: Lessons for Europeans in Asia (Part 2). *Euro-Asia Business Review.* Vol. 2, No. 1:38-46.

Hofstede, G. (1991): *Cultures and Organizations.* London: McGraw-Hill Book Company.

Hofstede, G. (1982b): Skandinavisk management i og uden for Skandinavien. *Harvard Børsen.* No. 2:96-104.

Hofstede, G. & Bond, M. (1988): The Confucius Connection: From Cultural Roots to Economic Growth. *Organizational Dynamics.* Spring, 1988:5-21.

Hoon-Halbauer, S. (1994): *Management of Sino-Foreign Joint Ventures.* Lund: Lund University Press.

Howard, P. (1992): China's Enterprise Management Reforms in the Eighties in *Advances in Chinese Industrial Studies.* Vol. 3:37-60. London: Jai Press.

Hsu, R.(1992): Industrial Reform in China in Jeffries, I. (ed.): *Industrial Reform in Socialist Countries – From Restructuring to Revolution.* Aldershot: Edward Elgar.

Ireland, J. (1991): Finding the Management Approach. *The China Business Review.* Vol. 18, No. 1:14-17.

Jackson, S. (1992): *Chinese Enterprise Management.* Berlin: Walter De Gruyter.

Kahn, H. (1979): *World Economics Development. 1979 and Beyond.* Boulder: Westview Press.

Kedia, B. og Bhagat, R. (1988): Cultural Constraints on Transfer of Technology Across Nations: Implications for Research in

International and Comparative Management. *Academy of Management Review*. Vol. 13, No. 4:4-9.

Kipnis, A. (1994): »What's a Guanxi«. Paper presented at Association for Asian Studies' Annual Conference. Boston.

King, A. (1992): Kuan-hsi (Guanxi) and Network Building: A Sociological Interpretation. *Dædalus*. Vol. 120, No. 2.

Kirkbride, P. & Tang, S. (1990): Negotiation: Lessons from Behind the Bamboo Curtain. *Journal of General Management*. Vol. 16, No. 1.

Lasserre, Ph. & Probert, J. (1994): Human Resource Management in the Asia Pacific Region. A Comparative Assessment. *Euro-Asia Centre Research Series*. No. 25.

Lasserre, Ph. & Schütte, H. (1995): *Strategies for Asia Pacific*. London: MacMillan Business.

Lee, B. (1993): The Fifth Dragon. *The China Business Review*. Vol. 20, No. 4.

Legge, James (1994): *The Chinese Classics. Confucian Analects*. Taipei: SMC Publishing Inc. First published Claredon Press, Oxford, 1893.

Lessem, R. & Neubauer, F. (1994): *European Management Systems. Towards Unity out of Cultural Diversity*. London: McGraw-Hill Book Company.

Liang, Shuming (1987): *Zhongguo Wenhua de Yaoyi* (The Essential Meanings of Chinese Culture). Hong Kong: Joint Publishing Company. Originally published in 1949 in Chengdu, Sichuan Province.

Liao, Kuang-sheng (1986): *Antiforeignism and Modernization in China*. Hong Kong: Chinese University Press.

Lin, Fang (1988): Chinese Modernisation and Social Values, in Sinha, D. & Kao, H. (eds.): *Social Values and Development*. New Delhi: Sage Publications.

Lin, Yutang (1989): *My Country and My People*. Singapore: Heinemann Asia. First published in 1936.

Lindkvist, L. (1991): *A Passionate Search for Nordic Management*. Copenhagen: Samfundslitteratur.

Lindsey, C. & Dempsey, B. (1985): Experiences in Training Chinese Business People to Use U.S. Management Techniques. *The Journal of Applied Behavioral Science*. Vol. 21, No. 1.

Liu, Yunbo (1990): *Zhongguo Rujia Guanli Sixiang* (Confucian Administrative Thought in China). Shanghai: Renmin chubanshe.

Lockett, M. (1988): Culture and the Problems of Chinese Management. *Organization Studies.* Vol. 9, No. 4:475-496.

China-EC Management Institute (1990): *Management of Equity Joint Ventures in China.* Beijing: China-EC Management Institute.

Maruyama, M. (1994): *Mindshapes in Management.* Aldershot: Dartmouth.

Mote, F. (1971): *Intellectual Foundations of China.* New York: Alfred Knopf.

Mun, Kin-Chok (1990): Characteristics of the Chinese Management: An Exploratory Study, in Clegg, Dunphy & Redding (eds.): *The Enterprise and Management in East Asia.* Hong Kong: University of Hong Kong Press.

Nathan, A. (1993): Is Chinese Culture Distinctive? – A Review Article. *The Journal of Asian Studies.* Vol. 52, No. 4:923-936.

Nee, V. (1992): Organizational Dynamics of Market Transition: Hybrid Forms, Property Rights, and Mixed Economy in China. *Administrative Science Quarterly* 37:1-27.

Ng, Sek-hong (1990): The Ethos of Chinese at Work: Collectivism or Individualism. *Advances in Chinese Industrial Studies.* Vol. 1. Part A. London: Jai Press.

Oxfeld, E. (1993): *Blood, Sweat, and Mahjong.* Ithaca: Cornell University Press.

Pearson, M. (1992a): A Muted Voice for Reform. *The China Business Review.* No. 5.

Pearson, M. (1992b): Breaking the Bonds of »Organized Depencence«: Managers in China's Foreign Sector. *Studies in Comparative Communism.* Vol. 43, No. 1:57-77.

People's Republic of China Year Book 1991/92. Beijing, 1991.

Perkins, D. (1992): China's »Gradual« Approach to Market Reforms. *UNCTAD Discussion Papers.* No. 52.

Punnett, B. & Yu, P. (1991): Attitudes toward Doing Business with PRC, in Shenkar, O. (ed.): *Organization and Management in China 1979-1990.* New York: M.E. Sharpe.

Punnett, B. & Zhao, Y. (1992): Confucianism, Needs and Organizational Preferences. *Advances in Chinese Industrial Studies.* Vol. 3:77-94. London: Jai Press.

Pye, L. (1991a): *China – An Introduction.* New York: Harper Collins.

Pye, L. (1982): *Chinese Commercial Negotiating Style.* Cambridge, Mass.: Oelgeschlager, Gunn & Hain, Publ.

Pye, L. (1991b): The Individual and the State: An Overview Interpretation. *China Quarterly*. No. 117:443-66.

Redding, S.G. (1980): Cognition as an Aspect of Culture and its Relation to Management Processes: An Exploratory View of the Chinese Case. *Journal of Management Studies*. May 1980:127-148.

Redding, S.G. (1993): Cultural Effects on the Marketing Process in Southeast Asia in Weinshall, Th. (ed.): *Societal Culture and Management*. Berlin: Walter De Gruyter.

Redding, S.G. (1990): *The Spirit of Chinese Capitalism*. Berlin: Walter De Gruyter.

Redding, S.G. (1986): The Psychology of Chinese Organizational Behaviour, in Bond, M. (ed.): *The Psychology of the Chinese People*. Oxford: Oxford University Press.

Redding, S.G. & Ng, M. (1983): The Role of »Face« in the Organizational Perceptions of Chinese Managers. *International Studies of Management and Organizations*. Vol. 13, No. 3:92-123.

Redding, S.G. & Wong, G. (1986): The Psychology of Chinese Organization Behaviour, in Bond, M. (ed.): *The Psychology of the Chinese People*. Oxford: Oxford University Press.

Robbins, S. (1991): *Management*. London: Prentice-Hall.

Rodzinski, W. (1988): *The People's Republic of China. Reflections on Chinese Political History since 1949*. London: Collins.

Ronan, A. & Needham, J. (1988): *The Shorter Science and Civilisation in China:1*. Cambridge: Cambridge University Press.

Schramm-Nielsen, J. (1993): *Dansk-Fransk samarbejde i erhvervsvirksomheder*. Ph.D.serie 2.93. Copenhagen: Samfundslitteratur.

Selmer, J. (1993): Sweden, in Peterson, R. (ed.): *Managers and National Culture. A Global Perspective*. Westport: Quorum Books.

Seligman, S. (1989): *Dealing with the Chinese*. New York: Warner Books.

Silin, R. (1976): *Leadership and Values. The Organization of Large-Scale Taiwanese Enterprises*. Cambridge: Harvard University Press.

Shaw, S. & Woetzel, J. (1992): A fresh look at China. *The Mckinsey Quarterly*. No. 3:37-51.

Smith, A. (1986): *Chinese Characteristics*. Singapore: Graham Brash (Pte) Ltd. First published in Shanghai in 1890.

Stone, B. (1994): Sino-Foreign Joint Ventures and Government Corruption, in Stewart, S. (ed.): *Advances in Chinese Industrial Studies*. Vol. 4. London: Jai Press.

Strand, D. (1993): Civil Society and Public Sphere in Modern Chinese History, in Des Forges, Luo Ning & Wu, Y. (eds.): *Chinese Democracy and the Crisis of 1989*. New York: State University of New York Press.

Tan, Chwee Huat (1990): Management Concepts and Chinese Culture. *Advances in Chinese Industrial Studies*. Vol. 1, Part A. London: Jai Press.

The Taoist I Ching (1991). Translated by T. Cleary. Kuala Lumpur: Eastern Dragon Books.

Tayeb, M. (1988): *Organizations and National Culture*. London: Sage.

Thompson, J. (1967): *Organizations in Action*. New York: McGraw-Hill.

Tretiak, D. & Holzmann, K. (1993): *Operating Joint Ventures in China*. Hong Kong: The Economist Intelligence Unit.

Trompenaars, F. (1993): *Riding the Waves of Culture*. London: The Economist Books.

Tu, Wei-Ming (1984): *Confucian Ethics Today*. Singapore: Federal Publ.

Tung, R. (1994): Strategic Management Thought in East Asia. *Organizational Dynamics*. Vol. 22, No. 4:35-65.

Tung, R. & Yeung (1996): Guanxi (connections) and Business Success in Confucian Societies. *Organizational Dynamics*. (forthcoming)

Tung, R. (1989): A Longitudinal Study of United States – China Business Negotiations. *China Economic Review*. Vol. 1, No. 1: 57-71.

Usunier, J. (1994): »Oral Pleasure and Expatriate Satisfaction: An Empirical Approach«. Paper presented at the EIASM workshop on Cross Cultural Perspectives: Comparative Management and Organisation. November 12, 1994 at Henley Management College.

Wagner, C. (1990): A Survey of Sino-American Joint Ventures: Problems And Outlook For Solutions. *East Asian Executive Reports*. (March).

Walder, A. (1986): *Communist Neo-traditionalism: Work and Authority in Chinese Industry*. Berkeley: University of California Press.

Walker, T. (1993): China Freezes Pay of State Enterprise Workers. *Financial Times*. March 18.

Wall, J. (1990): Managers in the People's Republic of China. *Academy of Management Excecutive*. Vol. 4, No. 2.

Wan, Xiang (1980): Cong guanliao dao jingli (From bureaucrat to manager). *Jingji Guanli* (Economic Management). No. 11:3-8.

Wang, Xiaodong (1993): A Review of China's Economic Problems: The Industrial Sector, in Des Forges, Luo Ning & Wu, Y. (eds.): *Chinese Democray and the Crisis of 1989*. New York: State University of New York Press.

Wee, Lee & Hidajat (1991): *Sun Tzu: War and Management. Application to Strategic Management and Thinking*. Singapore: Addison-Wesley Pub. Company.

Westwood, R. (1992): Culture, Cultural Differences, and Organisational Behaviour, in Westwood, R. (ed.): *Organisational Behaviour. Southeast Asian Perspectives*. Hong Kong: Longman.

Westwood, R. & Chua, B. (1992): Power; Politics, and Influence, in Westwood, R. (ed.): *Organisational Behaviour. Southeast Asian Perspectives*. Hong Kong: Longman.

White, G. (1993): *Riding the Tiger. The Politics of Economic Reform in Post Mao China*. Stanford: Stanford University Press.

Whithane, S. (1992): A Consensual Framework For Business Negotiation. *Advances in Chinese Industrial Studies*. Vol. 3. London: Jai Press.

Wong, Siu-Lun (1991): Chinese Entrepreneurs and Business Trust, in Hamilton, G. (ed.): *Business Networks and Economic Development in East and Southeast Asia*. Hong Kong: Centre of Asian Studies, University of Hong Kong.

Worm, Verner (1995): *Nordiske virksomheder i Kina*. Ph.D. Serie 2.95. Copenhagen: Copenhagen Business School.

Yang, Lian Sheng (1987): *Zhongguo Wenhua zhong Bao, Bao, Bao zhi yiyi* (The meaning of Reciprocity, Trustworthiness, and Integrity in Chinese Culture). Hong Kong: The Chinese University Press.

Yang, M. (1994): *Gift, Favors and Banquets: The Art of Social Relationships in China*. Ithaca: Cornell University Press.

Yau, O. (1994): *Consumer Behaviour in China. Customer Satisfaction and Cultural Values*. London: Routledge.

Zhongguo Tongji Nianjian (1994) (China's Statistical Yearbook). Beijing: Tongji chubanshe.

1995 nian guomin jingji he shehui fazhan de tongji gongbu (1995 Statistical Communiqué of Economic and Social Development of the PRC). *Renmin Ribao* (People's Daily). Overseas Edition. March 7, 1996.